ALFRED NORTH WHITEHEAD AND YI YULGOK

Toward a Process-Confucian Spirituality in Korea

Chung Soon Lee

University Press of America,® Inc.
Lanham · Boulder · New York · Toronto · Oxford

Copyright © 2006 by
University Press of America,® Inc.
4501 Forbes Boulevard
Suite 200
Lanham, Maryland 20706
UPA Acquisitions Department (301) 459-3366

PO Box 317
Oxford
OX2 9RU, UK

All rights reserved
Printed in the United States of America
British Library Cataloging in Publication Information Available

Library of Congress Control Number: 2005935101
ISBN 0-7618-3357-9 (paperback : alk. ppr.)

Scripture quotations are from the New Revised Standard Version
of the Bible, copyright © 1989 by the National Council
of the Churches of Christ in the U.S.A.
Used by permission. All rights reserved.

To Chang-Keum
My wife and friend
To Bo-Reum and Han-Earl,
My loved children

Contents

Acknowledgments

Introduction 1

Chapter 1: The Process Cosmology of Alfred North Whitehead ... 13

Chapter 2: The Neo-Confucian Cosmology of Yi Yulgok 43

Chapter 3: A Comparison of Whitehead and Yulgok on Cosmology ... 79

Chapter 4: A Process Cosmological Application to
    Interreligious Spirituality in the Context of Korea 91

Conclusion 141

Notes 149

Glossary of Korean Chinese and Terms 169

Bibliography 171

Index 189

Acknowledgments

I first deeply thank my former advisors, Dr. John H. Berthrong and Dr. Claire Wolfteich, for their excellent teachings and thoughtful guidance during my doctoral program at Boston University. My special thanks go to Dr. Robert C. Neville, Dr. James Nash, and Dr. Brian Stone for their meaningful comments on this book. I am very grateful to all the beloved members of the First Congregational Church of Waverley-Senuri. They not only offered me the precious opportunities to practice my theological thoughts, but also enabled me to grow as a more spiritual pastor and academic theologian. Finally, I express my thanks to my mother and mother-in-law, sisters and brothers, my former adviser Prof. Kee-Deuk Song Emeritus, Rev. Heung-Il Moon, Rev. Kee-Soo Kim, the late Rev. Kwang-Soo Lee, Min-Whan Lee, Rev. Dr. Tae-Yeon Cho, and Rev. Carolyn Clarke. They have supported my study and ministry with warm encouragements and good advices. I express my gratitude to Dr. Chae Young Kim who arranged the special meeting to present my dissertation, the first manuscript of this book, and gave me some useful suggestions. I will also not forget the hard work of Mary Hogan who proofread the manuscript of this book.

Most sincerely, I would like to express my deepest appreciation to my wife Chang-Keum and my two children Bo-Reum and Han-Earl for their unchanging love, enduring support, and wholehearted prayers for my doctoral study and parish ministry. Without them, my graduate studies and this book project would never have come to fruition. They have been patient and supportive of my double jobs as a student and pastor. I am also thankful for all the students of my religion class at Merrimack College who academically stimulated me to publish this book. Above all, I give many thanks to God for my Korean-Confucian-Christian heritage and leading me into a new world of comparative theology/religion and multicultural-racial ministry in the United States.

Finally, I am grateful to the Simon & Schuster, Inc. for the permission to quote copyrighted material from *Process and Reality*, Corrected Edition by Alfred North Whitehead. Copyright © 1929 by Macmillan Publishing Company; copyright renewed © 1957 by Evelyn Whitehead. Corrected edition copyright © 1978 by The Free Press. Reprinted with the permission of Scribner, an imprint of Simon & Schuster Adult Publishing Group.

INTRODUCTION

Statement of the Problem

This book is a study of Confucian-Christian dialogue in the context of Korea regarding spirituality by means of a comparative study of the cosmologies of Alfred N. Whitehead (1861-1947), a founder of contemporary process philosophy, and Yi Yulgok (1536-1584), a great scholar of Choson Dynasty (1392-1911) Korean Neo-Confucianism. More specifically, this book will analyze certain themes of the process cosmologies in a comparative perspective and investigate their applications to cross-cultural and interreligious spirituality—spirituality derived from both Christian and Confucian roots. As a result of ongoing Confucian-Christian dialogue in Korea, a new type of interreligious spirituality is emerging because of the interaction of these two cosmological visions.

Religious pluralism is one of the striking characteristics today in Korean society. This is, of course, a very natural phenomenon in East Asian societies in which many religions were born and developed together. All living religions are still streaming together, although they are in conflict as well as harmony and unity. As Diana L. Eck describes, "The religious traditions are more like rivers than monuments. They are not static and they are not over. They are still rolling--with forks and confluences, rapids and waterfalls."[1] This is the case in Korea where various living religions have existed together for over three thousand years. As religions have been introduced over the centuries, they were indigenized on Korean soil and have co-existed. Thus, it is hard to discern precisely the characteristics of each religion separately in Korea, as they have all influenced one another and mixed together. Christianity is no exception. Many elements of other religions, such as Confucianism, Buddhism, and Daoism, exist in Korean Christianity. Christianity, however, still remains the one western religion in Korea. This means that there are still many conflicts in the encounter between

Christianity and other traditional religions.

Confucianism, which served as the state religion for the Choson Dynasty for five hundred years, still exists and exerts strong religious and spiritual influence in Korean society.[2] Given its historic dominance in Korea, as well as its profound influence on the rest of Asia, Confucianism is an important partner in the Christian's encounter with the traditional religious culture of Korea. Confucian spirituality has often been defined as the practice of self-cultivation through which people obtain the Way/Dao in service to others. In spite of this positive, world affirming spirituality, the Confucian encounter with Christianity had not been successful in the modern period. Moreover, cosmology is one of the defining features of religious scholarship in both Confucianism and Christianity. It plays an important role by presenting a framework for religious worldview and also gives rise to a certain type of spirituality.

However, some questions arise with regard to Confucian-Christian dialogue concerning cosmology: Why, among the many religions in Korea, should a Confucian-Christian dialogue be initiated? Why is an interreligious spirituality needed? Why is cosmology essential in the making of spirituality? How are process cosmologies significant in the emergence of a new interreligious spirituality? Due to the lack of comparative study between Whitehead's Process philosophy and Yulgok's Neo-Confucianism in the Korean context, these questions have not been explored within the modern history of Korea.

Therefore, the central thesis of this book is based upon the following three arguments:

(1) Process philosophy/ theology provides a solid philosophical framework for a great diversity of human experience and belief in world religions and functions as a helpful means of comparing and synthesizing them in a creative new way. It can also be a useful instrument for dialogue among various religions. Above all, process theology, with its processive, organic, and relational cosmology, a sensibility shared by Choson Neo-Confucianism, can be used to reflect upon Christian spirituality and spiritual practices for a new era in the context of Korea.

(2) Confucianism, as a living religious tradition and culture, is a rich resource for enhancing Korean spirituality. Specifically, Neo-Confucianism represented by Yi Yulgok is not only a philosophy that deals with the origin of the universe and the essence of human nature, but is also a religion that has a spiritual dimension. This dimension is defined by the quest for the embodiment of the wisdom of the sages as profound and significant as any world religion. Above all, its similarities to process philosophy with respect to cosmology can produce meaningful suggestions and implications for spiritual formation in the Korean Church.

(3) The Confucian-Christian dialogue is an urgent task in the religiously pluralist society of Korea. Dialogue functions as a bridge between Western Christianity and Korean traditional religions introduced from China. Such dialogue will thus stimulate the development of mutual learning between Western

and Asian civilizations. It will further influence the emergence of a new type of interreligious spirituality, a process-Confucian spirituality, as a desirable way of peaceful coexistence among religious believers in the global context of religious pluralism.

Significance of the Study

This study is significant for four reasons. First, interreligious dialogue is an urgent task in a Korean society, particularly for Korean Christianity, which has many theological and practical problems with traditional living religions. This study is significant because it contributes to Confucian-Christian dialogue. It is important for Korean Christians to study other religions as living partners in Christian faith in order to make Christianity fruitful in the religiously pluralistic society of Korea. Interreligious dialogue enables Christians to live out their faith by fully understanding the essential meaning of Christianity as a living religion in the Korean historical context. Christianity exists in a complex web of relationships with other traditional religions in Korea because Christianity has been unconsciously influenced greatly by other religions as it has emerged in Korea.

Christianity in Korea, including both Catholicism and Protestantism, has a history of more than two hundred years. The Korean Church is growing rapidly and evolving its own theology and spirituality. It is still struggling with issues posed by Korea's unique heritage, present political position, and rapid economic development. Korean Christianity, however, has many theological and practical problems with traditional living religions, particularly Confucianism, Buddhism, Shamanism, and other new national religions. On the one hand, while Christianity, particularly Protestantism, was introduced to Korea by Western missionaries, traditionally Korea has been a religiously pluralist society. On the other hand, the Christianity introduced from Western countries is still not indigenized into Korean culture in a true sense. That is, Christianity in Korea does not fully understand or accept a religiously pluralistic culture, so it still regards other religions as heretical or ignores them altogether. According to the Korean theologian Kyoung-Jae Kim, "The exclusivistic prejudice of Korean Christians against non-Christian religions and their ignorance of other religions prevent interreligious dialogue, and in turn hinder the growth of Christianity in Korea."[3] Therefore, the Christian encounter with other religions, especially Confucianism, is crucial for reforming, deepening, and maturing Korean Christians' faith.

Second, Whitehead's philosophy can present meaningful insights for enhancing religious faith and spirituality. This study is significant because it contributes to the use of Whitehead's thought in the practice of faith, in this instance, spiritual practices. It is well known that Whitehead was one of the most profound and important philosophical minds of the twentieth century. His special philosophic contribution lies in the comprehensiveness of his synthesis of the process point of view, and the exactness of his analysis of the relationship between the sciences and humanities. His philosophic vision continues to be applied in many areas of science, theology, and philosophy. Process philosophy, beginning with Whitehead, can be one appropriate pole for this dialogue, because it is one of the major theological reformations of traditional Western Christianity. In particular, process theology is an appropriate tool for developing a new theological movement in Korea, especially because theologians have followed Western conservative theologies that allow for little positive dialogue. Process theology, which uses processive, organismic, and relational models to explain the Christian cumulative tradition inspired by Jesus Christ, is biblically rooted and philosophically appealing to many modern Koreans. In addition, it is significant that process theology effectively uses Whitehead's philosophy to express and integrate Christian belief into our contemporary perception of reality.

Specifically speaking, its processive, organismic, and relational cosmology resonates as well with Asian thought as any contemporary western philosophy and theology. This cosmology is effective and versatile enough to initiate a new way of peaceful coexistence and mutual learning among world religions. Thus, it can be well applied to the context of the Confucian-Christian dialogue, which is necessary in a Korean society. Furthermore, it can present meaningful insights for enhancing Christian spirituality and spiritual practices, because, for Whitehead, cosmology or world view gives rise to a certain type of religious spirituality.

Third, Neo-Confucianism, represented by Yi Yulgok, is the most common intellectual, moral and cultural heritage of Korea. It has greatly influenced the life and value system of the Korean people and religions; it has also fused its horizon with religious paradigms of other religions.[4] This study is significant because it contributes to the use of Yulgok in reflecting upon spiritual practices. Yi Yulgok was one of the greatest Confucian scholars in the history of Korea. Due to his scholarly activities, the Neo-Confucianism of Song dynasty China was revitalized in Korea three hundred years after the death of Zhu Xi (1130-1200), the great synthesizer of Neo-Confucianism in China. Yulgok's Neo-Confucian thought can play an important role in the Confucian-Christian dialogue because his thought manifests many themes similar to Whitehead's. In a sense, Yulgok is a precursor of Whiteheads process philosophy of organism. Even though Yulgok follows the Neo-Confucian tradition, he developed his own thoughts in the Korean context and remains one of Korea's most revered and influential thinkers. Yulgok upholds the tradition of Neo-Confucianism and develops it further in unique, creative, and enduring ways.

Fourth, spirituality is a fundamental way to express the existence of religions and their believers. This study is significant because it contributes to a contextual religious practice related to spirituality as manifested in interreligious dialogue. "Spirituality" refers to the whole of one's spiritual or religious experience in respect to God, the divine mystery and the ultimate or absolute in every religious tradition. It is achieved through diverse forms of self-cultivation, prayer, study, ritual, or a combination of all of these things. Although the term "spirituality" has often been associated with Christian theology, it can be used more generally from a comparative perspective in the case of Korean society. Hence, the study of spirituality in a comparative perspective is very appropriate for the religiously plural society of Korea.

In particular, the study of spirituality is important for the churches in Korea because, although Korean Christians affirm that their lives should be filled with the Holy Spirit, they have not yet achieved a good theological understanding of the Holy Spirit. Moreover, although as a result of its successful mission Korean Christianity experienced a remarkable growth in a short period of time, it has not yet achieved the state of a mature Christian spirituality that embraces other religions as living partners and friends; instead, many Korean Christians regard other faiths as evil enemies and sinners in the society of religious pluralism. Spirituality as a core of practical theology is a new theological field for Korean Christians. In this respect, spirituality in terms of comparative religious studies is necessary for spiritual development in the Korean Church.

Sources of the Study

This book will include wide and extensive research on the historical, philosophical, and theological literature written in English, classical Chinese, and Korean. The main sources of the study will be the written works of A. N. Whitehead and Yi Yulgok. In particular, this study will focus on the two thinkers' main works: for Alfred N. Whitehead, *Process and Reality: An Essay on Cosmology* (1978); *Science and the Modern World* (1926); *Modes of Thought* (1938); *Adventures of Ideas* (1933); *Religion in the Making* (1926; Reprint, 1996); and for Yi Yulgok, *Yulgok Chonso* [Complete Works of Yi Yulgok]. (1971); *Yulgokjip* [Collected Writings of Yulgok] (1985); *Kukyok Yulgok Chonso* 7 vols.[Korean Translations of Complete Works of Yulgok with Chinese Texts] (1984-1988); Michael C. Kalton et al. *The Four-Seven Debate: An Annotated Translation of the Most Famous Controversy In Korean Neo-Confucian Thought* (1994). This study will also use secondary resources and reference works with regard to process cosmology, process philosophy and theology, Confucianism, spirituality, spiritual practices, and the Korean Church.

Method of Investigation

The main focus of this book is a comparative study of two major philosophers and religious figures: A. N. Whitehead and Yi Yulgok. In a secondary sense, it can serve as an example of the emerging discipline of comparative theology between and among the religious traditions of Euro-America and East Asia. Along with theological and philosophical insights derived from the comparison of these two seminal thinkers, some practical applications concerning the formation of interreligious spirituality will be attempted in the context of Confucian-Christian interaction in Korea. More specifically, this book will focus on the origins and current practice of Confucian-Christian dialogue as a specific case in the broader field of comparative theology and religion.

Certainly, there is no scholarly consensus about the definition of the term "comparative theology" in the context of Korea. The term "comparative theology" seems strange to many Korean intellectuals because the term "theology" has been used mainly to define the intellectual activities of Christian intellectuals. While this term may seem strange, it is contextually meaningful in Korea for the simple reason that cumulative traditions such as Buddhism, Confucianism, Daoism, and Shamanism in Korea have defined themselves as ways of life or worldviews, but not as theologies. Therefore, people of other religious or spiritual traditions regard "theology" as a Christian term. Thus, the term comparative theology will be used in a broad sense as a subset of the vague category of the comparative study of religion.

In terms of specific methods of comparison, I will make use of comparative systematic cross-cultural studies in philosophy and theology, and I will use this comparative study to suggest ways of enhancing Korean Christian Spirituality and spiritual practices. For instance, by developing this dual methodology, this book suggests that, although these two great thinkers come from two radically different philosophic traditions and cultures, they articulate similar views of process cosmology. In other words, this book will analyze common terminology for mutual understanding and learning cross-culturally. Furthermore, in terms of the study of spirituality, Whitehead and Yulgok propose remarkably convergent strategies for the promotion of interreligious spirituality in the context of Korea.

In comparative philosophy and theology, it is important to understand one's religion on its own terms and perspective. One needs to describe accurately, explain and analyze what has been described, and then commend a comparative pattern of mutual recognition. Furthermore, in order to focus the initial descriptive selection, the main focus of the study will be on a set of key concepts based on both Christianity and Confucianism, because "Concepts are themselves material of a comparative nature from within a specific religious tradition."[5] I will identify a set of core texts and motifs in both traditions as the subject matter for comparison and analysis.

In other words, this book will compare and contrast terms, traits or concepts from Confucian and Christian discourses in order to suggest how Christian theology must attend to the Confucian heritage of Korea and vice versa. Comparison, which will be used as a main tool of study in this book, means "a process of making, evaluating, and correcting comparative assertions, not a merely the assertions themselves lifted from the process."[6] In order to refine the focus even further, this study will attend to cosmology or worldview analysis because cosmology, as Whitehead noted, suggests a religious perspective and contributes a great deal to the making of spirituality. In particular, Whitehead and Yulgok derive meaningful practical insights from their versions of process cosmology with regard to religion and spirituality.

Finally, the study will investigate how the result of the comparative study of two process cosmologies can be used to reflect upon interreligious spirituality in the Korean context. In other words, it will attempt to show how process cosmologies can play a role in the development of new type of spirituality in a religiously pluralistic culture. This study, therefore, engages in a diachronic and synchronic dialogue between two religious and philosophical traditions based on two major cosmological articulations of these traditions. This dialogue is then used to reflect upon the contemporary praxis of Christian spirituality within a pluralistic world.

With the comparative methodology procedure in mind, I will attempt a theoretical analysis of Whitehead's process philosophy and Yulgok's Confucian "Study of the Way" as the main body of this book. This analysis will be based on the main categories and concepts which are comprised of their cosmological articulations. In addition to the comparison of the process cosmologies of Whitehead and Yulgok, definitions of spirituality in a comparative perspective and the formation of interreligious spirituality in the context of Korea will be also investigated.

Structure of the Study

This book consists of five chapters divided into two different parts. While the first three chapters are a theoretical comparative study of process cosmology, the remaining chapters are a practical integration of those comparative studies in terms of the study of spirituality. Part one deals with the historical and theoretical explication of the two thinkers' philosophical thought from the comparative perspective. Part two deals with the implications of the comparative study of the process cosmologies and their application to the study of spirituality. Here we shall give a brief summary of each chapter.

In the first chapter, I will investigate the process cosmology of A. N. Whitehead, paying special attention to his theory of eternal objects and actual entities.

Those are key concepts for understanding Whitehead's philosophy and theology. Also, I will discuss how eternal objects and actual entities are concretized in the process of creativity by means of prehension and concrescence. Then, I will explicate the concept of God in terms of his role and meaning in process cosmology.

In the second chapter, I will investigate the Neo-Confucian cosmology of Yi Yulgok by investigating Yulgoks theory of *li* (理, principle) and *qi* (氣, material force). I will first discuss Zhu Xi's view of *li* and *qi* because of Zhu's strong influence on Yulgok. I will also examine T'oegye's emphasis on 'mutual issuance of *li* and *qi*' and Hwadam's '*qi* monism' because they help us understand Yulgok in a comparative perspective. Then, I will discuss Yulgoks famous phrases by means of which his philosophical system of *li* and *qi* is organized and systematized. These phrases are *ki-bal-yi-seung* (氣發理乘, material force issues and principle mounts it), *i-il-bun-su* (理一分殊, principle is one but its manifestations are many), *i-tong-ki-kuk* (理通氣局, principle pervades and material force delimits), and *i-ki-ji-myo* (理氣之妙, the marvel of principle and material force). I will then discuss how *li* and *qi* are interrelated and interdependent both in terms of theory and praxis. Moreover, I will discuss Yulgok's understanding of *taiji* (太極, the supreme ultimate) and its cosmological significance in terms of the creative mutuality of the *yin- yang* (陰陽) forces. Finally, I will explore how Yulgok's cosmological thought is applied to the doctrine of human nature in the famous philosophical debate called *Sa-Dan-Chil-Jong-Non* (四端七精論; The Debate on the Four Beginnings and Seven Feelings).

In the third chapter, I will discuss and compare Whitehead's organic and dynamic system of eternal objects and actual entities in relation to Yulgok's three famous rubrics concerning *li* and *qi.* I will explore the interrelations between *li* and *qi* in comparison with the eternal objects present in actual entities as the form of the entities. I will examine, in more detail, the dynamic and interdependent relationship between eternal objects and *li* as potentiality, and between actual entities and *qi* as actuality. Finally, I will compare the process concept of God with Neo-Confucian concept of *taiji.*

The purpose of the fourth chapter is to use the process cosmologies of Whitehead and Yulgok to suggest ways of enhancing Korean Christian Spirituality and spiritual practices. Furthermore, I will review the important issue of Confucian-Christian dialogue in the Korean context, focusing on the historical and theological understanding of the two systems of religious thought. In particular, I will develop this issue on the basis of contemporary studies of spirituality. I will first describe the religiously pluralistic situation of Korea in general, focusing on Christianity in relation to other religions. Second, I will discuss ancestor worship as a critical issue in the Confucian-Christian dialogue in the modern history of the Korean Church. I will describe how significantly the issue of ancestor worship shapes the Confucian-Christian dialogue in Korea. Third, I will define the term "spirituality" from a comparative perspective. Finally, I will engage in a preliminary discussion of spiritual formation in the context of the Korean Church from the process cosmological perspective.

In the final chapter, I shall discuss some general conclusions concerning the future of comparative theological studies and comparative spirituality studies. Future tasks for the study of the encounter between Christianity and Confucianism will be suggested. I will present some ideas concerning ways to contribute to a meaningful and successful interreligious dialogue.

Definitions

Process philosophy and theology

Process philosophy and theology is a school of thinkers rooted in the thought Alfred N. Whitehead. The earliest versions of process theology came out of the so-called Chicago School of liberal, empirical theism during the late 1920's and 1930's. The main figures were Henry Nelson Wieman and Bernard Meland followed by Bernard Loomer and Charles Hartshorne. The most influential representatives of the second generation of process theologians are John B. Cobb, Jr., Schubert M. Ogden, Lewis Ford, David Ray Griffin, William Christian, A. H. Johnson, David Day Williams, Marjorie H. Schocki, and many others.

Neo-Confucianism

Neo-Confucianism represents the second major epoch of the Confucian Way beginning in the Northern Song (960-1126) China, and hence is distinguished from classical Confucianism and New or modern Confucianism. Neo-Confucianism embarked both as a creative response to the Buddhist and Daoist challenge and as an imaginative reinterpretation of classical Confucian insights in the Song period. It is called "Neo-Confucianism" in Western scholarship, and remains as a living religious tradition in China and other Asian countries. Zhu Xi (1130-1120) and Wang Yang-Ming (1472-1529) are the most important representatives of Neo-Confucianism. Neo-Confucianism was introduced into Korea in the 13th century and influenced Yulgok's philosophy in the 16th century.

Li

Etymologically, *Li* means the veins in jade, or polishing jade. *Li* signifies meaning, pattern, reason, truth, discernment, and analysis. *Li* is translated as principle, pattern, order, meaning, or essence in English. In neo-Confucianism, all phenomena are manifestations of this primordial ideal principle (*li*). According to Zhu Xi, *li* is identified with the *dao*(way)of 'what is above shape'. *Li* is the source from which things are produced. In other words, each existent things has a reason for its existence, or essence or principle for its existence, which is known as *li*.

Qi

Qi literally means breath, ether, vital force, material force or matter energy. It is generally considered to be the concrete, material, differentiating principle of things. *Qi* constitutes all beings together with *li*. In neo-Confucianism, *qi* gives physical substance to metaphysical ideals (*li*). *Li* cannot exist without *qi*. According to Zhu Xi, *qi* is identified with the instrument of 'what is within shape.' It is the material means whereby things are produced. *Qi* is the motivating power of things that are subject to change, processing movement and quiescence, capable of producing forms and shape.

Taiji

Taiji is translated as 'great ultimate' or 'supreme polarity' in English. The first component of this term means the great, the supreme, while the second signifies the utmost or highest axis. In Chinese classics, *taiji* is often referred to as the First principle of the universe and human nature. Zhu Xi identifies it with the *Tianli*(way of heaven), the embodiment of all truth, wisdom, and virtue. In other words, *taiji* is described as immanent not only in the whole of the cosmos, but in each individual being as well.

Spirituality

Spirituality in its broadest sense refers to the whole of humankind's spiritual or religious experience in respect to what is ultimate or what defines the mystery of the divine. In general, spirituality is the human attempt to be united with the ultimate or the divine reality by transcending oneself in a fundamentally normative or religious orientation. In other words, spirituality means the "inner dimension of the person called by certain traditions 'the spirit.' This spiritual core is the deepest center of the person. It is here that the person is open to the transcendent dimension; it is here that the person experience ultimate reality."[7] Likewise, Christian spirituality is the striving for a radical union with God the

Father through Jesus Christ the Son by living in the Holy Spirit.[8]

Interreligious spirituality

Interreligious spirituality emerges as a result of the interreligious dialogue with special attention to the issue of spirituality. It is a new synthesized type of spirituality which can be applied to a certain context of religious pluralism. In the context of Korea, interreligious spirituality is developed by various dialogues or comparative studies among religions. It is unavoidable that such a new spirituality, based on dual or multiple religious identities, can and will emerge.

Limitations

The book will be focused only on two philosophical and religious thinkers: Alfred N. Whitehead and Yi Yulgok. Further, it will be limited to an analysis of their theories of cosmology based on selected comparative concepts, texts, and motifs. Both thinkers have many things in common; in particular, their understandings of cosmology are congruent and will be dealt with as the subject matter in this book. Thus, their cosmological articulations will be compared such that this study will be focused mainly on similarities. A limitation of this study is that the difference between the cosmologies of Whitehead and Yulgok will not be discussed in detail.

This book will make a practical application of comparative study of Whitehead's and Yulgok's cosmological thought regarding the issue of spirituality. Although this book first pursues a theoretical comparative study of religions, it also seeks practical applications in terms of normative and constructive religious practices, which will be presented as models of Confucian-Christian dialogue in the context of Korea. It will be based on a process-oriented Korean Christianity and Neo-Confucianism. Furthermore, it will be narrowed to the issue of interreligious spirituality, which should be helpful in the spiritual formation of the Korean Church in the context of religious pluralism.

Furthermore, the book will be limited to the specific context of historical and contemporary mainline Korean Protestant churches. This study will focus on both the specific circumstances that face the Korean Church and the task of spiritual formation that the Korean Church should undertake. This book will not deal with the circumstances of the Catholic Church and other religions.

Finally, the research for this book will be challenged by the scarcity of resources written in English related to Yulgok. Almost all resources regarding Yulgok are from writings in the classical Chinese and the Korean languages. Therefore, this study will help validate the need for a study which pursues an explication of the Korean Confucian-Christian dialogue in English for Western scholars.

Chapter 1

THE PROCESS COSMOLOGY OF ALFRED NORTH WHITEHEAD

Historical Background of Process Philosophy and Theology

Process philosophy and theology are new academic movements that have been influenced by the philosophies of Alfred North Whitehead and his followers. John Cobb and David Griffin say, "The position they hold in common is widely known as 'process philosophy' and the theological movement influenced by it is accordingly called 'process theology.' The term 'process' rightly suggests that this movement rejects static actuality and affirms that all actuality is process."[1] It generally emphasizes process and becoming rather than static beings or substances in the actual world.

On the other hand, the process philosophy initiated by Whitehead is also called "the philosophy of organism" or "the organismic philosophy" because it can be confused with other similar philosophies that focused on the term "process" in the history of Western philosophy. Whitehead himself frequently called his philosophy "a philosophy of organism," which is an interpretation of the world as an intricately connected whole. Whitehead's organismic worldview basically shows how the world is comprised of individual elements which are related to one another, and how the world is advancing creatively. Undoubtedly, this worldview paved a way for the development of a new philosophy and theology. Marjorie H. Suchocki points out, "Alfred North Whitehead's organismic philosophy gave Cobb the means to address more successfully the intellectual problems of Christian faith. A through-going relational base displaced the primacy of self-sufficient substance."[2]

Whitehead developed his philosophy of process or organism from his careful studies of modern sciences, philosophies, and literature. He often claimed that his philosophy was based on the analysis and rediscovery of modern philosophical thought emerging from Descartes and ending with Hume. First of all, as is well known, the philosophy of empiricism advocated mainly by John Locke and David Hume was critical of metaphysics and speculative philosophy, insisting that human knowledge came from the human senses only. Lock and Hume also denied any reality beyond the empirical real world. Empiricism gained popularity along with the growth of science and the growing concern about language itself in the nineteenth and twentieth centuries. More precisely, it was supported and developed by French positivism, the logical positivism of Vienna Circle, and English philosophical positivism in the nineteenth century.[3]

Whitehead, on the contrary, greatly advocated the importance of metaphysics in philosophical work. He maintains that apart from a metaphysical scheme, the proper theories of human experience cannot be established. In the preface to *Process and Reality*, he stated, "All constructive thought, on the various special topics of scientific interest, is dominated by some such scheme, unacknowledged, but no less influential in guiding the imagination. The importance of philosophy lies in its sustained effort to make such schemes explicit, and thereby capable of criticism and improvement."[4] For Whitehead, therefore, the construction of an inclusive cosmological framework is an inevitable task of proper philosophy and this leads him to emphasize speculative philosophy. He believes that apart from metaphysical reference, all abstraction in the final analysis is not correct. This means that the philosopher should possess a framework of thought (i.e., a metaphysical scheme) before approaching a specific matter.

The goal of philosophy, in this respect, is to construct a scheme of ideas and correct and improve them in light of other schemes of ideas and daily human experiences. Whitehead thus defines speculative philosophy: "Speculative philosophy is the endeavor to frame a coherent, logical, necessary system of general ideas in terms of which every element of our experience can be interpreted."[5] In order to exercise speculative philosophy well, Whitehead presents "the method of imaginative rationalization," using the metaphor of flight. "The true method of discovery is like the flight of an aeroplane. It starts from the ground of particular observation; it makes a flight in the thin air of imaginative generalization; and it again lands for renewed observation rendered acute by rational interpretation."[6] Therefore, Thomas E. Hosinski insists that "Whitehead is not a rigid empiricist; because he includes the roles of the imagination and reason as well as experience in his theory of knowledge, he might be called a rational empiricist."[7]

This definition includes the elements that are required of a proper speculative philosophy: coherence, logic, applicability, and being adequate. It has, on the other hand, close connection with his criticism of "sensationalist principle," which uncritically succeeded the philosophy of Hume. Whitehead believes that human experience is broader than the one insisted on by the sensational empiricism. He thus claims, "The sensationalist principle is, that the primary activity in the act of experience is the bare subjective entertainment of the datum, devoid of any subjective form of reception."[8] In addition, he criticizes the subjective principle in his careful analysis on modern philosophy from Descartes to Kant. For him, "The subjective principle is, that the datum in the act of experience can be adequately analyzed purely in terms of universals."[9] In particular, the subjective misconception was introduced to the modern philosophy by Descartes' substance theory.[10] Insisting that the demerit of the entire philosophical systems is originated from the subjective misconception, Whitehead points out three premises that are to be overcome: "(i) The acceptance of the 'substance-quality' concept as expressing the ultimate ontological principle. (ii) The acceptance of Aristotle's definition of a primary substance, as always a subject and never a predicate. (iii) The assumption that the experient subject is a primary substance."[11]

Whitehead's philosophy of organism denied both the doctrines of sensationalist principle and subjective principle. The goal of his philosophy is to organize a scheme through which all human experience can be interpreted. Unlike the concept of experience in English empiricism in the eighteenth century, his concept of experience is that of the actual entity. Thus the actual entities are "the final real things" and "the drops of experiences."[12] These actual entities are interdependent and interrelated. The world is not comprised of subjective ideas; it is comprised of real existing moments, like drops of experience, that are related to both one another and being as a whole.

In this respect, all existing beings, which influence and feel one another, are not only an entire dynamic unity but also a living organism. They are in process because they are alive. They are in process and becoming. "Thus nature is a structure of evolving processes. The reality is the process."[13] The theory that matter has simple location in space and time, which is "the foundation of the seventeenth century scheme of nature," is regarded as the error of "the Fallacy of Misplaced Concreteness."[14] Therefore, Whitehead's philosophy, which has been explored as a new alternative to traditional Western philosophy, is appropriately called "the process philosophy" or "the philosophy of organism." Whitehead summarizes this view by saying, "The concrete fact, which is the organism, must be a complete expression of the character of a real occurrence."[15] "Thus, concrete fact is process. Its primary analysis is into underlying activity of prehension, and into realized prehensive events."[16] He goes on to say, "The primary character of this process is that it is individual to the actual entity; it expresses how the datum, which involves the actual world, becomes a component in the one actual entity."[17]

Biographical Sketch of Alfred North Whitehead

Alfred North Whitehead (1861-1947) is called "one of the most profound and important philosophical minds of the twentieth century."[18] He was actively engaged in various fields of science for his entire life. He contributed to the development of mathematics, philosophy of science, and process thoughts in religion and theology. Due to certain periods of his academic activities, his entire life is usually divided into three periods. Lucien Price, who recorded frequent dialogues with Whitehead, explains, "Whitehead's is a three-volume life; Volume I, Cambridge University; Volume II, London; Volume III, Cambridge, Massachusetts. He also said that he had a sense of having lived three lives of successive epochs; the first, from 1861 to 1914; the second, during the war of 1914-1918; and the third, after that first war."[19]

Alfred North Whitehead was born in Ramsgate, Kent, in England, on February 6, 1861. He died in Cambridge, Massachusetts, in the United States, on December 30, 1947 at the age of eighty-six. He grew up in a Victorian middle class family and was influenced by his grandfather and father, who were involved in education and religion as teachers and clergymen. At the age of fourteen, Whitehead entered the Sherborne School, an ancient school founded by St. Aldhelm. There he studied Greek, Latin, and the classics as well as mathematics, to which he decided to dedicate his life.

In 1880, Whitehead entered Trinity College in Cambridge. Here, he became aware of politics, religion, philosophy, and literature. He was also a member of a free discussion group named "The Apostles," which influenced the development of his study. "It was this 'civilizing self-education' of undergraduates through informal conversation and discussion which was one of the best aspects of the university life in England."[20]

In 1885 Whitehead began to work as a Fellow of Trinity College. He then married Evelyn W. Wade who influenced Whitehead with her "vivid life." Whitehead confessed that throughout his married life he had "a great sense that he was fully alive and participating in the real world."[21] He also experienced an extraordinary deepening and strengthening of his mathematical career. As a result of that, he published his writing entitled *Principia Mathematica* in 1910 through 1913 with his co-author Bertrand Russell.

In 1910 Whitehead left Cambridge and moved to the University of London, where he began his new professorship. He became engaged actively in writing, teaching, and administration. Before his retirement, he also worked as President of the Senate at the University of London. During World War I one of his sons, Eric, was killed as a pilot in air combat in 1918. Whitehead experienced a great feeling of loss and dedicated one of his books to his lost son. As Russell points out, "The pain of this loss had a great deal to do with turning his thought to philosophy and with causing him to seek ways of escaping from belief in a merely mechanistic universe."[22] In this period at London, Whitehead published three important books about mathematics, logic, and physics: *An Enquiry Concerning the Principle of Natural Knowledge* (1919); *The Concept of Nature* (1920); and *The Principle of Relativity, with Applications of Physical Science* (1922).

In 1924, while he was preparing for retirement from the University of London, Whitehead accepted an invitation from Harvard University in the United States to work on the philosophy faculty. He moved to Cambridge in the United States and began to exercise his remarkable talent on philosophy. "At the age of sixty-three, Alfred North Whitehead, in a new land, begins a new life and by far, the most brilliant and productive part of his career."[23] Whitehead completed his new philosophy of organism at Harvard. He taught at Harvard from 1924 until his retirement in 1934.[24] During this period, he worked diligently to refine his philosophical thoughts. He then published seven important works: *Science and the Modern World* (1925); *Religion in the Making* (1926); *Symbolism: Its Meaning and Effect* (1927); *Process and Reality: An Essay in Cosmology* (1929); *The Function of Reason* (1929); *Adventures of Ideas* (1933); and *Modes of Thought* (1938). As noted above, Whitehead died in Cambridge, Massachusetts, in the United States, on December 30, 1947.

Whitehead's Process Cosmology

Quite contrary to the static worldview of traditional Western philosophy, Whitehead holds that the world must be understood in terms of the processes of change and becoming. The world is neither an unchanging substance nor a machinery part; it is instead dynamically and creatively alive and changing. The world is in the continuous process of becoming. Like a living organism, the world is always moving in creative advance, which is also called process. All actual entities in the world change and become new, persistently influencing one another. Whitehead describes this process of the world, making analogy to Hegelian philosophy:

> The universe is at once the multiplicity of *res verae* and the solidarity of *res verae*. The solidarity is itself the efficiency of the macroscopic *res vera*, embodying the principle of unbounded permanence acquiring novelty through flux. The multiplicity is composed of microscopic *res verae*, each embodying the principle of bounded flux acquiring 'everlasting' permanence. On one side, the one becomes many; and on the other side, the many become one. But *what* becomes is always a *res vera*, and the concrescence of a *res vera* is the development of a subjective aim.[25]

This constitutes a unique worldview of Whitehead's process metaphysics. Whitehead thus makes clear that, "This is the doctrine that the creative advance of the world is the becoming, the perishing, and the objective immortalities of those things which jointly constitute *stubborn fact*."[26] This unique worldview, which is also called 'process cosmology', has fundamental impact on the life of religion. Whitehead says, "The theme of Cosmology, which is the basis of all religions, is the story of the dynamic effort of the World passing into everlasting unity, and of the static majesty of God's vision, accomplishing its purpose of completion by absorption of the World's multiplicity of effort."[27]

In order to have a proper understanding of this dynamic, changing, and becoming world, we shall first discuss two important terms: actual entities and eternal objects. According to Whitehead, "the fundamental types of entities are eternal objects and actual entities. The other types of entities only express how all entities of two fundamental types are in community with each other in the actual world."[28] It is the case that "actual entities or actual occasions are the most primitive and basic units of actuality."[29] For him, the universe is entirely comprised of actual entities. However, actual entities are not static beings but dynamic and interactive beings in the process of becoming. So, the actual entity should be understood as a process or event. "The constitution of an actual entity is a process of becoming."[30]

Eternal objects, on the other hand, are relational elements for an actual entity to exist in the process of becoming. Eternal objects are the elements that express how one actual entity is related to other actual entities. For Whitehead, these two concepts depend on each other and interact together in the process of becoming. Furthermore, all actualities of the world are fundamentally interdependent. Due to this interdependence, his philosophy is called "the philosophy of organism," which is the basis of the process cosmology. As Thomas Hosinski appropriately points out, "Whitehead was convinced that actual entities and the universe as a whole are more like organisms than like machines."[31]

Furthermore, an actual entity has meaningful relationships with other actual entities by prehending the actual world and making it the datum into its internal elements. In other words, actual entities involve each other by prehending each other. In Whitehead's process cosmology, the actual world is a creative process which means the becoming of actual entities. This creative process has a rhythm: "the process of attaining actuality, of becoming, passes into process of transition from attained actuality to another in attainment."[32] In order to show this creative process of the actual world, Whitehead suggests his new terms such as "prehension," "concrescence," "the primordial nature and consequent nature of God," and "creativity." Whitehead, in particular, deals with the concept of God extensively in new ways in order to explain the fundamental structure of the world. Above all, God is considered to be a fundamental element in Whitehead's understanding of the universe. Therefore, Marjorie Suchocki summarizes a Whiteheadian cosmology as follows:

An actual entity comes into existence through the force of its past, a directive force from God, and its own emergent decision. It internalizes that which it experiences from others (both God and the world), and having done so it becomes an influence partially determining what its successors can be. Whitehead's way of summarizing this process was to say that "the many become one, and are increased by one." The many influences of the past evoke the becoming of the present, entering into that becoming. But the newly becoming entity unifies those influences, becoming a new "one" in the world of process.[33]

The basic scheme of Whitehead's process metaphysics and cosmology is presented in his most outstanding writing, *Process and Reality*. Whitehead explores his metaphysics in this book, placing emphasis on his eight categories of existence: actual entities, prehension, nexus, subjective forms, eternal objects, propositions, multiplicities, and contrast. Among these eight categories, I find four categories most fundamental: actual entities, eternal objects, prehension and concrescence, and God. These shall be discussed in the following.

Actual Entity: The Final Real Thing in Nature

The "actual entity" is the fundamental concept on which Whitehead's philosophy of organism is based. It is also one of the most important metaphysical categories on which his process cosmology is based. "The term actual entity in the primary sense, signifies the general metaphysical category of that which is."[34] Whitehead defines actual entity as follows:

> 'Actual entities'—also termed 'actual occasions'—are the final real things of which the world is made up. There is no going behind actual entities to find anything more real. They differ among themselves . . . . The final facts are, all alike, actual entities; and these actual entities are drops of existence, complex and interdependent.[35]

As indicated in the above passage, the actual entity is the most fundamental and primary reality of which nature is comprised. Actual entities or actual occasions are the concrete and basic elements of the world. For him, the universe is comprised entirely of actual entities. Like the atoms of Democritus, actual entities are microcosmic entities and form entities of our daily experience in the world. But the atoms of Democritus are inert, imperishable, and material stuff, while Whitehead's actual entities are vital, transient, complex, and interdependent things. This is why he termed actual entities as "drops of experience," which can be best understood as moments of experience.

The term "actual entity" enables Whitehead to present his ontological principle, which provides the ground for his process metaphysics. He said, "the actual world is built up of actual occasions (entities); and by the ontological principle whatever things there are in any sense of 'existence,' are derived by abstraction from actual occasions (entities)."[36] Here, the ontological principle for building Whitehead's metaphysical system is developed: "no actual entity, then no reason".[37] Since actual entities are the basic and ultimate reason of beings, they themselves will not perish, though their modes of existence are variable in an indefinite number of ways. In Whitehead's philosophical thought, however, actual entities are not the things created by God from nothingness. In other words, God is also an actual entity among other actual entities.

Whitehead uses his new concept of process rather than the traditional notion of substance. He rejected Descartes' concept of substance because they insist on a monism in which there is only one entity which is actual or existent in a full sense.[38] That is to say, criticizing Descartes as incoherent and inappropriate, he argues:

> In Modern philosophy Descartes' two kinds of substance, corporeal and mental, illustrate incoherence. There is, in Descartes' philosophy, no reason why there should not be a one-substance world, only corporeal, or a one-substance world, only mental. According to Descartes, a substantial individual requires nothing but itself in order to exist. Thus this system makes a virtue of its coherence. But, on the other hand, the facts seem connected, while Descartes' system does not.[39]

Instead, adopting pluralism, Whitehead maintains that the final facts are all actual entities. This is a formulation of the ontological principle on a pluralistic basis: there are many entities which are actual.[40]

However, all actual entities are generically of one kind. In other words, though there are gradations of importance, and diversities of function in principle, all actualities are on the same level.[41] This is a completely universal principle which applies to all actual entities whatsoever. Even God is not an exception. In other words, God is not treated as an exception to all metaphysical principles. "God is an actual entity, and so is the most trivial puff of existence in far-off empty space."[42] According to Whitehead's philosophy, God's existence is no different than that of other actual entities, except that God is primordial in a sense to be gradually explained.[43] In other words, God is one of the actual entities in the sense that he is consequent and really exists in the world.

Whitehead's term "actual entity" is similar to Leibniz's term "monad." However, there is a big difference between two terms. While Leibniz's monads are the windowless ones with their pre-established harmony, Whitehead's actual entities are the becoming realities which are open and accept other realities through process; they have dynamic movability and flexibility.[44] In other words, Whitehead's actual entities are dynamic and interactive things in the process of becoming. An actual entity is not a static thing but is always growing in the process of becoming. For him, being is becoming and becoming is being. Whitehead maintains that the actual entity is the "event in the more general sense of a nexus of actual occasions, inter-related in some determinate fashion in an extensive quantum."[45] That is, all actual entities exist in the nexus of organic systems. In this sense, his concept of the actual entity is also different from the Cartesian concept of substance as a thing that does not need anything except substance itself to exist as reality.[46] He certainly refuses the philosophical position of actual entity as the unchanging subject of change.

According to Whitehead, "the final facts are, all alike, actual entities; and these actual entities are drops of experience, complex and interdependent."[47] Actual entities are things which exist and are being experienced. As William Christian points out, "an actual entity is an experiencing subject and is constituted by its experience. Its experience is its real internal constitution."[48] According to Whitehead, an actual entity is called "subject-superject," which means more than the term "subject." He states,

> An actual entity is at once the subject experiencing and the superject of its experiences. It is subject-superject, and neither half of this description can for a moment be lost sight of. The term 'subject will be most employed when the actual entity is considered in respect to its own real internal constitution. But 'subject' is always to be construed as an abbreviation of 'subject-superject.'[49]

Actual entities are not framed and fixed things. They are referent to an external world. They have a vector character. That is to say, they involve emotion, purpose, valuation, and causation. Thus, the characteristics of an actual entity are reproduced in prehension. Actual entities influence one another, prehend the anteceding actual entities, and become datum for the next actual entities. Whitehead says:

> Actual entities involve each by reason of their prehensions of each other. There are thus real individual facts of the togetherness of actual entities, which are real, individual, and particular, in the same sense in which actual entities and the prehensions are real, and particular. Any such particular fact of togetherness among actual entities is called a 'nexus' (plural form is written 'nexus'). The ultimate facts of immediate actual experience are actual entities, prehensions, and nexus. All else is, for our experience, derivative abstraction.[50]

It is in this process that complex and interdependent experiences of actual entities take place. The process is the basic characteristic of actual entities. Hence, his thought is also called "process philosophy". Since actual entities are dependent on process, actual entities are in the process and the process determines the characteristics of actual entities. A new actual entity appears by the process of feeling, prehehending, and determining the given datum.[51] Whitehead clearly refutes the substantial view in which a fixed and unchangeable reality supports the phenomenal world. He emphasizes the process constituted by a stream of reality.

However, the process itself is not an actual entity. It does not mean the perpetual continuity but the atomic event which is understood as a non-temporal drop of experience. In this sense, the metaphysical characteristic of the actual entity is not perpetual immortality but the repeating process, which means a continuous temporal process. This kind of view can be explained in two species of process: macroscopic process and microscopic process or transition and concrescence. Whitehead writes:

> The macroscopic process is the transition from attained actuality to actuality in attainment; while the microscopic process is the conversion of conditions which are merely real into determinate actuality. The former process effects the transition from the actual to the merely real; and the latter process effects the growth from the real to the actual. The former process is efficient; the latter process is teleological. The future is merely real, without being actual; whereas the past is a nexus of actualities. The actualities are constituted by their real genetic phase.[52]

Each actual entity is related internally and externally to all other members of a society because of the characteristics of the process. It then makes its own microcosm that constitutes the whole universe. While each actual entity exists as a microcosm by opening itself to the macrocosm, it also participates in the constitution of the macrocosm by realizing values. Through this organismic process, all elements which are comprised of the macrocosm become constituents which are comprised of new actual entities. Of course, this process is not repeating the past. Instead, it is creating a novelty in every occasion, that is, creating a process. Whitehead writes:

> Each actual entity is itself only describable as an organic process. It repeats in microcosm what the universe is in macrocosm. It is a process proceeding from phase to phase, each phase being the real basis from which its successor proceeds towards the completion the thing in question. Each actual entity bears in its constitution the reasons why its conditions are what they are. These 'reasons' are the other actual entities objectified for it.[53]

According to Whitehead, in the process of concrescence and transition, actual entities constitute themselves in relationships with others through experience.[54] An actual entity is the acting and experiencing being. Each actual entity is a process of activity.[55] Activity means experiencing, receiving, and including other entities. This view is related to the process of becoming, which means the process of experiencing in this sense. By way of concrescence, this process of becoming is the process of acting, which receives and transforms other objects into a definite unity. This can be explained by the transforming of "many" into "one" in the process of concrescence. Whitehead writes: "Concrescence is the name for the process in which the universe of many things acquires an individual unity in a determinate relegation of each item of the 'many' to its subordination in the constitution of the novel one."[56] This shows well the dynamic relationship of an actual entity with other entities. In this sense, we can say that an actual entity is an individual entity in the process of concrescence in which many become one and one becomes many. Therefore, an actual entity always exists in the interrelationship with other objects in the process of becoming.

Eternal Object: The Form of Definiteness

"Eternal object" is also one of the crucial terms in the structure of Whitehead's process cosmology. Whitehead defines an eternal object in the following way: "Any entity whose conceptual recognition does not involve a necessary reference to any definite actual entities of the temporal world is called an eternal object."[57] William Christian states: "Eternal objects are pure potentials. They are in fundamental contrast with actual entities. In themselves they do not determine in what actual entities they are ingredient . . . . They are merely possible forms of definiteness."[58]

According to Whitehead, an actual entity is created by the process which is understood as prehension, feeling, identification and objectification. An eternal object should give to an actual entity a particular mode of becoming. This is the role of the eternal object. In other words, eternal objects are forms of definiteness capable of specifying the character of actual entities. They are potentials for the specific determination of fact.[59] Whitehead writes:

> That an eternal object can be described only in terms of its potentiality for ingression into the becoming of actual entities; and that its analysis only discloses other eternal objects. It is a pure potential. The term ingression refers to the particular mode in which the potentiality of an eternal object is realized in a particular actual entity, contributing to the definiteness of that actual entity.[60]

In other words, an actual entity's process of becoming is a process of acquiring definiteness by decisions to select or reject various forms of definiteness based on an eternal object. How is this possible? How does an eternal object determine the subjective form of an actual entity? Here, Whitehead emphasizes the interrelationship between an eternal object and an actual entity. It is the actual entity that selects and prehends an eternal object, because an eternal object is always a potentiality for actual entities. Accordingly, an eternal object functions as a determinant of the datum and as a determinant of a subjective form for an actual entity. In other words, an eternal object ingresses through its function of objectifying the actual world.[61] In this manner, an eternal object has an interrelationship with an actual entity. An actual entity cannot be an individual and concrete fact without an eternal object, while an eternal object without an actual entity remains a potentiality. Whitehead states:

> The actualities constituting the process of the world are conceived as exemplifying the ingression (or participation) of other things which constitute the potentialities of definiteness for any actual existence. The things which are temporal arise by their participation in the things which are eternal.[62]

On the other hand, William Christian clarifies the concept of "eternal object" in the following way: "eternal objects can be such things as colors (e.g., red or blue), emotional qualities (e.g., anger, or love), mathematical forms (e.g., triplicity), relationships (e.g., before, or greater), grades of generic abstraction (e.g., redness, or color), and the abstract essence of an actual entity. In fact, every constituent of an actual entity is capable of being analyzed as the exemplification of an eternal object."[63]

Whitehead's theory of eternal object sounds Platonic, because an eternal object as a form of definiteness is similar to the Platonic forms. Whitehead thus notes:

> We admit that in some sense or other, we inevitably presuppose this realm of forms, in abstraction from passage, loss, and gain. For example, the multiplication table up to 'twelve-times-twelve' is a humble member of it. In all our thoughts of what has happened and can happen, we presuppose the multiplication table as essentially qualifying the course of history, whenever it is relevant. It is always at hand, and there is no escape.[64]

These forms of definiteness are the Platonic forms, the Platonic ideas, and the medieval universals. However, since Whitehead's conception of them is different from those forms, he suggests the new term "eternal object."[65]

The being of actual entities is constituted by their process of becoming, acting, and changing. Unlike actual entities, however, forms are not novel creations. That is to say, their being does not consist in a process of becoming. Becoming, process, and transition are irrelevant to the nature of forms. In this regard, Whitehead says that they are "eternal." However, their being involves process, because they are the determinants of the definiteness of the process of becoming actual entities. Although they themselves are not new creatures, they come into existence in the sense of informing the actualities in the process of becoming. Whitehead uses the term "ingression" for this.[66]

It is important not to confuse an eternal object with the Platonic idea. It can be misunderstood that ingression of the forms means that they are antecedent to the actualities of actual entities. We cannot say that forms are antecedent in time by virtue of their eternity. "By the ontological principle, the antecedence cannot consist in the forms themselves being actualities, existing in some kind of Platonic 'world of forms.' Instead, they exist only as ingredients in actual entities."[67] Accordingly, an eternal object exists in the process of becoming. This is the difference between them and Platonic ideas. Here, it should be noted that there is nothing in their nature to determine which actuality they will have ingression into. In other words, in themselves they are neutral as to the particular actual entities into which they have ingression. Their natures are given, timeless, and eternal. Whitehead calls them "eternal objects," because they are given as objects to the actualities and they are eternal in their nature. He combines two words.[68]

It is also necessary to understand the concept of "eternal object" with regard to the concept "of actual entity." As we have indicated above, an eternal object, which is understood as pure potential or form of definiteness, consists of polarity of beings along with actual entities. It does not exist as reality on its own, but as a part of inner constituents in actual entities. While an actual entity can be called 'event' as a fundamental unit, an eternal object can be called 'form' or 'universal' as an unchanging occasion. Whitehead presented his philosophical argument about this issue in one of his early writings entitled *The Concept of Nature*.

> You cannot recognize an event; because when it is gone, it is gone. You may observe another event of analogous character, but the actual chunk of the life of nature is inseparable from its unique occurrence. But a character of an event can be recognized. We all know that if we go to the Embankment near Charing Cross we shall observe an event having the character which we recognize as Cleopatra's Needle. Things which we thus recognise I call objects. An object is situated in those events or in that stream of events of which it expresses the character. There are many sorts of objects. For example, the colour green is an object according to the above definition.[69]

As indicated in the quoted statements above, "event" has different quality from "object." According to Whitehead, an object is possible, abstract, and unchanging in nature, whereas an event is concrete and actual. Objects become real in events. The relationship between objects and events is well applied to the relationship between eternal objects and actual entities.

Prehension: Actual Entities' Process of Appropriation

The term "prehension" is a newly coined term in Whitehead's metaphysics by which other important terms such as "actual entity," "eternal object," and "God" can be rightly understood. In brief, "prehension" means a process by which varieties of data are appropriated into a unifying being. It is a method through which an actual entity becomes a subject of experience. An actual entity comes to enjoy itself as an individual through the process of prehension. In other words, prehension is a seizing and grasping process through which an actual entity appropriates other things. It describes appropriately the movement of all actual things in the universe. Whitehead thus notes, "To be actual must mean that all actual things are alike objects, enjoying objective immortality in fashioning creative actions; and that all actual things are subjects, each prehending the universe from which it arises."[70]

According to Whitehead, the term "prehension" comes from "apprehension" or "comprehend." It literally means "to grasp," "to seize," and "to take." Whitehead wants to descriptively avoid using the words "apprehension" or "comprehension" because they usually refer to experiences occurred already in human consciousness. He is also not satisfied with other traditional terms such as "awareness" or "perception." He wants to use more general and neutral terms which fit with his new metaphysical scheme. Thus, he describes:

> Leibniz can find no other connectedness between reals except that lying wholly within the individual experiences of the monads . . . He had employed the terms 'perception' and 'apperception' for lower and higher ways in which one monad can take account of another, namely for ways of awareness. But these terms are too closely allied to the notion of consciousness which in my doctrine is not a necessary accompaniment. Also they are all entangled in the notion of representative perception which I reject. But there is the term 'apprehension' with the meaning of 'thorough understanding.' Accordingly, on the Leibnizian model, I use the term 'prehension' for the general way in which the occasion of experience can include, as part of its own essence, any other entity, whether another occasion of experience or an entity of another type.[71]

He is, of course, cautious to use a new term because he wants to overcome the dualistic problem of the western philosophy. He claims,

> The perceptive constitution of the actual entity presents the problem, How can the other actual entities, each with its own formal existence, also enter objectively into the perspective constitution of the actual entity in question? This is the problem of the solidarity of the universe. The classical doctrines of universals and particulars, of subject and predicate, of individual substances not present in other individual substances, of the eternality of relations, alike render this problem in capable of solution, the answer given by the organic philosophy is the doctrine of prehension, involved in concrescent integrations, and terminating in a definite, complex unity of feeling.[72]

In another place, Whitehead insists, "I have adopted the term 'prehension,' to express the activity whereby an actual entity effects its own concretion of other thing."[73] That is to say, "prehension" is the term that effectively expresses the general process by which many things in the universe become one actual entity. To cite Ivor Leclerc's explanation: "For the generic activity constituting an actual entity is an act of 'grasping,' of 'appropriating' other entities so as to be the components of its concrescence."[74]

For Whitehead, on the other hand, prehension means that a subject feels an object and evaluates its meaning with regard to the future. In other words, a subject must be related to an object before taking and understanding it. This relatedness is more important than a subject's act of apprehension. In this respect,

Whitehead defines prehension as "concrete fact of relatedness."[75] The nature of prehension is well understood only by its relatedness. Whitehead argues: "Every prehension consists of three factors: (a) the 'subject' which is comprehending, namely, the actual entity in which that prehension is a concrete element; (b) the 'datum' which is prehended; (c) the 'subjective form' which is how that subject prehends that datum."[76] The subject, the datum, and the subject form are interrelated. Prehension happens through those three interrelated elements. Robert B. Mellert also explains the relational character of prehension in the following way:

> A child is related to his parents differently from the way in which his parents are related to him. Whereas parents are only externally influenced by their children, a child's very existence, his genetic inheritance, and parental influences during early childhood all help to determine how he is to mature and grow. He "takes" from his parents his very reality as an individual person. An emerging entities is similarly related to eternal object and past actual entities in that these are the elements out of which the new entity is to become. Prehension, therefore, also indicates that the relatedness of these elements to the emerging actual entity is determinative because the relatedness constitutes the entire data available to that entity in its process of becoming . . . . the relation of the things prehended to the subject prehending determines what that subject will become.[77]

Whitehead further gives us a more exact explanation of prehension by dividing it into two prehensions: "positive prehension" and "negative prehension." According to William Christian, "positive prehension includes its datum as part of the synthesis of the subject occasion, but negative prehensions exclude their data from the synthesis."[78] Whitehead clearly defined two kinds of prehensions:

> There are two species of prehensions, the 'positive species' and the 'negative species.' An actual entity has a perfectly definite bond with each item in the universe. This determinate bond is its prehension of that item. A negative prehension is the definite exclusion of that item from positive contribution to the subject's own real internal constitution. This doctrine involves the position that a negative prehension expresses a bond. A positive prehension is the definite inclusion of that item into positive contribution to the subject's own real internal constitution. This positive inclusion is called its 'feeling' of that item.[79]

First, positive prehension means that the actual entity as the subject clearly prehends the items in the universe in order that they can engage as the objective data in the internal structure of beings. Whitehead calls this "the feeling of the subject." For him, the word "feeling" is used synonymously with "prehension." Whitehead expresses the process of internal constitution of an actual entity in terms of "prehension" or "feeling." This shows us that he applies the category of "feeling" or "prehension" which belongs to human experience to all things in the nature. In other words, in Whitehead's process cosmology, all actual entities, from unperceivable atoms and electrons to the macro cosmos, are social realities that are related to each other, feelings of feelings, and societies of societies.[80]

The word "feeling" sounds like "experience" occurring in the level of sensation. But it has a different meaning. Whitehead explains "feeling" as follows:

> This word 'feeling' is a mere technical term; but it has been chosen to suggest that functioning through which the concrescent actuality appropriates the datum so as to make it its own.[81]

> Each actual entity is conceived as an act of experience arising out of data. It is a process of 'feeling' the many data, so as to absorb them into the unity of one individual 'satisfaction.' Here 'feeling' is the term used for the basic operation of passing from the objectivity of the data to the subjectivity of the actual entity in question. Feelings are variously specialized operations, effecting a transition into subjectivity.[82]

The subject of feeling receives the datum from the actual entity and whereby those data are transgressed and objectified, feeling arises and a new actual entity is concrescent. That is to say, an actual entity as the subject is created as a new being through those feelings. According to Whitehead, the process of feeling has complex structure. He insists:

> A feeling-i.e., a positive prehension-is essentially a transition effecting a concrescence. Its complex constitution is analyzable into five factors which express what transition consists of, and effects. The factors are: (i) the 'subject' which feels, (ii) the 'initial data' which are to be felt, (iii) the 'elimination' in virtue of negative prehensions, (iv) 'the 'objective datum' which is felt, (v) the 'subjective form' which is how that subject feels that objective datum.[83]

Feeling cannot be abstracted from the actual entity that embraces it. This actual entity is called the "subject." The subject of the feeling is an actual entity which entertains the feeling. Feeling is an aspect of the subject which is an individual actual entity. Whitehead here uses his new term "superject" because the term "subject" might be misleading. The positive prehension is clearly argued with this new term. Thus, he explains:

> The 'subject-superject' is the purpose of the process originating the feelings. The feelings are inseparable from the end at which they aim; and this end is the feeler. The feelings aim at the feeler, as their final cause. The feelings are what they are in order that their subject may be what it is. Then transcendently, since the subject is what it is in virtue of its feelings, it is only by means of its feelings that the subject objectively conditions the creativity transcendent beyond itself.[84]

The new term "superject" is also related to the scheme of his metaphysics. In an earlier page, he mentioned, "An actual entity is to be conceived both as a subject presiding over its own immediacy of becoming, and a superject which is the atomic creature exercising its function of objective immortality. It has become a 'being'; and it belongs to the nature of every 'being' that it is a potential for every 'becoming.'"[85]

How does "the initial data" become "the objective datum" through the process of feeling? According to Whitehead, the initial data means the actual entities which exist as the elements of the actual world before they are objectified. The initial data are objectified only through the "perspective," i.e., the medium, which is called "the objective datum." And the data left after the process of negative prehension are objectified and involved in the structure of the subject of feeling. He states:

> A feeling is the appropriation of some elements in the universe to be components in the real internal constitution of its subject. The elements are the initial data; they are what the feeling feels. But they are felt under an abstraction. The process of the feeling involves negative prehensions which effect elimination. Thus the initial data are felt under a 'perspective' which is the objective datum.[86]

Whitehead also talks about the "subjective form," which defines how the subject feels the objective datum. He maintains,

> The essential novelty of a feeling attaches to its subjective form. The initial data, and even the nexus which is the objective datum, may have served other feelings with other subjects. But the subjective form is the immediate novelty; it is how that subject is feeling that objective datum. There is no tearing this subjective from the novelty of this concrescence.[87]

Therefore, the subject form always involves the novelty of the feelings with regard to its data. Although the subject form of the feeling has relationships with reproduction of the data, it is not completely determined by the data. And all the feelings are the feelings toward the subject, so they must be felt with the subject form. In other words, the subjective form controls the progressive integration of feelings. According to Whitehead, "thus the subjective form embodies the pragmatic aspect of the feeling; for the datum is felt with that subject form in order that the subject may be the superject which it is."[88] Furthermore, an actual entity becomes the subject-superject through the subjective form. He goes on to say, "In the analysis of a feeling, whatever presents itself as also *ante rem* is a datum, whatever presents itself as exclusively in *re* is subjective form, whatever presents itself *in re* and *post rem* is 'subject-superject.' This doctrine of 'feeling' is the central doctrine respecting the becoming of an actual entity."[89]

Secondly, there is another kind of prehension: "a negative prehension." It usually means "an exclusion from feeling." In other words, "a negative prehension" is a definite act of exclusion from contribution. The subjective form of a negative prehension makes the data unable to be involved in the concrescence of the subject; it has an excluding character from the feeling. A negative prehension only presents such a subjective form that contributes the forming of new integrative prehensions. Thus, the negative prehension has its own meaning. It expresses a bond in the universe. Whitehead explains:

> The importance of negative prehensions arises from the fact, that (i) actual entities form a system, in the sense of entering into each other's constitutions, (ii) that by the ontological principle every entity is felt by some actual entity, (iii) that, as a consequence of (i) and (ii), every entity in the actual world of a concrescent actuality has some gradation of real relevance to that concrescence, (iv) that, in consequence of (iii), the negative prehension of an entity is a positive fact with its emotional subjective form, (v) there is a mutual sensitivity of the subjective forms of prehensions, so that they are not indifferent to each other, (vi) the concrescence issues in one concrete feeling, the satisfaction.[90]

A negative prehension has its own subjective form that contributes to the becoming of an actual entity. That is to say, "A negative prehension holds its datum as inoperative in the progressive concrescence of prehension constituting the unity of the subject."[91] In sum, both prehensions constitute an actual entity which has a definite bond with all items in the universe. "This determinate bond is its prehension of that item."[92] Both prehensions express a bond. Furthermore, they express the process of becoming actual entities in the universe. As he concludes, "All actual entities in the actual world, relatively to a given actual entity as 'subject,' are necessarily 'felt' by that subject, though in general vaguely. An actual entity as felt is said to be 'objectified' for that subject. Only a selection of eternal objects are 'felt' by a given subject, and these eternal objects are then said to have 'ingression' in that subject."[93]

Concrescence: A Creative Process of Becoming Actual Entities

As we have discussed above, an actual entity gains meaningful relationships with other actual entities by prehending the actual world and creating it as the datum into its internal elements. In other words, actual entities involve one another other by reason of their prehensions of one another. In Whitehead's process cosmology, the actual world is a creative process, which means "the becoming of actual entities." This creative process has a rhythm: "The process of attaining actuality, of becoming, passes into the process of transition from attained actuality to another in attainment."[94] In regard to this creative process of becoming, we need to pay attention to another concept called "concrescence," which was coined by Whitehead. He explains:

> The word concrescence is a derivative from the familiar Latin verb, meaning 'growing together'. It also has the advantage that the participle 'concrete' is familiarly used for the notion of complete physical reality. Thus Concrescence

is useful to convey the notion of the individual character arising in the concrescence of the aboriginal data.[95]

For Whitehead, the universe consists not of macro realities but of micro realities which are called "actual entities." Actual entities are not only self-centered atomic beings but also the beings of the subjective aim which is toward the satisfaction of the completed subject.[96] This also means that the world consists not of non-temporal entities but of their process of forming and persistence. It indicates to us that the traditional way of looking for the ground of being in substance must be changed into a new way of looking for the ground of being in the concrescent nature of actual entities. Here we come to his new term "concrescence" which means the process by which many things get an objectified unity as many things become subject to the structure of a new one. Thus Whitehead holds, "'Concrescence' is the name for the process in which the universe of many things acquires an individual unity in a determinate relegation of each item of the 'many' to its subordination in the constitution of the novel 'one.'"[97] It seems certain that Whitehead "uses the word 'concrescence' to signify this process of becoming which constitutes the new actual entity."[98]

In other words, "The many become one, and are increased by one. In their natures, entities are disjunctively 'many' in process of passage into conjunctive unity. . . . Thus the 'production of novel togetherness' is the ultimate notion embodied in the term 'concrescence.'"[99] Namely, an actual entity comes out of the many and the unified one becomes into the other many. We can say that an actual entity is the result of the concrescence of the antecedents and continues to be concrescented as the successor. Actual entities arise from a primary phase of the concrescence of objectifications which are settled in some respect.

Whitehead adds his further explanations by mentioning two kinds of fluency in this fluent world:

> One kind is the fluency inherent in the constitution of the particular existent. This kind I have called 'concrescence.' The other kind is the fluency whereby the perishing of the process, on the completion of the particular existent, constitutes that existent as an original element in the constitutions of other particular existents elicited by repetitions of process. This kind I have called 'transition.' Concrescence moves towards its final cause, which is its subjective aim; transition is the vehicle of the efficient cause, which is the immortal past.[100]

As shown in above passage, concrescence is a kind of entering point for concrete unity of actual entities. Those actual entities that are completed through the process of concrescence are not succeeded as the data for new concrescence but related to one another in a sense of cosmological solidarity. This is the process of becoming of the world. Whitehead thus said, "There is a rhythm of process whereby creation produces natural pulsation, each pulsation forming a natural unit of historic fact. In this way, amid the infinitude of the connected universe, we can discern vaguely finite units of fact."[101]

Whitehead explains the character of actual entities in the process of transition by presenting several steps:

> The four-stage constitutive of an actual entity . . . . can be named, datum, process, satisfaction, decision. The two terminal stages have to do with 'becoming' in the sense of the transition from the settled actual world to the new actual entity relatively to which that settlement is defined. . . . The 'settlement' which an actual entity 'finds' is its datum. It is to be conceived as a limited perspective of the 'settled' world provided by the eternal objects concerned. The datum is 'decided' by the settled world. It is 'prehended' by the new superseding entity. The datum is the objective content of the experience. The decision, providing the datum, is a transference of self-limited appetition; the settled world provides the 'real potentiality' that its many actualities be felt compatibly; and the new concrescence starts from this datum. The perspective is provided by the elimination of incompatibilities. The final stage, the decision,' is how the actual entity, having attained its individual 'satisfaction,' thereby adds a determinate condition to the settlement for the future beyond itself. Thus the 'datum' is the 'decision received,' and the 'decision' is the 'decision transmitted.' Between these two decisions, received and transmitted, there lie the two stages, 'process' and 'satisfaction.' The datum is indeterminate as regards the final satisfaction. The 'process' is the addition of those elements of feeling whereby these indeterminations are dissolved into determinate linkage attaining the actual unity of an individual actual entity.[102]

An actual entity, therefore, is always self-creating creation in the creative process. A new actual entity is becoming by taking the antecedent actual entity as the datum. An actual entity in the becoming means that the preceding data are growing as new units. Thus, Whitehead used the word "concrescence" to explicate the constitutive process that a new actual entity is becoming.

Concrescence works towards the final end called "satisfaction" which merges scattered constituents as the datum into actual togetherness. In Whitehead's words, "The production of novel togetherness is the ultimate notion embodied in the term 'concrescence.' "[103] The process of concrescence results in attainment of a final satisfaction. Here, creativity as an incessant process begins concrescence of a new actual entity by offering an actual entity of a final satisfaction as a datum for the concrescence of other actual entities. In other words, "In a process of concrescence, there is a succession of phases in which new prehensions arises by integration of prehensions in antecedent phases."[104] Satisfaction, the completion of actual entities, directly perishes but attains "objective immortality" by remaining as the elements of succeeding actual entities. An actual entity which loses its real immediacy becomes a real constituent for becoming of other actual entities and attains "objective immortality." He said, "Actuality in perishing acquires objectivity, while it loses subjective immediacy. It loses the final causation, which is its internal principle of unrest, and it acquires efficient causation whereby it is a ground of obligation characterizing the creativity."[105]

God and the World: A Panentheistic Approach

The concept of God is one of the large cornerstones on which Whitehead's metaphysics is based. For Whitehead, the concept of God is essential to explaining the fundamental structure of the world.[106] As Hosinski points out, "God is a necessary element in Whitehead's understanding of the universe and there is an important sense in which God can be called 'creator' of all entities."[107] Whitehead was also aware of the importance of this issue by claiming, "Today there is but one religious dogma in debate: What do you mean by "God"? And in this respect, today is like all its yesterdays. This is the fundamental religious dogma, and all other dogmas are subsidiary to it."[108] John Berthrong also states: "The concept of God becomes important for Whitehead not as a religious issue or faith crisis but as a problem in philosophic speculation."[109] Thus, in his main writings, "Whitehead dealt extensively with God as an indispensable part of his metaphysical system, as that without which there would be no order or novelty and, hence, no world."[110] The concept of God, in this regard, is the final one that completes his process cosmology and functions as a basis of his process metaphysics. His ultimate concern in the religious and metaphysical explorations is concentrated on the understanding of God.[111] In other words, he has attempted to formulate unique ideas of God which fit with his metaphysical scheme.

Whitehead's concept of God, of course, is quite different from traditional Christian concepts of God because it is based on his unique process metaphysics and cosmology, which perceives the world not as a static concept of being but as a dynamic concept of becoming. According to Whitehead, "The modern world has lost God and is seeking him."[112] The reason for this is applied to the whole history of Christianity. That is to say that the history of Christianity (in particular the history of the doctrine of God) made modern people face the loss or death of God. More precisely, in *Process and Reality,* he criticizes the representative notions of God which were applied to Western Christianity: the notion of God as an aboriginal, eminently real, transcendent creator; the notion of God as an imperial ruler; the notion of God as a personification of moral energy; the notion of God as an ultimate philosophical principle.[113] He argues that those traditional concepts of God are far away from the Galilean origin of Christianity. He claims:

> The history of theistic philosophy exhibits various stages of combination of these diverse ways of entertaining the problem. There is, however, in the Gali-

lean origin of Christianity yet another suggestion which does not fit very well with any of the three main strands of thought. It does not emphasize the ruling Caesar, or the ruthless moralists, or unmoved mover. It dwells upon the tender elements in the world, which slowly and in quietness operated by love; and it finds purpose in the present immediacy of a kingdom not of this world.[114]

In *Religion in the Making,* Whitehead, on the other hand, presents his position of God, generally analyzing the concepts of God that appeared in the world religions. According to him, there are also three concepts of God in the world.

1. The Eastern Asiatic concept of an impersonal order to which the world conforms. This order is the self-ordering of the world; it is not the world obeying an imposed rule. The concept expresses the extreme doctrine of immanence. 2. The Semitic concept of a definite personal individual entity, whose existence is the one ultimate metaphysical fact, absolute and underivative, and who decreed and ordered the derivative existence which we call the actual world. . . . It expresses the extreme doctrine of transcendence. 3. The Pantheistic concept of an entity to be described in terms of Semitic concept, except that the actual world is a phase within the complete fact which is this ultimate individual entity. The actual world, conceived apart from God, is unreal. Its only reality is God's reality. The actual world has the reality of being a partial description of what God is. But in itself it is merely a certain mutuality of "appearance," which is a phase of the being of God. This is the extreme doctrine of monism.[115]

Whitehead attempts to harmonize the Semitic transcendental God and the Asiatic immanent God, and the monotheistic God and the pantheistic God.[116] This is why we call his ideas of God a 'panentheism.' According to his panentheism, this universe is considered to be an appearance which expresses an aspect of the being of God; God is immanent as the order giver and value creator in all processes of creation. God is included in all creatures. Hence, the world and all things exist together with and in the being of God. John Cobb clarified the meaning of Whitehead's panentheism, defining it as the doctrine that all is in God: "It is distinguished from pantheism, which identifies God with the totality or as the unity of the totality, for it holds that God's inclusion in the world does not exhaust the reality of God. Panentheism understands itself as a form of theism, but it criticizes traditional theism for depicting the world as external to God."[117]

God as an Actual Entity and the Principle of Concretion

In Whitehead's process metaphysics, it is an actual entity in the universe that really exists as a final reality and is the fundamental unit of all things. This universe is regarded as the organism that is comprised of all kinds of actual entities. All actual entities are open to one another and operate all together; they are momentary and relational realities. All actual entities themselves have subjective and objective, mental and physical dipolars; they also have function of active perception and passive datum.[118] According to Whitehead, God as a concrete being is also an actual entity. God is not an exception to all metaphysical principles. For him, God is not an abstract being who is considered an absolute, perfect being. Thus, like all other actual entities, God is also dipolar, mentally and physically, and relational, formative, and societal. God is an actual entity that seeks its satisfaction with its feeling and subjective aim.[119]

However, God is different from all other actual entities in the sense that God not only prehends all other actual entities and relates to them; but God functions as a formative element in all the processes of creation. For Whitehead, "God is the infinite ground of all mentality, the unity of vision seeking physical multiplicity."[120] That is to say, God is both a temporal and non-temporal reality.[121] This means that, although God is the same concrete reality as other actual entities, God is not the actual entity in birth and death. God is always with all the processes of becoming, change, and novelty of actual entities. But God is the actual entity as a mediator who includes all of actual entities and makes them possible.[122] Whitehead's concept of God is the same as for other actual entities, but God is a special sort of actual entity, i.e., God is an imperishable actuality, such that in the case of God the mental pole is prior to the physical pole. It is God who gives the initial aim to all concrescent moments in the world. It is God who offers the origin of actual entities' subjectivity. It is God who provides the lures for the individual actual entities to actualize.

> In this sense God is the principle of concretion; namely he is that actual entity from which each temporal concrescence receives that initial aim from which its self-causation starts. That aim determines the initial gradations of relevance of eternal objects for conceptual feeling; and constitutes the autonomous subject in its primary phase of feelings with its initial conceptual valuations, and with its initial physical purpose.[123]

Dipolarity of God

According to Whitehead, like other actual entities, the nature of God is analogically dipolar. God as an actual entity has two natures: primordial nature and consequent nature. He asserts:

> Thus, analogously to all actual entities, the nature of God is dipolar. He has a primordial nature and a consequent nature. The consequent nature of God is conscious; and it is the realization of the actual world in the unity of his nature, and through the transformation of his wisdom. The primordial nature is conceptual, the consequent nature is the weaving of God's physical feelings upon his primordial

concepts.[124]

Thus, his position on God is called "dipolar theism" as well. That is to say, just as all actual entities have both subjective and objective sides, both mental and physical sides, God also has both conceptual and physical natures. But this does not mean that God has dual realities. Rather, it means that God has two aspects of one actual entity. In other words, Whitehead presents two natures of God in order to offer an effective explanation of God's transcendence and subjective activity. As Whitehead explicitly notes: "The notion of God . . . . is that of an actual entity immanent in the actual world, but transcending any finite cosmic epoch-a being at once actual, eternal, immanent, and transcendent. The transcendence of God is not peculiar to him. Every actual entity, in virtue of its novelty, transcends its universe, God is included."[125]

For Whitehead, the primordial nature of God means a pure ideal or mental nature. In other words, God is "the unlimited conceptual realization of the absolute wealth of potentiality."[126] The consequent nature of God, on the other hand, means the objectification of the world in himself, in other words, the nature operating in the creation of the world. Regarding primordial nature, God is separate from the concrete reality in the world. Thus, according to Whitehead, the primordial nature of God has no feeling or consciousness of fullness, and is not influenced by the love, hatred, suffering, and pleasure of the world. In other words, the primordial nature of God is neither directly related to the facts of the world, nor restricted by any actualities. This explains the selfness, eternity, and transcendence of God.

The primordial nature of God, on the other hand, has the role of including, ordering, and classifying eternal objects as pure potentials, so that those eternal objects can be used as datum by other actual entities. This refers to the function of God as the principle of concretion. According to Whitehead, "God is the principle of concretion, namely, he is that actual entity from which each temporal concrescence receives that initial aim from which its self-causation starts."[127] God gives all actual entities comprised of the world their subjective aims. In this sense, God is considered to be an original ground that limits all creations of actual entities. Whitehead argues for this: "Each temporal entity, in one sense, originates from its mental pole, analogously to God himself. It derives from God its basic conceptual aim, relevant to its actual world, yet with indeterminations awaiting its own decisions."[128] He goes on to say, "God is the aboriginal instance of this creativity, and is therefore the aboriginal condition which qualifies its action. It is the function of actuality to characterize the creativity, and God is the eternal primordial character."[129]

According to John W. Lansing, the functions of the primordial nature of God can be summarized in three points. "First, it grades the eternal objects in terms of their relevance to one another. . . . Second, it grades the eternal objects in terms of their relevance for inclusion in particular actual occasions. . . . Third, the primordial nature of God makes this graded relevance effective in the world through providing the initial aim for each concrescent occasion."[130] In order words, initial aims are derived from God. In these three functions, the primordial nature of God is manifested and realized.

For Whitehead, God as the primordial nature is not directly related to actual entities; rather, he is indirectly related to actual entities through eternal objects. Therefore, the primordial nature of God means conceptual evaluation, unlimited potentiality, initial aim, and effective power that relate actual entities to eternal objects. In this respect, God as the primordial nature is everlasting, non-temporal, and unchangeable.

In addition to the primordial nature, God has the consequent nature which is directly related to the world. The consequent nature of God refers to the concreteness of God in which actual entities in the world are objectified. Due to the consequent nature, God is able to have relationships with the world and accept results of various acts from the world. This explains the way that God has relationships with the world. However, God accepts the world as the subject and by his own way, i.e., his own decision. Both the activity and passivity of God are included.[131]

Most specifically, God as the consequent nature means that God has essential relationships with all things in the world. God prehends all actual entities as they are when they occur, takes them into himself, and relates them to the reality of God. This is why God is temporal. Due to the consequent nature, God continues to accept actual entities and is thus being changed. Everything we do in this world influences God's reality. So, it can be said that God is like an organism of organisms who prehends all organisms and includes them into God himself. All actual entities, at the same time, are prehended, memorized, and accepted by God and they are then immortalized in the consequent nature of God. In this context, God is called "the fullness of all actual entities," in which all actual entities are everlastingly preserved. On the contrary, all actual entities get objective immortality in the consequent nature of God and remain as data for next creation.[132]

God's consequent nature is also explained in terms of the relationship between the God and the world. In short, "God and the world move conversely to each other in respect to their process."[133] Whitehead makes it clear by saying,

> God and the World stand to each other . . . . God is the infinite ground of all mentality, the unity of vision seeking physical multiplicity. The World is the multiplicity of finites, actualities seeking a perfect unity. Neither God, nor the World, reaches static completion. Both are in the grip of the ultimate metaphysical ground, the creative advance into novelty."[134]

Hence, God's concrescence in the consequent nature of God means a process which leads various prehensions to ultimate unity. That is to say, God's consequent nature leads all feelings in the actual world into a unity of feelings. Thus, for Whitehead, "God is the great companion—the fellow-sufferer who understands."[135]

For Whitehead, the relationship between God and the world is expressed in a paradox. In other words, God is one in terms of a unity of feelings, but has concrescent diversity in process. On the contrary, the world consists of many but attains a consequent unity in the process. Therefore, while the world is one as well as many, God is many as well as one. This constitutes a basic structure of process cosmology. He holds:

> God is primordially one, namely, he is the primordial unity of relevance of the many potential forms; in the process he acquires a consequent multiplicity, which the primordial character absorbs into its own unity. The World is primordially many, namely, the many actual occasions with their physical finitude; in the process it acquires a consequent unity, which is a novel occasion and is absorbed into the multiplicity of the primordial character. Thus God is to be conceived as one and as many in the converse sense in which the World is to be conceived as many and as one.[136]

It is certainly for Whitehead that God of the consequent nature is inevitably related to the world and both God and the world are comprised of a unity. Of course, this does not mean that this world itself is God because God is immanent in the world as a function of aesthetic evaluation, formative factors of the actual world, and prior ground. In a similar way, all things in the world are supported, grown, and maintained by these functions of God. So, Whitehead maintains, "The power by which God sustains the world is the power of himself as the ideal. He adds himself to the actual ground from which every creative act takes its rise. The world lives by its incarnation of God in itself."[137]

Therefore, while God's consequent nature means that God is an actual entity directly related to the world, God is different from other actual entities because God is not a perishable or temporal entity. God is an everlasting entity because the consequent nature is inevitably connected with the primordial nature of God. In other words, the two natures of God are not the combinations of two different natures; they are two as well as one and, namely, the two natures of God mean two aspects of an undivided reality. Hence, "God is the primordial creature; but the description of his nature is not exhausted by this conceptual side of it. His 'consequent nature' results from his physical prehension of the derivative actual entities."[138]

God as Creativity

Another term that characterizes Whitehead's concept of God is "creativity." Whitehead prefers "creativity" to "creator," which is traditionally ascribed to

God. Whitehead does not agree to the concept of God as a transcendental and supreme being who creates from nothing. In his metaphysics, God as an ultimate being is "creativity" or "creating activity." The word "creativity," for him, is a fundamental principle of creation and formation. It indicates to us that the creation of God is involved in all processes of the universe. Thus, Whitehead claims that God does not exist before the creation but exists along with the creation.[139]

Creativity is the same as the concept of "matter" in Aristotle's philosophy. It does not have its own character. It cannot be explained by all other things. It is the "ultimate notion of the highest generality at the base of actuality."[140] He expounds on the functions of "creativity" in more detail:

> 'Creativity' is the universal of the universals characterizing ultimate matter of the fact. It is that ultimate principle by which the many, which are the universe disjunctively, become the one actual occasion, which is the universe conjunctively. It lies in the nature of things that the many enter into complex unity. 'Creativity' is the principle of *novelty*. An actual occasion is a novel entity diverse from any entity in the 'many' which it unifies. Thus 'creativity' introduces novelty into the content of the many, which are the universe disjunctively. The 'creative advance' is the application of this ultimate principle of creativity to each novel situation which it originates.[141]

In other words, the function of God as creativity is to get each actual entity ready for development by offering them initial aims and enabling a transition into novelty in the process of concrescence in terms of prehension, evaluation, selection, satisfaction, and determination. It can thus be said that without God as creativity, nothing is produced; without God as creativity, nothing exists. This means that God as creativity is engaged in all the processes of creation, evolution, and transition of all things. Therefore, Whitehead also said, "God is the one systematic, complete fact, which is the antecedent ground conditioning every creative act."[142]

God, however, does not exist without regard to the world. God is not the creator who created the world once for all in an ancient time. God is meaningful only with the world. In other words, "There is no meaning to 'creativity' apart from its 'creatures,' and no meaning to 'God' apart from the 'creativity' and the 'temporal creatures,' and no meaning to the 'temporal creatures' apart from 'creativity' and 'God.'"[143] So, it can be said that God is creativity who is always involved in all the processes of creation in and with the world. Whitehead makes this point clear in his famous antithetical statements:

> It is as true to say that God is permanent and the World fluent, as that the World is permanent and God is fluent. It is as true to say that God is one and the World many, and that the World is one and God many. It is as true to say that, in comparison with the World, God is actual eminently, as that, in comparison

with God, the World is actual eminently. It is as true to say that the World is immanent in God, as that God is immanent in the World. It is as true to say that God transcends the World, as that the World transcends God. It is as true to say that God creates the World, as the World creates God.[144]

In other words, God does not create the world; he is not a creator in the context of Judeo—Christian tradition. God as an actual entity is always engaged in the process of creation altogether with the world. Whitehead holds:

God's role is not the combat of productive force with productive force, of destructive force with destructive force; it lies in the patient operation of the overpowering rationality of his conceptual harmonization. He does not create the world, he saves it: or, more accurately, he is the poet of the world, with tender patience leading it by his vision of truth, beauty, and goodness.[145]

Just as both the primordial nature and consequent natures are inseparable elements in understanding God, both God and the world are engaged in the process of creation. "Both are in the grip of the ultimate metaphysical ground, the creative advance into novelty."[146] Whitehead explains how God and the world work together in the process of creation:

God and the world stand over against each other, expressing the final metaphysical truth that appetitive vision and physical enjoyment have equal claim to priority in creation. But two actualities can be torn apart: each is all in all. Thus each temporal occasion embodies God, and is embodied in God. In God's nature, permanence is primordial and flux is derivative from the world: in the World's nature, flux is primordial and permanence is derivative from God. Also the World's nature is primordial datum for God; and God's nature is a primordial datum for the World. Creation achieves the reconciliation of permanence and flux when it has reached its final term which is everlastingness—the Apotheosis of the World.[147]

According to Lewis Ford, God should be an actual entity among other actual entities in order to make Whitehead's metaphysical system coherent. This means that God also has physical prehensions, so that God directly experiences the world. Ford describes the relationship between God and the world in the following way:

Therefore, in this vision, God and the world form an ecosystem, wherein both contribute to each other. God provides each event with its aim or lure toward which it moves. The event actualizes itself, influenced by the possibilities that God has provided, but also becoming something in its self-production by appropriating elements out of its past. This result is then experienced by God. In this way, the world enriches God.[148]

Conclusion

In conclusion, Whitehead believes that the fundamental and final components of the universe are the actual entities, which are the potentialities of becoming and coming into being in relationships with eternal objects. The real world is the process of relatedness of those potentialities of actual entities. He refutes the idea that there are such things that have substance to endure in the universe. Whitehead rather presents the processive, organic, and relational philosophies rooted in his metaphysical system and by so doing, clarifies the framework of his new cosmology revolving around some basic motifs and concepts such as "actual entity," "eternal object," "prehension," concrescence," "God," and "creativity." In the remaining chapters, we shall discuss how much of his process cosmology has an affinity with Yulgok's Neo-Confucian thought and how significantly it is used to integrate Christian belief into our contemporary world and enhance its spiritual practices.

Chapter 2

THE NEO-CONFUCIAN COSMOLOGY OF YI YULGOK

Historical Background of Korean Neo-Confucianism

Confucianism has been one of the living religions, along with Buddhism, Daoism, and Christianity in Korea. This means that Confucianism has a place of representative religion in the history of religion in Korea. Confucianism is a traditional religion with a long history; it has influenced broad areas of Korean society for many years. Confucianism has been one of Korea's most important religious heritages providing a moral foundation for the entire society. In other words, the moral and ethical structure of the Korean people is deeply rooted in Confucian tradition, although many still refuse to be official Confucian believers.

Spencer J. Palmer points out the continuing influence of Confucianism in the light of its rituals nationally still observed in Korea. He notes: "Confucianism is alive among Koreans today in large measure because of the continuing impact of that people's ritual traditions, as carried out for centuries in the family, in local Confucian schools, and in the great state ceremonies at the National Confucian Academy."[1] Korean Confucian scholar Jang-Tae Keum also argues that Confucianism has strongly influenced Korean society. He makes note of four things: first, Confucianism provides Koreans with moral norms; second, Confucianism has made Koreans greatly concerned about education; third, Confucianism influences the way that Koreans practice rites in their daily lives. (They came to express filial piety to the ancestors through Confucian teachings);

and fourth, Confucianism has been deeply involved in the ways that Koreans philosophically understand humanity and the cosmos. (i.e., Koreans may have Confucian anthropology and cosmology.)[2]

Korean Confucianism was introduced from China. Since the Korean peninsula is geographically connected to mainland China, Korea has naturally been influenced by Confucian thoughts developed over a long period of time in China. Although it is hard to say when Confucianism was introduced into Korea, many scholars insist that Confucianism was accepted at least before 372 C.E. during the period of three kingdoms. Historian Ki-Baik Lee says: "All three kingdoms laid great stress on inculcating the Confucian ethos as a means of maintaining their aristocratic social orders. Already in 372 Koguryo had established a National Confucian Academy called "T'aehak"(Great Learning) at which Confucianism was taught."[3]

In Paekche, the south kingdom of this period, A Jikgi and Wang In handed over Confucius' *Analects* and *One Thousand Chinese Characters* to Japan. Confucian education was exercised and numerous Chinese classics, including Confucian classics, were read by the people. In Silla, another kingdom of this period, a famous youth's school called "Wharang" followed Confucian moral norms such as filial piety, loyalty, and courage. Confucian values were widely practiced by people.[4] In all three kingdoms, Confucianism was taught at schools during this period and was regarded as an important religion and ethic for government and society, along with Buddhism.

Strictly speaking, however, Confucianism as a systematized type of state religion did not start until the Koryo Dynasty (918-1393, C.E.). In other words, Korean Confucianism was completely formed by Chinese Neo-Confucianism during the Koryo Dynasty. Although Buddhism still prevailed, it was Confucianism which functioned as a political ideology in the Koryo Dynasty. Unlike the peaceful coexistence of two religions throughout the periods of three kingdoms, Confucianism was considered to be opposed to Buddhism by civil officials and gradually became a central governing ideology in the Koryo Dynasty. Ki-baik Lee states:

> Confucian political ideology rejects the Buddhist doctrine of reward for good works and takes as its ideal a centralized state governed by an elite whose rule is sanctioned by a morality grounded not in religious belief, but in a rational view of the cosmos and man's place within it. This political vision gradually received wide support among the Koryo aristocracy. The result was that Confucianism, which had little appeal in comparison with Buddhism in the Silla Era just past, would develop to the point where it someday would be able to suppress Buddhism as an institutionalized religion.[5]

The first civil service examination based on Confucian classics was exercised in 958 C.E. King Taejo ordered the building of a university in which Confucianism was taught. King Songjong built local Confucian schools nationwide to expand Confucian education and Oh In-Yu established "*jongmyo*" (宗廟, the Royal Ancestor's Shrine) and "*sajik*" (社稷, the guardian deities of the State) in this period. Several Confucian scholars such as Ahn Hyang, Chung Mong-Ju, and Gil Jae tried to actively accept Zhu Xi's Neo-Confucianism. In particular, it was historically An Hyang (1243-1306 C.E.) who went to China and first brought Zhu Xi's writings to Korea in 1290 C.E. As a result of An Hyang's lifelong effort, Songgyun'gwan, the national Confucian Academy, was established in Kaesong in 1304 CE. An Hyang, as "the first of many champions of Confucianism" in Korea, devoted himself to the establishment of a reformed kingdom based on Confucian ideals, openly criticizing Buddhism as a popularized ideology. His yearning for a Confucian kingdom at that time was expressed in these moving lines of his poem: "Buddha is prayed to in every lighted house. Ghosts are served with drums and flutes. But, lo! The shabby shrine of Confucius stands untended in its yard, rank with autumn weeds."[6]

Later, Paik I-Chung also went to China and brought Cheng and Zhu's writings to Korea. These two scholars made great contributions to the development of Neo-Confucianism in the Koryo Dynasty. In this process, the famous book, Zhu Xi's *Chia-li* (朱子家禮, family rites) was also introduced to the Korean people. Thereafter ancestor worship was established as the core rite of Neo-Confucianism. Furthermore, Chung Mong-Ju, a leading Confucian scholar in the late Koryo Dynasty, established "the rule of three years mourning period for the dead parents" and built the ancestor shrine to worship ancestors' gods according to Zhu Xi's *Chia-li*.[7]

Zhu's Neo-Confucianism, which was initiated in the Koryo Dynasty, became a state religion during the Choson Dynasty (1392-1910 C.E.). Confucian political ideals and moral doctrines became deeply embedded in every aspect of people's lives during Choson Dynasty.[8] Unlike Buddhism, which tried to harmonize with other religions in the former periods, Zhu's Neo-Confucianism in the Choson Dynasty criticized and opposed other religions including Buddhism, and became an orthodox religion in the society. Many Confucian scholars who participated in the creation of the new dynasty placed the governing ideologies of the Choson Dynasty squarely within Confucian orthodoxy. Hence, numerous Buddhist temples were destroyed and many Buddhist monks were excommunicated at the beginning of the Choson Dynasty.

There were many attempts made to establish Confucianism as an official state religion and orthodox ideology in the Choson society. Chung Do-Jun (1342-1398 C.E.) first presented logical criticism against Buddhist doctrines based on the view of Zhu's Neo-Confucianism and further wrote important works about Confucian governing principles. Kwon Gun (1352-1409 C.E.) commentated on Confucian classics and wrote an introduction to Confucianism in the form of diagrams. The Great King Sejong (1418-1450 C.E.) raised numerous Confucian scholars in the special institute called "*Chiphyonjon*" (集賢殿, the Hall of Worthies) and let them commit themselves to studying National rites and rituals. He also tried to expand Confucian morality and ethics such as humanity (*in,* 仁), filial piety (*hyo,* 孝), and loyalty (*chung,* 忠) to ordinary people. The famous Confucian hymn called "*yongbiochonga* " composed by him, in which he praised the validity of the Choson Dynasty in Confucian terms, is a good example of those efforts. Later, his Confucian project was finalized and five national rites were established by King Songjong (1407-1498 C.E.).

In sixteenth century, Neo-Confucianism produced a great abundance of philosophical theories in Choson Korea. Many important scholars scattered over the nation vigorously participated in philosophical debates. These scholars included Suh Hwadam, Yi Unjok, Cho Sik, Yi Hang, Ki Daesung, Ugye, Yi T'oegye, and Yi Yulgok. They concentrated their debates on the central issues of Zhu's Neo-Confucianism, such as the Great Ultimate, the theory of principle and material force, and the problem of human nature. They took a further step philosophically in Zhu's Neo-Confucianism by more carefully focusing on those issues. In particular, T'oegye and Yulgok made the most significant contributions to the development of Neo-Confucianism in the Choson Dynasty by starting two great Confucian schools in Korean history: the Yongnam School and Kiho School.[9]

Biographical Sketch of Yi Yulgok

It is no wonder that Yulgok is highly respected as a great Confucian philosopher in Korea. But it is also true that he lived a very unique life, not only as a philosopher but also as a great statesman and politician. He was a very rare person who was able to balance the philosophical theories and political practices of his time. He attempted to apply his Confucian philosophy to both his personal life and to the public arena. Edward Chung makes a good point when he compares Yulgok with T'oegye:

> T'oegye and Yulgok are often mentioned together as the two great minds of Choson Korea. Modern Koreans respect Yulgok not only as a great Neo-Confucian scholar, but also as a distinguished politician and reformer. As a thinker, statesman, and educator, his short life of forty-nine years was filled with many remarkable accomplishments. No other Korean Neo-Confucian before and after Yulgok can match his far-reaching vision of history, practical learning, and politics. As an original and liberal political thinker, he advocated Confucian principles to reform the contemporary political, economic, social, and military institutions of the Choson dynasty.[10]

Yulgok was born on December 26 in 1536 C.E.in Kangreung, Korea.[11] As a baby, he was given the name "Hyunryong," which means "to see a dragon," because his mother saw a dragon before giving birth. His family moved to Seoul when he was five years old. He began his study of classics with his mother, Sinsaimdang, who is also highly respected by Koreans for her character and education. He began to read and understand four Chinese classics—the *Analects*, the *Book of Mencius*, the *Great Learning*, and the *Doctrine of the Mean*—not long after that. People praised him as a genius when he wrote a poem in Chinese at the age of eight.

Yulgok became famous by passing the first civil service examination at the age of twelve. However, the death of his mother was a shock to him when he was fifteen years old. With the loss of his great teacher, he was forced to study by himself. This led him to think about the meaning of life and go to the Kumgang mountain in order to explore Buddhism. After getting involved in the study of Buddhism for one year, he returned to his hometown, Kangreung, and resumed his extensive study of Confucian classics.

At the age of twenty-two, he began to have a relationship with master T'oegye by visiting his school in Andong. In the winter of the same year, Yulgok passed the highest civil service examination with highest ranks. He submitted a philosophical thesis entitled *Ch'ondo ch'aek* (天道策, Treatise on the Way of Heaven) for that exam, which was his first major philosophical work on the Neo-Confucian cosmology and metaphysics. Then, his career as a government official began in 1564 C.E. at the age of twenty-eight. He served many important positions in government from 1564 to 1583 C.E., such as minister of home affairs, minister of justice, minister of civil affairs, and minister of national defense.

His official careers, however, were sometimes interrupted by health problems. He withdrew to his hometown and dedicated time to his scholarly life. He diligently discussed philosophical issues with other scholars. He also finished *Songhak Jipyo* (聖學輯要, Essentials of the Sage Learning), which was a great philosophical commentary on Chinese Confucian six canons and the Four Books, and dedicated it to the king in 1575 C.E. After the age of thirty-nine, Yulgok did not return to his official career because he was not in good health. He therefore stayed in a rural area named the Sukdam, Whanghae province of northern Korea. He did not recover from his disease and finally died at the age of forty-eight in 1584 C.E.

Yulgok's Neo-Confucian Cosmology

Philosophical Impacts on Yulgok

Yulgok is well known as a devout follower of the Cheng-Zhu School of

Confucianism. He diligently studied all classics of Confucianism throughout his life. He emphasized the importance of Confucian tradition. He says in *Sunghakjipyo* [Essentials of the Sage Learning] that, since the Four Books and six canons and all the theories of former Confucian scholars such as Zhu Xi are significant to the sage learning, we should study these books extensively.[12] On many pages, he states that his writings and ideas are not his own, but come from former Confucian scholars. This means that he developed the essence of Confucian philosophy within its own traditions. In particular, it is important to note that Zhu Xi's Chinese Neo-Confucianism had a great impact on Yulgok. Although Yugok developed his Confucian thoughts in a unique way, he was a diligent student of Zhu Xi's Neo-Confucian thoughts. Yulgok had a great respect for Zhu Xi (1130-1200) as his Confucian master, but didn't hesitate to criticize him. He states: "If Master Zhu insists that principle and material force issue separately, he will be wrong. How could we say he is Master Zhu?"[13] Such an open attitude to the tradition enabled him to expand his study more deeply and broadly.

On the one hand, Yulgok's thinking was deeply rooted in the traditions of Classical and Neo-Confucianism. He remained, on the other hand, open to dialogue with other philosophical thoughts such as Buddhism, Daoism, and Yangming Studies. It is well known that, in addition to his critical succession of Master Zhu, he undertook philosophical dialogues with T'oegye (1501-1570 C.E.), the other great scholar of Korean Neo-Confucianism, and Whadam (1489-1546 C.E.), another advocate of *qi* (material force) philosophy. Moreover, Yulgok studied Buddhism for one year in the Buddhist temple at the age of nineteen. Thus, it is true that many elements impacted the development of his unique Neo-Confucian thoughts.

Zhu Xi's Chinese Neo-Confucianism

Zhu Xi had the greatest impact on the formation of Yulgok's philosophical thoughts. Zhu Xi , a great Confucian philosopher, developed a pattern of interpreting and transmitting the Confucian Way that would define the Confucian project for centuries not only in China but also in Korea and Japan. In his famous book entitled *A History of Chinese Philosophy*, Yu-lan Fung describes Zhu Xi:

> With Chu Hsi (Zhu Xi) we now reach the man who synthesized the ideas of all these predecessors into one all-embracing system and who, indeed, is probably the greatest synthesizer in the history of Chinese thought. Through his prolific writings and his commentaries on the classics, he brought the Rationalistic school to full maturity, and in the process created a version of Confucianism that was to remain orthodox until the twentieth century.[14]

In other words, Zhu Xi "reconstituted the Confucian tradition, giving it new meaning, new structure, and new texture. Through conscientious appropriation and systematic interpretation, he developed a type of new Confucianism," which is called Neo-Confucianism.[15] Wing-Tsit Chan states this in more details: "Up to this time, Neo-Confucianism was characterized by six major concepts advocated by different philosophers, namely, the Great Ultimate, principle (*li*), material force (*qi*), the nature, the investigation of things, and humanity. All of these were developed, systematized and synthesized in the greatest of Neo-Confucianists, Master Chu (Zhu)."[16] John H. Berthrong also writes: "Chu (Zhu) is second to Confucius and Mencius as a Confucian thinker. Chu is often compared to St. Aquinas in the West, and here again, there is a great deal of merit in the comparison. Chinese thought would never be the same after Chu Hsi (Zhu Xi) reworked and arranged the records of his beloved Northern Sung masters."[17]

Zhu's Neo-Confucianism,[18] which is different from Chinese Classical Confucianism, was introduced into Korea in the thirteenth century and deeply influenced Yulgok's philosophy in the sixteenth century.[19] Furthermore, Zhu Xi's Neo-Confucianism strongly influenced even modern Korean philosophy. Min-Hong Choi maintains: "The main subject of modern Korean philosophy was Neo-Confucianism, especially as outlined by Zhu Xi. At times it seemed to comprise the whole of Korean philosophy."[20] It is evident that Zhu "gave Confucianism new meaning and for centuries dominated not only Chinese thought but the thought of Korea and Japan as well."[21]

Broadly speaking, Zhu's metaphysical system is fundamentally based on Chou Tun-yi's cosmology expressed in the *Diagram of the Great Ultimate Explained* (太極圖說). Zhu, however, clarified and expanded Zhu's cosmological thoughts based on the Great Ultimate, and Yin-Yang by exploring in depth the concepts of principle and material force. Zhu completed a unique cosmology from his own philosophical viewpoint that other Confucian scholars never recognized.[22] His main cosmological thoughts can be thus articulated in the following ways:

First, it is important to mention that the notion of *Li* (principle) and *Qi* (material force) is the central theme of Zhu's Neo-Confucianism. In other words, Neo-Confucianism initiated by master Zhu perceives the universe as having two fundamental philosophical concepts called "*li*" and "*qi*." As Yung Sik Kim comments, Among the most fundamental and frequently used concepts in Chu Hsi (Zhu Xi)'s discussion of natural phenomena are *li* and *ch'i* (*qi*). In fact, in the standard Neo-Confucian schemes of classification, these concepts, grouped into one word, *li-ch'i* (*qi*), designate a category covering basic topics in what can be called cosmology ad natural philosophy.[23] Therefore, Zhu Xi first provides definitions of the two concepts *li* and *qi* by making a comparison: "what is above shape"(刑而上者) and "what is within shape"(形而下者). He also uses the term "instruments" (器) for things which have shapes and forms, and "the

Way" (*dao*, 道) for the "principle" of these instruments. And he identifies the Way of "what is above shape" with the principle (*li*) and the instrument of "what is within shape" with material force (*qi*). Zhu also differentiates between the two concepts as follows: "As for *li*, it simply is a clean and spacious world. It has no physical form or traces. It cannot operate. As for *ch'i* (*qi*), it can brew, congeal, and aggregate to produce things."[24] These two terms, "principle" and "material force," are metaphysical concepts by which the physical world may be explained.[25] Zhu Xi writes:

> Within the cosmos there are *li* (principle) and *ch'i* (*qi*, material force). *Li* constitutes the *dao* (the way) that is 'above shapes'; it is the source from which things are produced. *Qi* constitutes the 'instruments'(*ch'i*, 器) that are 'within shapes'; it is the material means whereby things are produced. Hence men or things, at the moment of their production, must receive this *li* in order that they may have a nature (*hsing*) of their own: they must receive this *qi* in order that they may have form.[26]

Here, the Way (*dao*) is the first principle of Zhu Xi's philosophy. The Way is also called the "Great Ultimate"(*taiji*, 太極), which is also characterized by principle. Zhu also identifies the Great Ultimate, which was advocated by Chu Tun-I, with principle, which was advocated by Cheng brothers. For him, "It is the principle of things to be actualized, and actualization requires principle as its substance and material force as its actuality."[27] "Principle," which is another name for the Great Ultimate, has priority over all things, including material force. Moreover, Zhu identifies the one principle (*li*) with "the heavenly principle"(*t'ien-li*). He said:

> The heavenly *li* flows and moves. Wherever one touches, it is the heavenly *li*. Hot weather goes and cold weather comes: rivers flow and mountains stand erect. Fathers and sons have love; rulers and subjects have righteousness and things like that. There is nothing that is not this *li*. . . . That 'filial piety and brotherly respect are the root of the humanness' also is in substance this *li*.[28]

Since Zhu Xi vigorously emphasizes principle (*li)*, he is often regarded as a representative of the school of Rationalism.[29]

Second, Zhu Xi believes that each existent thing has a reason for its existence, or has an essence or principle for its existence, which is known as *li* (principle). Thus, he writes: "When a certain thing is made, there is in it a particular Principle (*li*). For all things created in the cosmos, there is in each a particular Principle."[30] He continues: "When considered from the standpoint of principle, before things existed their principle of being had already existed. Only their principles existed, however, but not yet the things themselves . . . . There is principle before there can be material-force."[31]

Therefore, Zhu Xi's principles (*li*) are the ontological beings which are prior to the actual existence of objects. That is to say, the principle of a thing is the supreme archetype of that thing; it is the essence and the norm of that thing.[32] Zhu Xi calls this *chi* (極, Ultimate). He writes: "For every thing or object there is an Ultimate, which is the normative principle (of that thing or object) in its highest ultimate form."[33] However, besides these Ultimates in everything, Zhu Xi also acknowledges that there is one single principle which constitutes the Great Ultimate. Zhu Xi writes:

> These are the ultimates of a single thing or a single object. But the Principle (*li*) of all the myriad within the cosmos, brought into one whole, constitutes the Great Ultimate (*taiji*, 太極). The Great Ultimate did not originally have this name. It is simply an appellation applied to it. . . . The Great Ultimate is simply an utterly excellent and supremely good normative Principle.[34]

Although the Great Ultimate cannot be described in terms of forms and shapes, it basically includes a system of principle. The Great Ultimate includes the principles of the whole cosmos because it is the ground of the whole cosmos. Thus, all things that exist are particular things because they have their own principles: For without principle, it would be impossible for a thing to exist. All existent things exist because there is a cause of existence and a normative form or essence of existence, which is none other than principle.[35]

Third, according to Zhu Xi, all things, which are made of principle and material force, are never separated from each other. As Robert Neville points out, "Neither category has a determinate character without the other, and the presence of one entails the presence of the other. Neither can be reduced by the other."[36] However, Zhu affirms that principle precedes material force. Thus, he writes:

> Principle has never been separated from material-force. However, principle is what is above shape whereas material-force is what is within shape. Hence when spoken of as being above or within shape, is there not a difference of priority and posteriority? Principle has no shape or corporeal form, but material-force is coarse and contains impurities. Fundamentally principle and material-force cannot be spoken of as prior or posterior. But if we must trace their origin, we are obliged to say that principle is prior.[37]

Although Zhu Xi maintained the inseparability of principle and material force, he still insisted on the logical priority of principle over material force. Namely, principle itself already exists, even though its object does not yet actually exist. This is characteristic of his rationalism. Of course, the priority of principle is a logical one rather than a temporal one. It is like "Aristotelian form or actuality has a logical priority over matter or potentiality."[38]

Fourth, Zhu Xi states that principle, which is the metaphysical reality, is a changeless, motionless, and eternal principle, a reality that is perfect without deficiency. In other words, principle as the ultimate reality transcends forms and shapes, and all other limiting conditions. However, material force is the motivating power of things that are subject to change, processing movement and quiescence, capable of producing forms and shapes.[39] He writes:

> It would seem that the Ether (material force) is dependent upon Principle for its operation. Thus when there is a condensation of such Ether (material force), Principle is also present within it. It is the Ether (material force) that has the capacity to condense and thus create, whereas Principle lacks volition or plan and has no creative power. Yet the fact simply is that whenever the Ether (material force) condenses into one spot, principle is present within it.[40]

Fifth, according to Zhu, the physical world is created by the dynamic operation of principle and material force, and it moves continually in the cycle of movements and quiescence. In other words, "The world could be explained as the ceaseless unification of principle with matter-energy (material force) in some definite event or thing."[41] Of course, principle containing the Great Ultimate governs the movements and quiescence of all things, and material force undergoes all phases of those movements. In these processes of rotating movement, material force appears as "yin material force"(陰氣) in quiescence (or tranquility) and "yang material force" (陽氣) in movement (or activity). Zhu contends:

> Movement and quiescence, in their alteration, are each the root of the other. There is movement and then quiescence; quiescence and then movement. They open and close, come and go, succeeding each other without pause. There is a division into the yin and the yang, and the Two Forms (*liang yi*) are thus established. These forms are Heaven and Earth. . . . The transformations of the yang and congealing of the yin thus produce water, fire, wood, metal, and earth. The yin and yang, which is Ether (material force), in this way produce the Five Elements, which are 'corporeal matter'(*chih*, 質). . . . These seven—the Five Elements and the yin and yang—as they boil forth and combine with one another, form the material from which objects are created.[42]

As John Berthrong clearly pointed out, "Zhu saw the world as a constant changing pattern of the integration of the dynamics of matter-energy, the form of principle, and their ceaseless unification."[43] Likewise, the whole world cannot be explained without mentioning the dynamic combination of principle and material force. These two concepts have mutual interdependence and respective importance. In Zhu Xi's philosophy, however, the concept of principle is the primary and fundamental thing. It is the Great Ultimate that plays a role of a governing principle in the world. His strong emphasis on principle penetrates all aspects of his philosophy and makes him a representative of the Studies of Rationalism.

On the contrary, the concept of material force arises from the physical world which is the secondary and derivative. It is realized only by the initiation of principle and constitutes the physical world by its cycling movement in development and quiescence, yin and yang. According to Young-Jo Han, this is regarded as a perspective of circulation in understanding the cosmos. All phenomena of creation and changes in the cosmos are understood as the cycling movement between two poles: yin and yang. Yin and yang are not two separate forces but one force in the same pattern of principle. Yin and yang are nothing but two aspects of material force.[44] Thus, Zhu also states: "Yin and yang are the same material force. The retreat of yang is the emergence of yin. It is not true to say that yang retreats and then yin separately emerges."[45]

T'oegye's Emphasis on *Li* and Mutual Issuance of *Li* and *Qi*

It is sure that Yulgok belongs to the tradition of Chinese Ch'eng-Zhu Confucian School. In addition, he was also influenced by T'oegye (1501-1570)'s Neo-Confucian philosophy in Choson Korea. This does not mean Yulgok imitated T'oegye; he developed his own philosophical thoughts through the philosophical debates with T'oegye. That is, Yulgok presents different interpretations of the important concepts in Neo-Confucianism from T'oegye. Although Yulgok admired T'oegye as a great teacher, he often criticized T'oegye's thoughts. Yulgok was thirty five years younger than T'ogye and at the age of twenty-two first visited T'oegye's Confucian local school in Andong with a profound respect. They had time for a philosophical talk but didn't establish a master-disciple relationship. Young Chan Ro states: "In later years, Yulgok would challenge T'oegye on a number of key philosophical issues. Still, T'oegye must be recognized as the preeminent influence on Yulgok's thought, the thinker in opposition to whom Yulgok defined himself."[46] Therefore, in spite of their same memberships of Chinese Song Neo-Confucianism, they are different in exploring their philosophical theories in many ways.

T'oegye represents the School of Principle in the history of Korean Neo-Confucianism, primarily based on Zhu's Neo-Confucian thoughts. T'oegye, like Zhu Xi, understands that the cosmos and all things consist of principle and material force. Even the human body consists of principle and material force. Four beginnings and seven feelings in the human mind and heart consist of principle and material force. It is also important to point out that there is no principle without material force or material force without principle. For T'oegye's Confucian thoughts, principle and material force are two important pillars. In particular, principle is considered as more important than material force in his thoughts. T'oegye weighs more on principle than on material force by actively advocating the meaning and role of principle, sometimes more than Zhu's original thought.

According to him, principle is the basic way and the way of all beings and 'exists above forms' (形而上者), whereas material force is the vessel and 'exists below forms' (形而下者). Principle has the same meaning as the Great Ultimate and the Way, just as material force is understood as yin and yang.[47] Material force as a vessel contains principle within itself. While principle has no forms, or activity or limit, material force has form, activity, temporality, and limit. For T'oegye, principle is clearly different from material force. In his analogy, principle is treated like a king, whereas material force is like a king's subject. Thus, T'oegye says that principle should be more highly respected than material force.[48] This, of course, comes from his ethical concern and perspective: that is, it is like the position of moral human beings should be different from other animals or beings. It is sure that he intends to be a rationalist who concentrates on the value and function of principle in the society of his times.

Furthermore, principle is explained in two different subcategories: 'absolute principle' (絕對理) and 'relative principle' (相對理). The absolute principle means the transcendental principle which is apart from material force. The absolute principle is like a heavenly master who commands all things. This understanding of principle means that he acknowledges the transcendental character of principle. On the other hand, the relative principle means the principle which exists in a relationship with material force, and the principle which exists within material force. In the case of the absolute principle, material force cannot give any influence to principle; in the case of the relative principle, principle is also limited by material force. T'oegye focuses more on the absolute principle than on the relative principle, and thereby admits the transcendental, absolute characteristics of principle.[49]

In addition, he insists that principle exists prior to material force and 'principle produces material force' (理生氣). Here he takes a further step on the study of Zhu's Study of Principle (理學) by arguing that principle has its own dynamic activity. T'oegye explicates the movement of principle as follows:

> Generally, when principle moves, material force is subsequently generated, and when material force moves, principle subsequently emerges. When Chu Tun-I said that 'yang is born by the government of the Great Ultimate,'[50] he meant that material force is created by the movement of principle. Chou also speaks of seeing heaven and earth, which means that principle emerges from the movement of material force.[51]

Likewise, T'oegye understands the dynamic reality of principle, which has transcendental and active character. He believes that material force is generated from principle, and principle is the foundation of production of material force in the cosmos. In other words, the cosmos and the world are understood as the constant manifestation of principle in material force. He tries to keep the priority of principle over material force. Thus, it seems that T'oegye's thought is often criticized as a *Li* (principle) monism because for him material force is considered as secondary while principle is considered as primary.

T'oegye's emphasis on principle is expressed more vigorously by his theory of *'ibal'* (理發, principle issues). He states that principle does not issue in the aspect of its substance (*che*, 體) but in the aspect of its function (*yong*, 用). He writes:

> What has no emotion or volition is the original substance of principle. It deploys in all things and appears in everywhere; this is the marvelous use of principle. One considered it as a dead thing because he did not see its marvelous use and appearance but the non activity of its substance. Is this too far away from the way?[52]

T'oegye, like Zhu and Yulgok, argues for the issuance of principle, but broadly applies it to material forces as well and his differentiation between the substance and the operation of principle becomes ambiguous. He first says that 'principle issues and material force follows it' (*i-bal-ki-su*, 理發氣隨) and then identifies the issuance of principle with that of the material force. Finally, he acknowledges 'the mutual issuance of principle and material force' (*i-ki-ho-bal*, 理氣互發). This position is expanded to the 'Four-Seven Debates'(四七論爭) and the theory of sage learning. Edward Chung pointed out, "Unlike Zhu Xi who emphasized the rationalistic 'investigation of principle,' T'oegye has a stronger tendency for self-realization of principle. And his conviction was to take principle as the ultimate foundation of the Neo-Confucian learning for sagehood."[53]

Yulgok deeply admireds T'oegye as a great master and undoubtedly got big influence form his thoughts. Although Yulgok acknowledged the importance of principle in Cheng-Zhu Neo Confucian tradition, however, he did not agree to T'oegye's extreme emphasis on principle and theory of mutual issuance of principle and material force. Instead, Yulgok explored the equal and dynamic relationship of these two concepts. Yulgok basically did not agree to the activity of principle without material force. Yulgok contended,

> How could what T'oegye speaks of as mutual issuance really be as your letter describes it, saying it means that principle and material force are each in their own place mutually issuing as function? It's just that they are rolled up into a single thing, but there is the predominance of principle and the predominance of material force, that which emerges from within and that which is stimulated from without—beforehand, there are these two proclivities.[54]

> As for T'oegye's two words "mutual issuance," it seems that they were not just a mistake in expressing himself: I'm afraid it was a matter of his not being able to see deeply enough into the mystery of the inseparability of principle and

material force.⁵⁵

Hwadam's *Qi* Monism

Unlike the *li-qi* cosmology of Cheng-Zhu Neo-Confucianism, Hwadam (1489-1546) insists that *qi* (material force) is the ultimate substance of the cosmos. Hwadam was a famous advocate for *Qi* monism in Korea. He regards material force as the ultimate origin of the cosmos, focusing its dynamic activities and roles in the cosmos. According to him, the cosmos consists of material force, which is not perished. All things in the cosmos can be understood only in terms of coagulation and disintegration of material forces. Even principle and the Great Ultimate, which are transcendental and ultimate beings in Neo-Confucian traditions, are part of material forces in the cosmos.

Following the philosophies of Chang Tsai (1020-1077), one of Chinese Neo-Confucian thinkers, he presents this position in terms of the 'Great Vacuity'(太虛) as the original form(原形) of material forces which existed before all things under heaven were created and transformed. According to Hwadam, the Great Vacuity is empty but is not non-being; it fills all spaces in the cosmos. Thus, The Great Vacuity is vacuity as well as non vacuity. It is like 'the Non Ultimate is the Great Ultimate' which is argued by Master Chou Tun-i. Although it appears that the Great Vacuity has no voice or smell, it really exists, and it thus can be said that 'vacuity' is material force(虛卽氣).⁵⁶ Likewise, he identifies material force with great vacuity. On the basis of this position, Hwhadam criticizes Lao Tzu's theory that being comes from non-being and vacuity produces material force because Lao Tzu does not know that vacuity is material force.

How do all things in the cosmos come into being? Hwadam explicates this in terms of the theory of 'Prior and Posterior Heaven'(先後天). The 'Prior Heaven'(先天) means one material force and the Great Vacuity, which existed as the original substance of the cosmos before all things were created and generated. It is 'One Material Force because it is pure, empty, and quiet. It is also the Great One because it forms all things in the world. He states: "The Great vacuity is deep and formless and thus called the 'Prior Heaven.' It is too big to have no extension or beginning. It has no origin. It is deep, empty, and quiet. So, it is the origin of material force."⁵⁷ Hwadam indicates here that the Great vacuity is transcendental and ultimate. It is the same as the concept of the Great Ultimate advocated by Zhu Xi. Hwadam replaced it with the Great Vacuity.

On the contrary, the 'Posterior Heaven'(後天) means phenomena of material forces, which causes Yin and Yang as well as movement and quiescence. This is what we understand material force from the view of its function(用). When material force is dispersed into all kinds of forms, it is called the 'Posterior Heaven.' For Hwadam, although this cosmos consists of only material forces, the original substance of the cosmos is called 'the prior Heaven' when material force is not issued, and its phenomena is called 'the Posterior Heaven' when material force is already issued. After all, all things come into being when the Prior Heaven moves to the Posterior Heaven.[58]

Hwadam states in further detail how material force issues. He insists: "Material force suddenly rises up and opens in the cosmos. What causes it to do that? It occurs naturally by itself and cannot help do that. Thus, this is called 'the timing of principle'(理之時)."[59] This means that material force issues and cycles in development and quiescence under self-principle. This is what he calls 'the timing of principle' which belongs to the dimension of material force's self issuance. Hwadam does not agree to the original role of principle; instead, he argues that material force itself plays the same role of issuance as the one of principle. For Hwadam, principle does not exist apart from material force. But it plays a role of the lordship over material force, which means that principle directs the role of material force from within, not from outside. Principle does not exist prior to material force. Material force has no beginning; neither has it principle. If principle is prior to material force, then material force will have a beginning.[60] Therefore, for Hwadam principle is a principle of movement for material force, which as a principle of self-control and regulation rightly directs material force in movement and quiescence. In other words, principle is an internal quality of material force that is not developed in the Prior Heaven until material force becomes active in the Posterior Heaven. So, Hwadam's concept of principle is different from the one in Cheng-Zhu Neo-Confucianism. It is 'principle existing in the midst of material force'(氣中理).[61] In other words, principle exists only in material forces and principle then becomes another form of material force.

It is no doubt that Yulgok was influenced by Hwadam's *Qi*-monism. He praised Hwadam's originality of his philosophical thoughts and deep understanding of material force. Hwadam's emphasis on material force surely gave Yulgok a new moment of reviewing the *li-qi* theory and reconsidering of the importance of material force. Yulgok, of course, criticized that Hwadam confused material force with principle in philosophical debates with other Confucian scholars. Yulgok tried to move his philosophy beyond Hwadam. He said that Hwadam was a genius in discussing the inseparability of principle of material force but did not understand exactly their roles and movements.[62]

Yulgok's Neo-Confucian Cosmology

Theory of *Li* and *Qi*

As we have indicated above, Confucianism has served over a long period as the dominant religious paradigm in Korea ever since An-Hyang (1243-1306)'s introduction of Neo-Confucianism from China. As a Taiwanese scholar Tsai-chun Chung notes, "The earliest of the Neo-Confucianists were chiefly interested in cosmology, because cosmology is the first and most convenient way to display a new world-view."[63] Unlike classical Confucianism that emphasizes practical moral principles, social relations in human life and community, and self-discipline, "Neo-Confucianism was a philosophical religious Way searching after the essence of the human mind and the primordial principles of the universe. In other words, Neo-Confucianism is a philosophical Confucianism that explains the origins of man and the universe in metaphysical terms."[64] According to Chinese Cheng-Zhu Neo-Confucianism, there is a necessary reason behind movement of all things and a moral "oughtness" (German: "Söllen") behind a human being's moral behavior in the world and the cosmos. This reason, or moral oughtness, exists as an apriori metaphysical paradigm inherited in the movement of life of all things before the formation of the heaven and the earth. It is called "principle" or "Heavenly principle." In order to be realized as a concrete being, this apriori principle needs material, which is called "material force." The world has proceeded throughout history due to the constant mutual movement of principle and material force.[65]

Korean Neo-Confucianism is exactly centered on this Neo-Confucian cosmology which understands the cosmos in terms of the theory of *li* (principle) and *qi* (material force).[66] In other words, Korean Neo-Confucianism sees human beings and things, nature and society, substance and phenomena, and all other things in the perspective of both principle and material force. Therefore, the theory of principle and material force is not only the substructure on which Korean Neo-Confucian cosmology and ontology are built, but also the fundamental philosophical and ethical concept by which all philosophical thoughts of Neo-Confucianism are maintained. Furthermore, the theory of principle and material force affected views on various cultural aspects such as politics, economics, and history in the society of Choson Korea. In other words, it constituted the core of anthropology, worldview, ethics, and spirituality for Koreans for a long period of time.[67]

Yulgok's cosmology begins with this context. For Yulgok, the theory of principle and material force plays the most important role in the formation of his Confucian thought. Yulgok believes that the cosmos consist of principle and material force. These two elements have equal importance in understanding all beings in the cosmos. Beings cannot be understood by either the principle or material force alone. Although principle and material force are two different things, they together produce beings in the world under an inseparable relationship. In Yulgok, it is evident that principle and material force are the fundamental concepts for exploring his ideas of the world and human beings. Therefore, it is necessary to first explicate his theory of these two terms before presenting the Neo-Confucian Cosmology of Yulgok.

Yulgok first presents his own system of principle and material force. He primarily accepts the position of Zhu Xi's Neo-Confucian philosophy. In order words, Yulgok's theory is based on the dynamic interrelationship between principle and material force initially presented by Zhu Xi. He does not accept the cosmological theory "*Qi* monism" which is based only on material force without acknowledging the significance of principle. "*Qi* monism was advocated by Hwadam (1489-1546) in Choson Korea, a follower of Chang Tsai (1020-1077) who is one of Chinese Neo-Confucian cosmologists. Yulgok rather focuses on Zhu's *li-qi* theory. As mentioned above, Zhu Xi insisted that principle did not exist as a substance apart from material force. Material force produces all things by operating through them, whereas principle does not have any particular action or volition. Principle always adheres to material force, because principle is the principle which has no active function. On the contrary, material force has no value and order without principle. In other words, principle is the source of the movement of material force. Material force moves only according to principle.[68] "Principle is the master of material force and material force is the instrument of principle."[69]

In this way, two basic concepts of all things, principle and material force, depend upon each other. This means that there is a dynamic interrelationship of principle and material force. In other words, without material force, principle does not have any function or meaning as the principle of the cosmos. And without principle, material force does not have energy as the material force of nature. This is a common notion in both Zhu Xi's and Yulgok's philosophical thoughts. Principle and material force are two different elements in the cosmos, but they cannot be separated from each other in being and action, although they can be distinguished conceptually.

In another place, Yulgok adequately presents his definitions of two concepts in the following way:

> Principle is above shape and material force is within shape. These two things cannot be separated from each other. If they cannot be separated, then their issuances and functions are one. We can not say that principle and material force have alternate issuances and functions separately. If principle and material force have separate issuances and functions, then this would mean that there is some time when principle issued and functions, but material force does not, as well as times when material force is issued and functions, but principle does not. Thus there would be separation and union, priority and posteriority of principle and material force, and then there would be the beginnings of movement and tranquility and the beginnings of yin and yang. The error in this theory is indeed great.[70]

Yulgok undoubtedly accepts Zhu's basic definitions of principle and material force. He, however, does not consider principle and material force to be two individuals, emphasizing both their inseparability (不相離) and their unmixability(不相雜).[71] According to Yulgok, "Principle's inseparability from material force is really like the water's being inseparable from the vessel."[72] He neither agrees to the dualism of two concepts (理氣二元論) nor the monism of two concepts (理氣一元論). On the other hand, he seeks the proper understanding of two concepts in their inseparable dynamic interrelationship. In this case, he does not agree to the theory of "mutual issuance of principle and material force" (理氣互發) which was presented by T'oegye and refers to the two separable realities and their activities. He rather concentrates on the inactivity of principle and its mastership over material force. According to T'oegye, there is a simultaneous movement in both principle and material force; that is, principle and material force have mutual issuance. *Qi* as material force follows *li* as an active entity. Principle and material force are considered to be two individual things.[73] This indicates to us his dualistic tendency in understanding the two concepts.

Quite contrary to the T'oegye's theory, Yulgok gives us a clear understanding of the two concepts. Yulgok argues that "All things issued are of material force and the reason for issuance is principle. Without material force, there will be no issuance; without principle, there is no reason for issuance."[74] He does not agree to the activity of principle itself apart from material force. But he emphasizes the inactivity (無爲性) of principle itself, which is generally advocated by Zhu's Neo-Confucianism. According to Yulgok, principle exists as a principle in nature like "thus-so of things"(*jayon*, 自然). And the principle's characteristics of "thus-so of things" makes it possible to preside material force. He thus states:

> What moves once and stops once in quiescence is material force. The ground that causes things to move and stop is principle. . . . The 'thus-so of things' is material force and the reason of 'thus-so of things' is principle. I have no idea of who does this. I cannot help but say that it is done as the way things really are.[75]

Although principle is understood as the reason and source for material force, it does not move alone; rather, it operates only with regard to material force and plays a role of the master over material force. Yulgok writes about the basic functions of those two concepts:

> Generally speaking, what is manifest is material force (*balja / fa-che*), and the reason for its manifestation is principle (*soi balja / so-i fa-che*). Without material force, nothing can manifest; without principle, there is nothing manifested. (*Even a sage who is born again could not change this phrase of twenty three words.*) Although there is no priority and posteriority, and no separation and union between them, we cannot say that this could apply to mutual issuance.[76]

He further presents his unique understandings of principle and material force. It can be elaborated in his famous statements: *ki-bal-yi-seung* (氣發理乘, "material force issues and principle mounts it"); *i-il-bun-su* (理一分殊, "principle is one but its manifestations are many"); *i-tong-ki-kuk* (理通氣局, "principle pervades and material force delimits"); *i-ki-ji-myo* (理氣之妙, "the marvel of principle and material force").

Ki-Bal-Yi-Seung (氣發理乘, *"material force issues and principle mounts it"*)

Yulgok shows us his genius in explicating the relationship between principle and material force. He tries to define it more adequately and logically than any other Confucian scholar. According to Yulgok, "That which does the arousing- issuing is material force; that whereby there is the arousing-issuing is principle."[77] This fundamental view is elaborated very well by his famous statement "*ki-bal-yi-seung,*" which means that "material force issues and principle mounts it" (氣發理乘). He writes:

> In general, principle is master of material force; material force is what principle mounts upon. Without principle, material force has no root; without material force, principle has nothing to depend on. They are neither two [separate] things nor one thing. Not being one thing, they are one-yet-two; not being two things, they are two-yet-one.[78]

He goes on to say:

> Principle and material force are originally inseparable from each other and look like a single thing. The difference between them is that principle has no shape, but material force has shape; principle is non-active, but material force is active. That which is shapeless and non-active and the master of that which has shape and is active is principle. That which has shape and is active and is the instrument of that which is shapeless and non-active is material force. Principle is shapeless, and material force has shape. . . . Principle is non-active, and material force is active; therefore, material force issues, and principle mounts it.[79]

As we have discussed above, it is evident that Yulgok emphasizes the active movement of material force more than principle as a potential being.[80] While material force has concrete manifestation and embraces principle, principle rides material force and is thus realized in relationship with material force. That is what he means when he says that material force issues and principle mounts it. In this regard, it is also true that both are interdependent. However, this does not mean that material force is prior to principle. Instead, it means that material force is active, but principle is non-active. In other words, material force is always with principle and presupposes principle, but principle as non-activity is transmitted by material force as activity. Therefore, these two concepts are equally emphasized in Yulgok's philosophy.

On the other hand, the dynamic interrelationship between principle and material force is realized in the harmony of heaven and earth. Yulgok maintains that harmonies of heaven and earth are parallel to the functions of the mind and that there is no distinction between the changes of principle and material force in our minds.[81] The cosmos is composed of the totality of principle and material force. This harmony of heaven and earth comes from the process in which "material force issues and principle mounts it." Material force has the function of feeling in our mind, but cannot issue without principle as its source and ground.

I-Il-Bun-Su (理一分殊, "principle is one but its manifestations are many")

Yulgok's theory of "*i-il-bun-su*" (理一分殊), which means that "principle is one but its manifestations are many" is one well known characteristic in the *li-qi* theory in Neo-Confucianism. It was, however, not fully argued cogently with regard to material force until Cheng Yi and Zhu Xi.[82] Although Zhu did not use this phrase, he tried to present this theory in his argument for the Great Ultimate. He said: "Fundamentally there is only one Great Ultimate, yet each of the myriad things has been endowed with it and each in itself possesses the Great Ultimate in its entirety."[83] According to Zhu's thought, all things are generated from one Great Ultimate which is the origin of all things. This is exactly applied to principle and its relation to all things because, for Zhu, the Great Ultimate is nothing other than principle. Thus, it is right to say that principle is one, but it is manifested in many ways. Yulgok develops his theory of *i-il-bun-su* out of this background.

Yulgok first explicates *i-il-bun-su* by dividing the Great Ultimate into its substance and use. He states: "The original condition is that of principle's oneness and the condition of having become manifest is that of its varied differentiation";[84] "One fundamental principle is the substance of principle and diverse manifestation is the function of principle."[85] For him, it is clear that principle is understood in the dialectic of one and many. It is the same meaning as one of Zhu's famous statements: "There is the one Great Ultimate in all things in its entirety."[86] That is, there is one universal principle in the world but it appears in numerous ways by the issuing of material force. It is well understood by the relationship between principle and material force as well. He writes:

> Although principle is one, it takes on myriad variations when it is mounted on material force. Thus, in Heaven and Earth, it becomes the principle of Heaven and Earth; in the myriad things, it becomes the principle of the myriad things; in us humans, it becomes the principle of us human . . . . Although Heaven and Earth, men, and other things each have their own principle, the principle of

Heaven and Earth is the principle of the myriad things, which, in turn, is also the principle of us humans. This is what is described as the one universal Great Ultimate.[87]

Yulgok's theory of *i-il-bun-su* gives us a proper understanding of various phenomena in the world. Acknowledging one unified principle as a fundamental substance in the world, he states that this uniformity of principle varies, depending on the myriad movement of material force. He tries to understand all things in the world from the perspective of both *"i-il"* (one principle) and *"bun-su"* (its many manifestations). For him, all phenomena in the cosmos happen through the relationship of *i-ll* and *bun-su*.

According to Yulgok, it is not right to argue only for either *i-ll* or *bun-su*. He criticizes this view as being one-sided and extremist. He says: "Understanding only the unity of principle and not recognizing its diversity amounts to the Buddhist [mistake] of taking function for the nature and madly giving oneself over to dissoluteness. Understanding only diversity and not recognizing the unity of principle is the same as Hsün Tzu and Yang Tzu regarding the nature as evil or as a mixture of good and evil."[88]

On the other hand, this theory must be understood with regard to material force, which means another dimension of the relationship between principle and material force. This is also rightly called "the dialectic of one and many": one principle becomes many through the various movements of material forces in the world and many maintain one universal principle as a substance. Through this dialectic, all things come into being in various ways. This is a Neo-Confucian way of creation. He says:

> Indeed, principle is one, and that is all. In it, there is originally no differentiation into the partial and the fully correct, the penetrating and the blocked up, the clear and the turbid, the pure and the mixed. But the material force on which it is mounted rises and falls and flies about unceasingly, becoming mixed and variegated with numerous differences. It gives birth to Heaven and Earth and the myriad creatures, some blocked, some clear and some turbid, some pure and some mixed.[89]

The theory of *i-il-bun-su* is further applied to human nature. Unlike Zhu's division of human nature into "the original nature" and "the psychophysical nature," Yulgok analyzes only the psychophysical nature as human nature in terms of *i-il-bun-su*. For him, there is no need to mention either good or evil in human nature itself; it is necessary to discuss it only in terms of the theory of *i-il-bun-su*. We can just say that that human nature can have good and evil because it is a composite of principle and material force. While principle is originally pure and good, it mounts material force and then can appear as evil. One principle creates psychophysical endowment by material force, which is called "human nature." Yulgok speaks not only of one principle in human nature but also of its various manifestations in human nature. Human nature is one human nature and therefore the original nature contains the psychophysical nature.[90] He writes:

> Master Ch'eng said: "In the psychophysical endowment with which man is born, principle has good and evil.". . . What he speaks of as principle refers to principle as it mounts on material force and becomes active; it does not refer to principle in its original condition. In its original condition, principle is certainly purely good, but when it mounts material force and becomes active, it is differentiated in countless ways. Since there is both good and evil in the psychophysical endowment, principle likewise has both good and evil. Indeed, principle in its original condition is purely good, but when it has mounted material force it is disparate, not uniform. From the purest, cleanest, most noble of things to the filthiest and most base, there is nothing in which principle is not present.[91]

I-Tong-Ki-Kuk (理通氣局, "principle pervades and material force delimits")

Yulgok's harmonious view of principle and material force proceeds to another theory of his entitled "*i-tong-ki-guk*" (理通氣局, "principle pervades and material force delimits"). In fact, he expanded his theory of *i-il-bun-su* by discussing it in relationship with diverse activities of material force. He reinforces this by saying, "Material force has one origin because of the pervasiveness of principle and principle has many manifestations because of the delimitation of material force."[92] Along with his other theories, this theory of *i-tong-ki-guk* presents very uniquely the relationship of those two concepts. According to Yulgok, this theory is original in terms of its expression, even though his general system of thought is similar to Zhu Xi's.[93] Yulgok asserts:

> 'Principle pervades and material force delimits' (*i-t'ong-ki-kuk)*—I found these four [Chinese] words. I believe that this is my own discovery. However, I am afraid that, since my reading and study are not extensive, these four words may already be someplace but I have not yet seen them. Taking the Dao mind as material force in its original disposition seems to be a new expression; although it is what is meant by the sage, I have not yet seen it in classical texts.[94]

Michael Kalton also writes:

> Yulgok is finally driven to present his thinking in its most personal and original form: 'I will now empty out all I have.' What he has reserved until now is his own interpretation of the meaning of the distinction of principle and material force. The conventional description speaks of principle as being 'above'(or before) the world of actual phenomena ('form') and hence non-active, while material force belongs to that concrete level and so is active. His personal expres-

sion of the relationship is '*i-t'ong ki kuk,*' which I have rendered as 'principle pervades and material force delimits.'[95]

Yulgok investigates the meaning of *i t'ong ki kuk* in two ways. First, the phrase "*li* pervasives" (*i t'ong,* 理通) means "the universal character of principle." Principle appears all over the cosmos, mounting material force because principle itself has no shape or action, no origin or root, and no priority or posteriority. Yulgok writes:

What is it said that principle pervades? Principle has neither origin nor end, neither priority nor posteriority. Having no origin or end, no priority or posteriority, therefore what is unmoved is not prior and what is moved is not posterior. Thus as principle mounts material force and is involved in its circulating activity, it makes innumerable varieties and nonuniformities. But the mystery of its original condition exists everywhere . . . . Principle is everywhere present, even in dregs, ashes, excrement, and filth. It is the reason for each having its own nature. Yet, principle suffers no injury in the mystery of its original condition. This is what I meant by saying "principle pervades."[96]

Second, the phrase "material force delimits" (*ki kuk,* 氣局) means that "material force has a beginning and an ending in space, anterior and posterior in time because material force has shape and action." It is the particular character of material force that ascends, descends, and flies incessantly, and is pervasive over all things. He writes:

Why is it said that material force delimits? Material force is already involved with its physical form; therefore, it has beginning and end, priority and posteriority. The fundamental condition of material force is originally one and clear and pure. How can we say that there is the material force of dregs, ashes, excrement, and filth! But since it moves without ever ceasing, ascending and descending, flying and fluttering, it becomes uneven and irregular, and thus produces the myriad changes. As material force becomes active, some does not lose its original condition and others lose its original condition. When it has lost its original condition, then the original condition of material force is not present in any way. The one-sided thing is one-sided material force, not integral material force. The clear thing is clear material force, not turbid material force . . . . It is different from the presence of principle in the myriad things, wherein the mystery of its original condition is present in all things. This is what I meant by saying 'material force delimits.'[97]

In the above paragraph, principle pervades because it has no shape or limits, which means the characteristics of universality. However, material force delimits and is always changed because it has shape and action, which means the character of particularity. In other words, principle pervades because it belongs to "what is above shape," that is, general as well as one, whereas material force delimits because it belongs to "what is below shape," that is, concentrating as well as changing, growing as well as diminishing.[98] Principle pervades in the world as a universal and transcendental being, but it is realized and involved in the creation of all things in the world as material forces delimits in specific forms and shapes in time and space. All things in the world are understood in these dynamic activities of principle and material forces. I think that this theory of "the pervasiveness of principle and delimitation of material force" enables us to more adequately understand the world in this dynamic perspective of those two concepts.

It is surely here that Yulgok concentrates more on the particularity of material force than any other place. According to him, translucent material force appears as both general material force and specific material force. Material force is present in all kinds of things and appears as myriads forms. It is well applied for the activity and concreteness of living organisms. It also shows us his emphasis on the reality of philosophical thoughts. For him, both the normativity of principle and the delimitation of material force (*ki-guk*) have equal importance. In other words, "*ki guk,*" which meant "the issuance and dynamic activity of material force," was the symbol of actuality of all things.

In another place, Yulgok explains the characteristics of *i t'ong ki kuk* with some illustrations. He argues:

> '*I t'ong ki kuk*' should be stated in terms of the substance. We cannot enjoy talking of it without regard to substance. Human nature is not a thing's nature because material force delimits. Human principle is a thing's principle because principle pervades. The water in vessels is the same, though a round vessel is different from a square vessel in shape. The air in bottles is always the same, even though bottles differ in shape and size. An origin of material force is one because principle pervades. Principle manifests in ten thousand ways because material force delimits.[99]

According to Yulgok, human nature is different than other animal or plant nature because material force delimits differently in human beings and things in the world. Thus, it gives rise to human beings, animals, plants, or other things in the world. Human beings, however, have similarities to other animals and plants in the sense that all of them are living things because principle pervades over all of them. Likewise, *i-tong-ki-kuk* is one of the effective ways of all things in the cosmos.

I-Ki-Ji-Myo (理氣之妙, "*the marvel of principle and material force*")

In discussing principle and material force, Yulgok introduces a theory which is called "the marvel of principle and material force" (理氣之妙). This is one of many unique theories in Yulgok's philosophy. Through this theory, his other theories such as *"i-tong-ki-kuk"* and *"ki-bal-i-seung"* are well explicated with regard to the relationship of principle and material force. Furthermore, *"i-ki-ji-myo"* is a penetrating and fundamental philosophical framework throughout Yulgok's philosophy. It is a grounding perspective from which we can understand all of his philosophical thoughts. It is basically rooted in Yulgok's conviction of the "marvelous unity" (*myohap*, 妙合) of all things. His *i-ki-ji-myo* clearly presents to us the characteristics of Yulgok's Neo-Confucian cosmology; that is, both principle and material force are in a marvelous unity and the cosmos and nature have this kind of relationship as well. Even human beings have this relationship.

I-ki-ji-myo, above all, is the statement that exactly expresses the relationship of principle and material force. For Yulgok, both concepts have a marvelously united relationship. This is what *i-ki-ji-myo* ("the marvel of principle and material force") means. In order to be one being, there should be not only principle as the thing which is above shape but also material force as the thing which is below shape. Principle and material force are always in a marvelous unity. This means that, in a being, principle and material force are related to each other without any temporal priority and posteriority or spatial gap. Principle and material force are not separated or combined at any temporal moment. Principle and material force are simultaneously and respectively coexisting in a marvelous way.

Frequently, Yulgok states this marvelous characteristic of two concepts: "principle and material force are not mixed together and originally not separated from each other"[100]; "In general, the origin of principle is one and the origin of material force is one as well.... Material force is not separated from principle and principle is not separated from material force."[101] He continues:

> Principle and material force are not two things because they are in the midst of a perfect harmony without gaps between them and they are originally not separated from each other.... Although they are not separated, they are not mixed together in the midst of a perfect harmony; we cannot say they are not one thing.[102]

Unlike T'oegye who solely emphasized the unmixibility of principle and material force, Yulgok emphasized both the unmixibility and the inseparability of them by presenting his unique theory of *i-ki-ji-myo*. For Yulgok, this means that principle and material force are neither two nor one; they are two as well as one because they exist together in a marvelous unity. As one and two they are related to each other. Furthermore, for him, all other things in the world are related to each other. In this sense the world is understood not as exclusive and isolated but as an interrelated and organic structure. Yulgok calls this "marvel."

This is what he interprets as a marvelous combination or unity of all things including principle and material force.

Why does Yulgok express the marvel of principle and material force? It is primarily because, in Yulgok's view, it is very hard to see and talk about the right relationship of principle and material force and all other beings. He needed an appropriate metaphor for the relationship of two concepts. He also wanted to avoid two extremes. Some philosophers focus on the dominance of principle, while others focus on the dominance of material force. Yulgok refuted those two extreme positions. It seems that he is one of the only Confucian scholars to grasp the correct meaning of principle and material force in the world. He realized the truth of the marvelous unity of principle and material force from his careful study on classics and incessant self-cultivation. According to him, it is a sort of religious enlightenment to experience human encounters with heaven. That is, he had first experienced this truth deeply in himself before he stated this theory. He claims:

> The marvel of principle and material force is difficult to understand and difficult to explain. Principle has only a single source, and material force likewise has only a single source. Material force actively manifests and becomes uneven and irregular; likewise, principle actively manifests and becomes uneven and irregular. Material force is not separated from principle, and principle is not separated from material force. This being the case, therefore, principle and material force are one thing. Where can we find any difference?[103]

For Yulgok, the word "marvel" (妙) is not logic but a metaphor that symbolizes the harmonious dimension of principle and material force. Therefore, he once expressed the marvel of principle and material force in his poem that was sent to his friend Ugye. It shows us his exact understanding of principle and material force in the perspective of *i-ki-gi-myo*.

> Where does the primal material force take origin? The formless is within the form. As we investigate the sources, we realize that they are originally united. (*Principle and material force are originally united: there is no a moment when they began to be united; those who would try to treat principle and material force as two entities would not understand the way.*) In the diverging flow of the streams we can get the varied feelings; (*Principle and material force are originally one but are divided into the two forces and the five agents.*) Water takes the shape of square or round utensils; Space makes itself small or big in the vessels.[104]

This unique theory can be explored in another way. According to Jun-Yon Hwang, Yulgok's theory of the wonder of principle and material force can be understood in the light of Buddhist view of a "middle way"(*joongdo*, 中道) because Yulgok had learned Buddhism in depth before his Confucian studies. Hwang insists that Yulgok's theory is very similar to the Buddhist theory that "emptiness"(*kong*, 空), a formless world, is "color"(*saek*, 色), a phenomenal world, and vise versa, and they can be understood in the world of middle way. Likewise, the marvel of principle and material force refers to an inseparable dynamic relationship which can only be understood in the world of middle way.[105]

Yulgok further applied the theory of *i-ki-ji-myo* to the relationship between human nature and heavenly way. He points out:

> What the heavenly way imparts to human beings is called human nature. From whence human nature is derived is called heaven. All principles are in shaped material forces. There is secrecy in broadness. Truly, if we are not the ones whose wisdom goes deep into the ultimate principle, how can we understand an exceedingly marvelous dimension of all things? [106]

Second, for Yulgok, *i-ki-ji-myo* means "beings themselves as a whole." Just as *i-ki-ji-myo* refers to "a relationship of beings," it also presents the characteristics of all beings themselves. In other words, human beings, nature, all things, and cosmos exist in a marvelously organized structure. As stated above, *ki-bal-i-seung* expressed a relationship of principle and material force as "material force issuance" and "principle mount." Similarly, *i-ki-ji-myo* also means that "the actuality of material force should be coherent to the lordship of principle."

Third, *i-ki-ji-myo* means that "principle has a complementary relationship with material force". Both concepts need each other. Both concepts are not complete alone. He states: "Although principle has no form or motion, material force has no origin without principle. Therefore, principle is formless and motionless, but it is the master of the things which have form and motion. Material force has form and motion, and is the vessel of the things which have no form or motion."[107] In brief, what one is able to realize is material force. The reason whereby one is able to realize is principle.[108] He goes on to say: "Generally, principle is the master of material force. Material force is the thing on which principle mounts. Without principle, material force has no place of basis. Without material force, principle has no place of dependence."[109]

Principle and material force always exist together in all things. This is a fundamental structure of the cosmos. In a sense, these two concepts are self-complementary concepts but need their counterparts in consisting of all things. With only one element, either principle or material force, being doesn't exist. Both have equal importance. In Yulgok's philosophy, it is not possible to discuss material force without principle or principle without material force. This is the point that Yulgok makes in his theory of the marvel of principle and material force. Further, as the most fundamental of his philosophical thoughts, this theory is applied to all of his theories such as cosmology, doctrine of human nature, and social thoughts.

Fourth, *i-ki-ji-myo* means "the dialectical logic of principle and material force". This is well expressed when he mentions that principle and material force are one thing as well as two things. This dialectical logic between principle and material force is beyond both dualism and monism of two concepts. This is what '*i-ki-ji-myo*' exactly means. He states:

> Principle and material force are not two [separate] things, but again they are not one thing. Not being one thing, they are one-yet-two; not being two things, they are two-yet-one. What does it mean when I say they are not one thing? Although principle and material force are inseparable from each other, "*in the midst of their marvelous unity,*" principle is principle and material force is material force; they are never intermingled and therefore are one thing. What does it mean to say that they are not two things? Although it is said that principle is principle and material force is material force, they are interrelated with no space, no priority or posteriority, no separating or conjoining; we cannot perceive them as two [separate] things."[110]

According to him, this dialectical relationship which is expressed in the marvelous unity of principle and material force was derived from his careful studies on Confucian masters. He argues:

> There was a question of principle and material force: are they one thing or two things? I replied to it. As I thought about the above lessons, principle and material force are two as well as one, or one as well as two. Principle is not separated from material force because there is no distance between them, so we cannot say that principle and material force are two things. Master Ch'eng said, 'Instrument is also *dao* (the way), and *dao* is also instrument'. And we cannot say that principle and material force are one because both are not to be mixed together although they do not depart from each other. Therefore, Master Zhu said, "Principle and material force are not to be mixed together because principle is naturally principle and material force is naturally material force." If we think carefully of what the two Masters said, "we will see the marvel of principle and material force."[111]

Yulgok therefore very adequately combined master Zhu's two theories: principle and material force cannot be separated; principle and material force cannot be mixed. As a result of that, he presented the theory of the marvel of principle and material force. He wanted to show that the origin of principle and material force are the same, saying that principle and material force are not two things or one thing. They are two as well as one because they are not one thing. They are one as well as two because they are not two things. His phrases clearly show that principle and material force cannot be separated from each other nor can they be mixed together. Principle and material force, therefore, maintain this special dialectic relationship; they are in the midst of the marvelous unity (妙合). Since this view of principle and material force is hard to understand and explain, Yulgok uses the phrase "the marvel of principle and material force" to make it more understandable to people. Therefore, the marvel or wonder (妙), here, expresses the relationship between principle and material force.

When Yulgok says that "one is one" and "two is one," "one" means that "principle and material force exist together in a marvelous unity," and "two" means that "principle and material force are radically distinguished." On the contrary, if we say that principle and material force are one, it does not mean that principle and material force are the same identities. Also, if we say that principle and material force are two, it does not mean that principle and material force have any priority and posteriority. In this sense, Yulgok criticizes both the theory that regards principle and material force as one and the theory that takes the temporal priority of principle of material force.

For Yulgok, both concepts are equally important in understanding all things in the cosmos. His theory of the marvel of principle and material force express very adequately and rightly the harmonious interrelationship of principle and material force of which all things are comprised. It offers a lot of significant insights in harmoniously understanding the cosmos and all things.

Tae-Geuk-Um-Yang (太極陰陽, "the Great Ultimate and Yin-Yang")

Yulgok's understanding of principle and material force is developed into the theories of the "Great Ultimate" and "yin and yang," which concludes his Neo-Confucian cosmology.[112] As it is well known, the understanding of the "Great Ultimate" is an important issue in the history of Chinese philosophy. That is, there were numerous debates about the expression of the "Great Ultimate" in the *Book of Changes*: "Therefore in the system of Change there is the "Great Ultimate." It generates the "Two Modes" (yin and yang). The "Two Modes" generates the "Four Forms" (major and minor yin and yang). The "Four Forms" then generate the "Eight Trigrams."[113] Although there are various interpretations regarding this expression of the "Great Ultimate," it is generally agreed that the "Great Ultimate" means the "origin of all things in the cosmos."

Traditionally, the Great Ultimate is conceptually the same as the "Great Vacuity" (太虛), which also refers to the "origin of the cosmos." In the history of Chinese Confucian philosophy, we see two different ideas of the "Great Ultimate." First, Chang Tsai (1020-1077 C.E.) regarded material force as the origin of all things and the cosmos. He states: "The Great Vacuity (*hsü*) has no physical form. It is the original substance of material force. Its integration and disintegration are but objectifications caused by Change."[114] On the contrary, Zhu Xi insists that principle is nothing other than 'the Great Ultimate.' He states:

The Great Ultimate is merely the principle of Heaven and earth and the myriad things. With respect to heaven and earth, there is the Great Ultimate in them. With respect to the myriad things, there is the Great Ultimate in each and every one of them. Before heaven and earth existed, there was assuredly this principle. It is the principle that through movement generates the yang. It is also this principle that through tranquility generates the yin.[115]

Yulgok's theory of the Great Ultimate is based on the traditional ideas in Cheng-Zhu Neo-Confucianism. He defines principle as the Great Ultimate, and material force as the yin and yang on which the Great Ultimate is dependent, following Zhu Xi's Neo-Confucian thoughts. He said, "The Great Ultimate is called the way (*dao*) in heaven and nature in humanity."[116] This means that the Great Ultimate is an ultimate truth that penetrates heaven and humanity, and has a meaning of heavenly way and human nature. For Yulgok, both the Great Ultimate and yin-yang are essential elements in constituting all things. They are involved in the formation of all things. Above all, the Great Ultimate causes yin-yang to act in movement and quiescence. It is the ultimate principle that exists in all things and the cosmos. As the basis of all things, it presides over all movements and changes of yin and yang. It has a central role in the cosmos.

On the other hand, the Great Ultimate is always followed by yin and yang. It would be an abstract principle or a theoretical concept without yin and yang. It should have a place of dependence: yin and yang. It always accompanies yin and yang as a counter partner. More exactly, the Great Ultimate is also in a marvelous unity with yin and yang. Here, Yulgok's central thesis of *ki-bal-yi-seung* (material force issues and principle mounts it) is applied to the Great Ultimate and yin-yang as well. Yulgok argues: "The transformative process of Heaven and Earth is completely a matter of material force issuing and principle mounting it. This is also true in the case of the human heart and mind. Therefore, yin and yang cycle in activity and tranquility, and the Great Ultimate mounts it. Here we cannot say that there is priority or posteriority."[117]

How does yin and yang act in the cycle of rest and movement? Yulgok presents his answer on the basis of Cheng Yi's important thesis: "Activity and tranquility have no beginning and yin and yang have no starting point."[118] This means that yin and yang have no beginning or ending of movement; they are cycling, starting from each other. This is related to the preexistence of material force before the formation of yin and yang. While some scholars insisted that tranquil and pure material existed force before the formation of yin and yang, Yulgok criticized this type of thinking, saying,

> Is tranquil and pure material force yin or yang? If it is yin, will there be yang before yin? If it is yang, will there be yin before yang? So, tranquil and pure material force cannot be the beginning of material force. Nowhere in the classics do we find discussion of any material force, existing separately from yin and yang, taking control over yin and yang. What is empty, broad, and motionless is principle. If we seek material force from principle, it is like all empty, broad, and motionless phenomena are put in order. If we seek principle

from material force, it is like we are saying that being a yang or being a yin is the way. This is what we express in language. However, in reality, we can not say that principle independently exists and there is the time when it is empty and broad without yin and yang.[119]

Likewise, Yulgok doesn't postulate any priority or posteriority of yin and yang. He seeks the relationship of yin and yang in a marvelous unity, generally agreeing with Zhu Xi's ideas. In other words, those two concepts influence each other, and thus changes and transformations are produced by their cycling movements.

Yulgok, further, presents the interplay of the Great Ultimate and yin and yang by interpreting the famous statement in the *Book of Changes* from his philosophical perspective: "In the system of Change there is the Great Ultimate. It generates the Two Modes (yin and yang)." He argues for the relationship between the Great Ultimate and yin and yang in the following statement:

> There is flaw in the Sages' words because they only said the Great Ultimate generates yin and yang; they didn't say that yin and yang originally existed and were never produced. Therefore, those who read this literally say that 'there is only principle before material force is produced.' This is a mistake. Some says that 'tranquil and clean material force in the Great Vacuity produces yin and yang.' This is also a one- sided idea and mistake because they don't know that yin and yang originally exist. In general, yin and yang are circulating and have no beginning. If yin is extinguished, yang will be produced. If yang is extinguished, yin will be produced. The Great Ultimate always exists when yin is produced and yang is produced. Therefore, the Great Ultimate is the pillar of changes of all things and their roots.[120]

Yulgok tries to correct some mistake in expressions in the *Book of Changes*. For clarity, he adds his point that "yin and yang originally existed and were never initially produced." Emphasizing the original and natural coexistence of yin and yang, he maintains that only the Great Ultimate independently exists as the original substance in all other things in the world. He also insists that the Great Ultimate always existed along with the constant movement of yin and yang. This, of course, does not mean any priority or posteriority of those concepts. According to him, there is neither beginning nor ending in movement and quiescence of yin and yang. Yulgok points out a possible misunderstanding of the relationship between the Great Ultimate and yin-yang. Yulgok contends:

> Master Chou [Tun-i] said, 'The Great Ultimate through movement generates yang. And through tranquility the Great Ultimate generates yin.' Is there anything wrong with these two phrases? But if we misinterpret them, we will certainly believe that originally there was no yin and yang, and the Great Ultimate existed before them. Then after the Great Ultimate moved, yang arose, and after

the Great Ultimate became tranquil, yin arose. To read it that way is a great misunderstanding of the original meaning, but as a literal interpretation it is quite in accordance with the sentence structure and the words, and so would present no problem.[121]

For Yulgok, there was no the great vacuous material force before yin and yang existed; similarly, there was no tranquil and pure material force before the movement and quiescence of yin and yang. Only the Great Ultimate exists by itself as the fundamental substance in the cosmos. It is the foundation of all beings in the cosmos. It is also called the principle which functions as the ground of yin and yang as well as movement and quiescence. It is always with two phases of the movement of material force: yin and yang. In this respect, it is evident that Yulgok lays more weight on principle as the Great Ultimate than material force in understanding the movement of all things in the cosmos.

Chil-Jong-Po-Sa-Dan (七精包四端, "the Seven Feelings Include the Four Beginnings")

Yulgok's cosmological thoughts are further applied to the doctrine of human nature expressed in the famous philosophical debate called "*Sa-Dan-Chil-Jong-Non* "(The Debate on the Four Beginnings and Seven Feelings or The Four-Seven Debate). Michael C. Kalton points out the importance of this debate: "Above all the famous controversy associated with them (T'oegye and Yulgok), the 'Four-Seven Debate,' addressed issues at the core of the great Ch'eng-Chu (Cheng-Zhu) synthesis in a way that set an important and distinctive philosophical agenda for subsequent generations of Korean thinkers."[122]

To the "Four Beginnings" and the "Seven Feelings" in human nature are described in Confucian classics. The Four Beginnings and the Seven Feelings have both theoretical and practical significance regarding human nature in Neo-Confucian anthropology. It is well known that the Four Beginnings (四端) are derived from Mencius' definitions of four human feelings arising in special circumstances. In support of human goodness, Mencius talks about the Four Beginnings as the original nature and good feelings of humanity. He claims:

> Here is a man who suddenly notices a child about to fall into a well. Invariably he will fell a sense of alarm and compassion. And this is not for the purpose of gaining the favor of the child's parents, or seeking the approbation of his neighbors and friends, or for fear of blame should he fail to rescue it. Thus we see that no man is without a sense of compassion, or a sense of shame, or a sense of courtesy, or a sense of right and wrong. The sense of compassion is the beginning of humanity; the sense of shame is the beginning of righteousness; the sense of courtesy is the beginning of decorum; the sense of right and wrong is the beginning of wisdom. Every man has within himself these four begin-

nings, just as he has four limbs.¹²³

That is, according to Mencius, the "Four Beginnings" means "the feelings of commiseration, shame and dislike, deference and compliance, and right and wrong." These are the feelings that reveal the original nature of humanity: humanity, righteousness, propriety, and wisdom. In the *Book of Rites,* on the contrary, human feelings are described as seven words: desire, hate, love, fear, grief, anger, and joy.¹²⁴ That is, all human beings have the "Seven feelings"(七情) from birth. It has been important for Confucians to control these feelings successfully through continuous self-cultivation, because these feelings hinder the ability to be a sage. Thus, the *Doctrine of Mean* teaches us similarly, "The state before delight, anger, sorrow, joy are aroused is called equilibrium (*zhong, joong,* 中). When those emotions have issued forth and all of them do so in a measured (not extreme) way, [the resulting state] is called harmony (*he, hwa,* 和). Equilibrium (of the cosmic forces corresponding to human emotions) is the great root of the world. Harmony is the most excellent dao (way of functioning) of the world."¹²⁵

Surely it is here that the seven or the four feelings must be well controlled. It was important for Confucian scholars in the Choson dynasty to argue these notions of the Four Beginnings and the Seven Feelings in the context of '*li-qi*' philosophy, because they thought the Confucian masters were not clear about these concepts with regard to the Confucian anthropology. Therefore, the debates on the Four Beginnings and the Seven Feelings began through philosophical correspondents by Choson Neo-Confucian Scholars such as T'oegye (1501-1570), Kobong (1527-1572), Yulgok, and Ugye (1535-1598). Here, I will focus on Yulgok's position.

Yulgok expressed his philosophical positions on the Four-Seven Debate nine times in his correspondences with T'oegye and Ugye. Yulgok's unique philosophy of *li-qi* deeply influenced his whole understanding of the Four Beginnings and Seven Feelings. Above all, his theory of *ki-bal-yi-seung* (氣發理乘, which means that material force and principle mounts it), was fully applied to the relationship between the Four Beginnings and Seven Feelings. Yulgok's *ki-bal-yi-seung* is different from T'oegye's thought. It is well known that T'oegye believes that principle is principle itself and material force is material force itself. He then presents the theory of "*i-ki-ho-bal*" (理氣互發), which means "the mutual issuance of principle and material force." However, Yulgok refutes T'oegye's theory of mutual issuance of principle and material force; he further does not agree to the issuance of principle or the dynamics of principle itself. For Yulgok, "That which gives issuance is material force and that whereby there is issuance is principle; without material force, there would not be the power of issuing; without material force, there would not be that whereby it issues."¹²⁶

Yulgok firmly holds to the theory of *ki-bal-yi-seung*. For him, the Four Beginnings and Seven Feelings can be explained by the philosophical structure of *ki-bal-yi-seung*. That is to say, for him, both the Four Beginnings and the Seven Feelings are all human feelings; however, the feeling is nothing more than that which nature arises and amounts on material force. The feeling is nothing but the issuance of nature. In the same way, the Four Beginnings are nothing but that which purely comes out of the Seven Feelings without being contaminated by human desires.[127] Just like principle and material force, the Four Beginnings and the Seven Feelings are not separated from each other. Yulgok also believes that the human nature of original disposition is in the midst of the human nature of psychophysical disposition. He explains the Four Beginnings and Seven Feelings with regard to the nature of original disposition (本然之性) and the nature of psychophysical disposition (氣質之性), the human mind (人心) and the Dao (tao) mind (道心) in the following way:

> The 'nature of original disposition' refers exclusively to principle and does not touch on material force. The 'nature of psychophysical disposition' refers to material force that includes principle in it. So, in this case, it is not possible to generalize with a contrastive division that explains it by the theory of principle-domination or material force-domination. If one makes a dichotomy of the nature of original disposition and the nature of physical disposition, will not the ignorant believe that there are two separate natures? Moreover, it is permissible to say that the four beginnings are mainly principle; but it is wrong to say that the Seven Feelings are mainly material force. The Seven Feelings include both principle and material force; they are not a matter of the domination of material force. (*The human mind and dao mind can be explained in terms of the theory of principle-domination or material force-domination. But the Four Beginnings and Seven Feelings cannot be explained in that way because the Four Beginnings are already included in the Seven Feelings and the Seven Feelings have both principle and material force.*)[128]

Yulgok basically agrees with Mencius that the Four Beginnings and the original nature are good. "The human nature is originally good, but the influence of the psychophysical disposition may cause it to devolve into evil."[129] In regard to the origin of the Four Beginnings and Seven Feelings, he maintains that they come out of one nature of humanity. On the basis of his belief that human nature are one and not two, he makes clear that the Seven Feelings include the Four Beginnings (七精包四端). In other words, while the Seven Feelings are the whole feelings of humanity, the Four Beginnings are good feelings among them. He maintains, "The Four Beginnings are the good side of the Seven Feelings, and the Seven Feelings are the totality of the Four Beginnings."[130] Thus he argues:

> Human nature consists of humanity, righteousness, propriety, wisdom, and fidelity—these five and that is all. Outside of these five, there is no other human

nature. The feelings consist of pleasure, anger, sorrow, fear, love, hatred, and desire—these seven and that is all. There are no other feelings than these seven feelings. The Four Beginnings are just alternative names for the good feelings. If we talk about 'the Seven Feelings,' the Four Beginnings are already contained in them. This is not like the human mind and Dao mind, which are contrastive to each other. Why do you try to compare these two [the 'four' and 'seven']? Generally speaking, the human mind and Dao mind are opposites to each other. When we talk about Dao mind, it is no longer the human mind; when we talk about the human mind, it is no longer Dao mind. Therefore, we can explain the mind from either side [the human mind and Dao mind]. But, in the case of the Seven Feelings, they already include the Four Beginnings in themselves. So, we cannot say that the Four Beginnings are not the Seven Feelings, or that the Seven Feelings are not the Four Beginnings. How could they be divided? Didn't you already see that the Seven Feelings include the Four Beginnings?[131]

In the statements quoted above, we find that Yulgok clearly opposes T'oegye's theory that the Four Beginnings and the Seven Feelings have respectively different origins: principle and material force. Instead, Yulgok is convinced that both have one origin and the Seven Feelings include the Four Beginnings (*chil-jong-po-sa-dan*, 七精包四端). The relation between the Four Beginnings and the Seven Feelings is the same as the one between the original nature and the psychophysical nature. The original nature is in the psychophysical nature. He firmly believes that, as the human nature is one, the human feeling is one; the human feeling is nothing but the issuance of the human nature. While the Four Beginnings refer to the dao (tao) mind, the Seven Feelings refer to the whole matrix of both the human and the dao mind. The dao mind and the human mind are one, but their names are different because they become different as they arise and are influenced by the psychophysical endowment and various orientations of the human mind. Some arise for the will of dao and become the dao mind; the others arise for the human body and its desires and become the human mind. It is the problem of the issuance to be pointed out here.

Therefore, Yulgok's position on human nature enables us to practice self-cultivation through the concept of "sincerity"(Chinese *cheng*; Korean *sung*, 誠). According to Yulgok's anthropological positions rooted in his Neo-Confucian metaphysics, we might be able to change human nature from the psychophysical nature to the original nature and from the human mind to the dao mind through sincere self-cultivation. This is the significance of Yulgok's creative position in the Four-Seven debate: "*chil-jong-po-sa-dan*"(七精包四端), which means that "the Seven Feelings include the Four Beginnings."

Conclusion

In conclusion, although Yulgok's Neo-Confucian cosmology was strongly influenced by Zhu's Song Chinese Neo-Confucianism and his followers both in China and Korea, it is considered to be unique and creative in many ways. Yulgok laid equal emphasis both on principle and material force, whereas T'oegye gave the priority to principle in Zhu's metaphysical scheme. Yulgok was not a *qi* (material force) advocate; rather, he realized the dynamic movement of two formative elements in a wondrous and harmonious way. Hence, he made more clear explanations of the interrelationship between the two philosophical concepts than any other Neo-Confucian scholar in China or Korea. Such a philosophical position had a large impact on many areas in his time. Kyoung-Jae Kim's assessment is very pertinent to this point, comparing Yulgok to T'oegye.

> One wonders how this kind of pedantic discussion of ontology may affect social norms and human ethicality. Yet the consequence is great. Lee Hwang's position is more conservative, normative, conceptual, and tradition-holding, yet that of Lee Yi is more progressive, revolutionary, and experimental. In the practical matter of policy, Lee Yi proposed a social renewal policy in amending the legal systems of the sixteenth century for the people. For Lee Yi, the positive laws as the actual manifestation of the *li* (principle) in social life must be subordinated to the people's life situation which is the concrete manifestation of the *ch'i* (material force).[132]

We shall examine how Yulgok's philosophical system was actively deployed in Choson society of sixteenth century and the implications it provides for the prompting of enhanced and reformed Christian spirituality and spiritual practices, along with Whitehead's process metaphysical system in the next two chapters.

Chapter 3

A COMPARISON OF WHITEHEAD AND YULGOK ON COSMOLOGY

Whitehead and Yulgok proposed remarkably parallel views on the cosmos and the world. Although they came from totally different philosophical contexts, it becomes evident that there are strong resemblances between Whitehead's process philosophy and Yulgok's Neo-Confucian philosophy. It is basically because both thinkers understand the universe and the world as an interrelated organism in the process of change and becoming. Although their philosophical contexts and terms are different, their modes of thoughts are very similar in terms of the organismic perspective of nature. I am convinced, above all, that there are similarities between the two thinkers on cosmology, more specifically, Whitehead's theory of "eternal object—actual entity" and Yulgok's theory of "principle-material force" (*li-qi*).[1] This is because Whitehead's "eternal object" and Yulgok's "principle" basically function as universal principles and sources of cosmological harmony, whereas Whitehead's "actual entity" and Yulgok's "material force" are phenomenological realities in the world. Accordingly, Whitehead's concept of God in terms of his panentheism has similarity to Yulgok's Neo-Confucian concept of the Great Ultimate. The two concepts suggest a balanced structure of God or the absolute and the world, transcendence and immanence, and the one and the many.

In his *Science and Civilisation in China*, Joseph Needham points out that "Chu Hsi (Zhu Xi)'s philosophy was fundamentally a philosophy of organism, and that the Sung Neo-Confucians thus attained, primarily by insight, a position analogous to that of Whitehead."[2] Needham's comment is very pertinent to the issue we deal with in this study. In the same way, Chung-ying Cheng also insists that Cheng-Zhu Neo-Confucianism shares the organic views of philosophy with Whitehead's process metaphysics.[3] Zhu Xi himself clearly expressed the organismic quality of his philosophy and even applied this philosophy of organism to family and society. Thus, in opposition to the Buddhists, he maintained,

> Under heaven, only the principle of *Tao* and *Li* exist, and we cannot but follow them unto the end. The Buddhists and the Taoists, for example, even though they would destroy the social relationships (i.e. by becoming monks and cutting themselves off them from the world) are nevertheless quite unable to escape from them. Thus, lacking (the relationship of) father and son, they nevertheless pay respect to their own preceptors (as if they were fathers) on the one hand, while they treat their novices as their sons on the other. The elders among them become elder-brother preceptors, while the younger become younger-brother preceptors. And yet (in so doing) they cling to something false, whereas it is the (Confucian) sages and worthies who have preserved the reality.[4]

Zhu Xi's organismic philosophy is rightly applied to Yulgok's thought because Yulgok was a faithful student of Zhu Xi and the frame of his philosophy was formulated under the influence of Zhu's Neo-Confucianism. Fundamentally, Yulgok's metaphysical system is formally similar to Whitehead's. It is well known that Whitehead preferred to call his philosophy "a philosophy of organism." Whitehead also maintained the similarity of his thought to Oriental thoughts. He claimed, "In the general position the philosophy of organism seems to approximate more to some strains of Indian or Chinese thought, than to western Asiatic or European thought. One side makes process ultimate; the other side fact ultimate."[5] These similarities enable us to do a comparative study between Whitehead and Yulgok, which can be significant in building a bridge between West and East today. As Ching describes, more precisely, "The richness and profundity of the Chinese macrosm / microsm outlook allows comparison with Western philosophers known for their dialectical logic and synthetic genius."[6]

We can find many good reasons for analyzing similarities between two thinkers. In particular, this kind of comparative study is very helpful to beginning the Confucian-Christian dialogue in the world of religious pluralism today. And through this dialogue, as Whitehead foretold, "They can learn from each other, borrow from each other, and individuals can make imperceptible transitions. Above all, they can learn to understand each other and to love."[7] Furthermore, the encounter and the dialogue among religious traditions can offer fresh opportunities for growth and vigor. As John Cobb notes, the purpose of dialogue is to learn from others about transforming ways, in order to cease threatening our planetary home. It must be a process of mutual learning and transformation which leads to the building of a global community. Therefore, the motivation for the interreligious should be "to increase the likelihood that both communities would become more effective in countering the forces that endangered the future."[8]

As a theoretical system of such a dialogue, the comparison between Yulgok and Whitehead can initiate a specific model of Confucian-Christian dialogue in the Korean context. It is, of course, not an easy job in the global community where hatred, conflicts, tensions, and war among the people of various religious backgrounds still exist. Similarly, it is not easy to compare Whitehead to Yulgok because their general schemes of philosophical thought and their historical, cultural backgrounds are not the same. It means that large differences exist between two thinkers. As Ching notes, "Their philosophies grew out of different cultural matrices with divergent basic concerns."[9] So, in order to reveal the similarities and differences between two thinkers more exactly, it is necessary to make a thorough comparative study in various ways. Here, our comparison will revolve around the two thinkers' cosmological thoughts, focusing on their key terms and motifs. We will focus more on their similarities than their differences, so that this comparative study may offer meaningful implications in the formation of the interreligious spirituality in the context of religious pluralism.

Actual Entity and Material Force (*Qi*)

According to Whitehead, the phenomenal world is composed entirely of actual entities in the process of changing and becoming. He defines "actual entities" as final realities. He maintains: "'Actual entities'—also termed 'actual occasions'—are the final real things of which the world is made up. There is no going behind actual entities to find anything more real."[10] Even God is one of the actual entities. That is, for Whitehead, actual entities are the fundamentals of the metaphysical system and the least elements of the universe. Hence comes the ontological principle of his process metaphysics: "No actual entity, then no reason."[11] This principle indicates to us that actual entities as ultimate things do not perish in the universe, although their modes and forms of existence are changed in many different ways. All actual entities have no differences in quality; instead, all actual entities are ontologically on the same level. All things are part of the society of actual entities in the universe. Also, actual entities are born, become, and change on their own. Furthermore, every actual entity is related to one another and surrounded by other entities. In particular, all actual entities form themselves and influence one another in the process of concrescence. However, in order to be an individual, concrete fact, an actual entity must have the form of definiteness. Actual entities always exist in relation to the form of definiteness. Here, an eternal object plays the role of the form of definiteness. Ingression is the manner in which eternal objects are present in actual entities as the form of definiteness or the pure potentials for specific determination.

In Yulgok's Neo-Confucian Cosmology, "material force" (*qi*) is the equivalent term to "actual entity." Along with "principle," "material force" is one of the fundamental concepts on which the Neo-Confucian cosmology is built. Like actual entities, material force is the final thing and element of which the universe is comprised. According to Yulgok's Neo-Confucianism, the universe is full of material forces. Material force, which is called "what is within shape," permeates all things in the universe. As Zhu said, "In the beginning of heaven and earth, there was only the *ch'i* of yin and yang, in heaven and earth. This *ch'i* moved and turned around continuously."[12] In the same manner, Yulgok also maintains, "All things issued are of material force."[13] Without material force, the universe cannot exist. Even principle has meaning only in relation with material force. All things, organism or non-organism, come into being by means of material force. They become various things depending on differences of their material forces. Furthermore, material force produces all things in the universe by operating through them. This means that, similar to Whitehead's actual entity, material force continually acts in the rotation of quiescence and movement: incessant movement of yin and yang in the universe. Yulgok thus states: "What moves once and stops once in quiescence is material force. . . . 'Thus-so of things' is material force."[14] And, material force is divided into the two modes of yin and yang, the two forces of quiescence and activity. Here "Yin and yang are the same material force. The retreat of yang is the emergence of yin. It is not true that yang retreats and then yin separately emerges."[15]

Eternal Object and Principle (*Li*)

In Whitehead's process cosmology, "eternal object" is understood as "universals." An eternal object is "eternal" because it is non-temporal; eternal objects are "objects" because they are given as pure potentials. Unlike actual entities, eternal objects have nothing to do with concrescence, process, and transition in essence. An eternal object functions as a determinant which determines definiteness in concrescence of all actual entities. In other words, an eternal object determines the realization of actual entities by having ingression into actual entities. Eternal objects are prior to actual entities because they ingress into actual entities. This is true if we are speaking not temporally but logically. This does not mean eternal objects exist apart from actual entities; rather, eternal objects function as datum of past actual entities in the process of concrescence. An eternal object plays its role only with an actual entity. Eternal objects cannot be separated from actual entities. Thus, eternal objects are potentialities which are realized in actual entities.

For Yulgok, "principle" is a similar concept to Whitehead's eternal object. "Principle," which is called "what is above shape," is the ontological being which is prior to the actual existence of objects. The principle of a thing is the supreme archetype of that thing; it is the essence and the norm of that thing. In other words, it is the principle of things to be actualized, and actualization requires principle as its substance and material force as its actuality. Principle has priority over all things, including material force. That is to say, all existent things have reasons for their existence, or have an essence for their existence, which is called "principle." Yulgok clearly states that principle is the reason for all things, which can be called the formal principle of all things.[16] Thus, he claims, "All things issued are of material force and the reason for issuance is principle. Without material force, there will be no issuance; without principle, there is no reason for issuance."[17]

The Dynamic Interrelationship of the Eternal Object -Actual Entity And the Principle-Material Force

A good way to explore and compare the cosmologies of Whitehead and Yulgok is to investigate the dynamic interrelationship of eternal object-actual entity and principle-material force. Interestingly, both Whitehead and Yulgok maintain that all things are constituted by the interrelationship between eternal object and actual entity and principle and material force.

First, there are systematical similarities between Whitehead's theory of eternal object-actual entity and Yulgok's theory of principle-material force. For Whitehead and Yulgok, the actual entity and material force have activity and function, while the eternal object functions as the form of definiteness and principle functions as the source of activity. Material force has artificiality, but principle has no artificiality. The eternal object and principle always exist in relation to the actual entity and material force. They are necessary in forming actual entities and material force.

Principle always adheres to material force because principle is the principle which has no active function. Likewise, an eternal object has ingression into actual entities. Material force is moving only according to principle.[18] "Principle is the master of material force and material force is the instrument of principle."[19] In this regard, Wanne J. Joe's comment is right: "Although all things were created by the two cosmic forces of *i* (*li*) and *ki* (Chinese *ch'i*; *qi*), the *i* as an immaterial and immutable principle did not participate in creation through action as such. It is the *ki* alone that creates through its ability to change and act."[20] By the contrary, material forces cannot begin to change and act without principles, which are the source of all movements of material forces. In other words, material force has no value and order without principle. Likewise, eternal objects play the role of determinants that determine the becoming of actual entities. Actual entities don't come into being without eternal objects. That is to say, principle and eternal objects are the sources of the movements of material force and actual entities.

According to Whitehead, actual entities take on a form of definiteness (i.e., eternal objects) and specific characteristics of movement and activity. Without having these forms of definiteness, actual entities cannot exist and function. In a similar way, according to Yulgok, the thing that gives issuance is material force, but material force is impossible without principle as the source of issuance. The eternal object and principle enable the actual entity and material force to have particular activities. Change, development, and transition do not belong to the activities of eternal objects or principle but to the activities of actual entities or material force. Since eternal objects and principle remain as the factors of definiteness in the changing process of actual entities and material force, the eternal object and principle exist only in the relationship of definiting and determining actual entities and material force.

Second, Yulgok maintains the theory that "material force issues and principle mounts it." This means that all things are moving and changing, which is possible not by the external controller, but by the function of material force in relation to principle. Actual entities and material force can be understood only in relation to the activities of eternal objects and principle as the ultimate realities. Actual entities also are moving and changing. Whitehead places identity and permanence on the process of actual entities interacting with other entities. Here, an eternal object has ingression into actual entities with the same characteristics. Thus, the eternal object has a role of "identity" and "permanence." In other words, the eternal object relates to all separated, individual entities. "The universe of many things acquires an individual unity in a determinate relegation of each item of the many to its subordination in the constitution of the novel one."[21] In other words, "The many, which are the universe disjunctively, become the one actual occasion, which is the universe conjunctively."[22]

Yulgok also presents the same basic format for principle and material force. He insists that principle is one, but a number of appearances are formed by material force.[23] It is expressed by the famous axiom of Cheng Yi and Zhu Xi that "principle is one but its manifestations are many." Here, "principle" refers to "one" and "material force" refers to 'many.' "Principle" as "one" has an interaction with material force as "many." As a result of that, principle appears in a number of ways in relation to material force. In other words, principle as formless is immanent in the actuality of material force and is concretized into many realities. This dynamic relationship between principle and material force is expressed by the theory "principle pervades and material force delimits."

Third, Whitehead's concept of "definiteness" corresponds to Yulkok's concept of "delimitation." For Yulgok, material force appears in various forms by the process of movement and change, which means that it delimits. Yulgok maintains that principle has no form but material force has form, and principle has no activity but material force has activity. Principle exists in all things, even in ashes, dregs, mud, and muck, because it pervades and penetrates. However, principle is realized according to its immanence in the actuality of material force. All things are related to one another in the organic system. In the same way, for Whitehead, eternal objects participate in all events of actual entities and play the role of universal characters for actual entities. That is, eternal objects function as ingredients in the given realities, and give them the objective form of definiteness. In other words, the actual entity must have some determinate forms in order to be a concrete reality. Thus, eternal objects are involved in the process of determining the specific character for the given actual` entities. This is the eternal object's role of specifying the character of an actual entity.

Fourth, like eternal objects, principle has the quality of universality over all actualities. Of course, this universality of the eternal object and principle is different than the Platonic "Idea" which is prior to all things. Instead, it is originally interrelated to actual entities and material force. There is no priority or posteriority between eternal objects and actual entities, principle and material force. Principle always exists along with material force. According to Yulgok, "Principle and material force are interfused with no interstice, no anterior or posterior, no separating or conjoining."[24] The two are never separated in reality. Principle can be prior to material force if we speak logically, but this does not refer to any temporal priority or posteriority. While principle is never manifested except through material force, material force is never issued except by principle. In a similar way, Whitehead's eternal objects and actual entities are also interrelated. Whitehead also writes: "That the fundamental types of entities are actual entities, and eternal objects; and that the other types of entities only express how all entities of the two fundamental types are in community with each other in the actual world."[25] Eternal objects and actual entities take part in the process of change, becoming, and determining each other. The two adequately present their interrelatedness and interdependence.

God and the Great Ultimate

God is the final term that completes Whitehead's process cosmology and functions as a ground for his process metaphysical system. The concept of God is based on his process metaphysics and cosmology, which fundamentally considers a reality of the world not a static concept of being but a dynamic concept of changing and becoming. In other words, Whitehead's process philosophy speaks of God and the world in very dynamic, developmental terms. Whitehead's concept of God is often called "panentheism," which means that God is included in all creatures. This is a new synthesized concept of God beyond theism and pantheism. Hence, God is characterized both as being transcendental and immanent. According to panentheism, this universe is an appearance which expresses an aspect of the being of God. Along with the character of God's transcendence over all other things, God is immanent as the order giver and value creator in the whole processes of creation as well. God enters into the world very intimately and transforms it by leading it into the future. Moreover, "God is the great companion—the fellow-sufferer who understands."[26] That is to say, in Whitehead's philosophical system, God suffers the pain of the world and people by virtue of an intimate relationship with all aspect of life. God attempts to build such a relationship with all things in the world in a persuasive way by the divine lure. God lures the world and people into the future by offering the choices that are made at all levels of existence. God lures people into making choices that morally or positively advance the created order. Lewis Ford describes the characteristics of the process theism developed by Whitehead:

> Process theism revises our understanding of divine power. Classically, God's power is seen in terms of omnipotence, and God is creator as the sole primary efficient cause of the world. In process theism, God is primarily persuasive, creating more indirectly by providing the lure for each occasion whereby it can create itself.[27]

On the other hand, the world and all things exist together with and in the being of God. Both God and the world participate in the whole process of creation together. God as an ultimate being, in this regard, is called "creativity" or "creating activity" rather than "creator." The word "creativity," for Whitehead, means "a fundamental principle of creation and formation." It indicates that the creation of God is continuously involved in all processes of the universe. Thus, Whitehead claims that God does not exist before creation but exists along with all creation. God is not the sole creator of the traditional Christian theism any longer in his metaphysics; instead, God is newly understood in terms of the scheme of Whitehead's process metaphysics. That is, with the world as his/her partner, God is considered to be co-creator in continuous creation of all things.

For Whitehead, more specifically, God is understood as a dipolar concept. That is to say, God as an actual entity has two natures: primordial nature and consequent nature. This means that God has two aspects as one actual entity. This explains the transcendence and immanence of God very adequately. The primordial nature of God refers to a pure ideal or mental nature of God. The primordial nature of God means that God is away from the concrete reality of the world. The primordial nature of God also has the role of including, ordering, and classifying eternal objects as pure potential, so that those eternal objects can be used as the datum by other actual entities. This means that God functions as the principle of concretion in the process of concrescence. On the other hand, God as the consequent nature means that God has essential relationships with all things in the world. God prehends all actual entities as they are when they occur, takes them into himself, and relates them to the reality of God. Thus Whitehead clarifies: "God is the infinite ground of all mentality, the unity of vision seeking physical multiplicity. The World is the multiplicity of finites seeking a perfected unity. Neither God, nor the World, reaches static completion. Both are in the grip of the ultimate metaphysical ground, the creative advance into novelty."[28]

In the Neo-Confucian cosmology, the Great Ultimate has a comparable place to God in Whitehead's process cosmology. In a word, the Great Ultimate means not only the principle but also the principle that includes all principles of heaven and earth and the myriad things. The Great Ultimate is often characterized as "limitless" because is not bound by space or shape. Ching's description of the Great Ultimate based on Zhu's philosophy is very helpful for our understanding:

> The Great Ultimate is full of *li* (principle), that which constitutes the myriad things, that which also determines good and evil. It is prior to things and yet also after the creation of things; it is outside yin and yang and yet operates in the midst of yin and yang; it penetrates all things, is absent nowhere, and yet originally was without sound, smell, shadow, or echo.[29]

Following Zhu Xi, Yulgok defines principle as the Great Ultimate, and material force as the yin and yang on which the Great Ultimate is dependent. In Yulgok's Neo-Confucian cosmology, the Great Ultimate is an ultimate truth that penetrates all things, including humanity, in the universe, and has a meaning of heavenly way and human nature. In other words, all things comes from the Great Ultimate and return to the Great Ultimate. It is a principle of unity and of wholeness in all things. He agrees with Zhu on the famous discourse that "the 'Limitless' or 'No Ultimate' (Chinese *wu-chi*; Korean *mu-geuk*, 無極) and yet the Great Ultimate"[30] is prior to things and yet is also after the creation of things. There is no doubt that this presents the transcendental character of the Great Ultimate like Whitehead's God of primordial nature. On the other hand, the Great Ultimate becomes manifest and immanent through material force, which indicates the immanent character of the Great Ultimate like the Whitehead's God of consequent nature. Therefore Whitehead also states: In God's nature, permanence is primordial and flux is derivative from the World: in the World's nature, flux is primordial and permanence is derivative from God. Also the World's nature is a primordial datum for God; and God's nature is a primordial datum for the World.[31] Similarly, in Yulgok's Neo-Confucian cosmological system, the Great Ultimate plays a role as the principle of permanence amid flux and brings multiplicity into unity. But material force plays a role as the principle of change and multiplicity.

It should be noted that both the Great Ultimate and the yin-yang forces are essential elements in constituting all things. They are like the relationship between God and the world. They are involved together in the formation of all things. However, it is the Great Ultimate as the ultimate principle that exists in the all things and the cosmos. As the basis and ground of all things, the Great Ultimate causes yin-yang to act in movement and quiescence. It further presides over all movements and changes of yin and yang. It has a central role in the cosmos. It is the origin of all things in the cosmos. Therefore, master Zhu emphasizes, "Fundamentally there is only one Great Ultimate, yet each of the myriad things has been endowed with it and each in itself possesses the Great Ultimate in its entirety."[32] This leads us to the dynamics of creativity between "one" and "many" in Whitehead's and Yulgok's process metaphysical systems.[33] That is, "The one is actually also many, since one is but manifested in many, while the many is also one, as its manifestations. Being is the principle of becoming, and becoming is also transmuted into being;"[34] Or Whitehead writes, "The many, which are the universe disjunctively, become the one actual occasion, which is the universe conjunctively."[35]

The Great Ultimate, on the other hand, is always followed by the yin and yang forces, the two appearances of material force. It would be an abstract principle or a theoretical concept without yin and yang. It should have a place of dependence: yin and yang. It always accompanies yin and yang as a counter partner. It does not initiate its activity without regard to material forces. This shows another aspect of the Great Ultimate in relation to the world. Thus, it seems clear that both the God in Whitehead's cosmology and the Great Ultimate in the Neo-Confucian cosmology have the dual natures in a similar way. That is to say, these two concepts are transcendental as well as immanent, primordial as well as conceptual. These two concepts stand for the absolute and the ultimate or the divine. These two concepts are found in panentheism, which is different than the traditional theistic concept of God. Furthermore, they can lead us to a cosmic religious feeling which functions as the foundation of spirituality in religion and paves the way to a mysticism that is common in all religions. Investigating Yulgok's cosmology in respect to its ecological implication, Young Chan Ro thus makes a very pertinent claim:

> Yulgok believed that the universe could not be completely comprehended by human intelligence or through human thought processes. He believed that the universe is a 'mystery' not to be reduced to the rational or conceptual framework of a human intellectual system. This dimension of mystery causes us to feel that the universe is sacred; hence, we have a sense of awe toward the universe. The universe 'manifests' itself to us as much as it 'conceals' itself from us.[36]

Therefore, Julia Ching's comments on the concept of the absolute in Neo-Confucianism also have much relevance for this issue. She first claims that the absolute in Neo-Confucianism, which is called "the Great Ultimate," "the Heavenly Way," and "Principle," is the origin of all things, presides over the universe, and explains the internal and ultimate meaning of the universe. She believes that it is very similar to the mystery of God in western medieval mysticism and the philosophical expressions of Schelling, Hegel, and Whitehead.[37] She goes on to say,

The notion of the Great Ultimate approximates most the notion of God in Western theistic philosophy, and it serves as foundation and center of Chu (Zhu)'s entire metaphysical system, the explanation of the organic interrelatedness of all things. I see Chu Hsi (Zhu Xi)'s philosophy of the Great Ultimate as an effort to present the notion of God as the chief exemplification of his metaphysical principles, an effort similar to Whitehead's.[38]

Chapter 4

A PROCESS COSMOLOGICAL APPLICATION TO INTERRELIGIOUS SPIRITUALITY IN KOREA

General Situation of Korean Christianity

It should be first noted that Korean Catholicism was founded not by foreign missionaries but by Confucian intellectuals who became aware of the Catholic faith through their study of Chinese translated materials on Christianity imported from the Ming and Ching dynasties in China. That is, the history of Korean Catholicism began due to some Confucian scholars' intellectual curiosity. According to the historian Ki-Baik Lee, Already in the reign of Kwanhaegun (1608-1623), Yi Su-Gwang made reference to Matteo Ricci's *True Principles of Catholicism* (*Ch'onju sirui*) in his *Chibong yusol*. Later, *Sirhak* scholars such as Yi Ik and An Chong-bok also were curious about Catholicism and discussed it in their writings.[1] Although there were different positions regarding Christianity among Confucians, young Confucians came to accept Christianity on the basis of the position that Christianity complements Confucianism.

It is important to point out that a significant event happened when Seung-Hun Yi (1756-1801) went to China and became the first baptized Christian in the History of the Korean Catholic Church. Jung-Young Lee explains this well: "In 1784 he (Seung-Hun Yi) returned to Korea with books, crucifixes, images and information about Catholic rituals. He and his friends founded a small Catholic lay congregation, the first Christian church in Korea."[2] David Chung describes this unique origin of Catholicism in Korea as follows: "It was a spontaneous birth, without direct evangelization, like a sprout that came out of the soil in a field where none was expected. The earliest converts were ones who had made themselves Christians."[3]

In 1885, on the other hand, as Horace G. Underwood, an American Presbyterian (Northern) missionary, and Henry G. Appenzeller, a Methodist Episcopal (North) missionary, arrived in Korea, the history of the Protestant Christian mission officially began. "They were quickly followed by representatives of a number of other Protestant sects who joined them in actively carrying on a variety of missionary works."[4] In general, their missions were very successful. As Ki-Baik Lee claims, in Korea, "Protestantism was most warmly received by the new intellectual class and by the business community, and this was particularly the case in religions of developing economic activity, such as P'yongan province."[5] Protestantism became one of major living religions in Korea. In the same manner, Duk-Whang Kim has already stated in 1963, "Today, not even a 100 years later, Protestant missionaries propagated in Korea so extensively that the number of its adherents can be counted at more than eight million. Protestantism not only occupies the premier position among the religious in Korea, but it also contributes much to the development of our culture."[6]

However, it should be noted that most American missionaries represented very pious faith and conservative theology. They had a great influence on the development of a very conservative Christianity. In this respect, Jung-Young Lee's comment is correct. He says, "Most Korean Christians are pietistic fundamentalists. New England pietism brought by early missionaries underlies the theological thinking of Korean Christians. The systematization of Korean fundamentalism must be understood as a continuation of that tradition."[7] It was therefore natural that early Korean Christians strongly opposed Korean traditional religious cultures. Ancestor worship is a typical example, which has been regarded as heresy by most Korean Christians.

Christianity in Korea has a history of more than two hundred years. But it has had a unique experience of church growth and theological movement. Donald Clark states: "The Korean Church is growing very fast and evolving its own theology. And it is still struggling with issues posed by Korea's unique heritage, present political position, and rapid economic development."[8] Although Korea's Christian history is not long, it has enjoyed remarkable growth. According to Harvey Cox, at the end of World War II, Christians still accounted for only about eight percent of the population. But by 1994 Christian churches had recruited over one-third of the population of South Korea.[9]

The survey presented by the South Korean Government in 1995 verifies the rapid growth of Christianity in Korean society. According to national statistics taken in 1995, over fifty-one percent of the Korean populations practices an organized religion (See Diagram 1). These statistics show that Buddhists number 10,388,000(23.31%), Protestants 8,819,000 (19.80%), Catholics 2,988,000 (6.7%), and Confucians 193,000 (0.43%). In other words, Christianity (Protestant and Catholics) is the most widely practiced major religion in Korea.

Diagram 1. The National Statistics of Korean Religion in 1995

Religion	Number of believers	Rate of Believers	Rate of Population
Buddhism	10,388,000	45.60 %	23.31 %
Protestantism	8,819,000	38.72 %	19.80 %
Catholicism	2,988,000	13.12 %	6.70 %
Confucianism	193,000	0.84 %	0.43 %
Won Buddhism	85,000	0.37 %	0.19 %
Chundokyo	30,000	0.13 %	0.07 %
Taejongkyo	11,000	0.05 %	0.02 %
Others	265,000	1.16 %	0.60 %

* Population of South Korea in 1995: 44,551,000 [10]

A typical example of the Christian Church's growth is the Yoeuido Central Full Gospel Church in Seoul, with more than 800,000 members. This symbolizes church growth in Korea. Yong-Gi Cho, the founder and senior pastor of Youido Full Gospel Church describes well the strong desire for growth of Korean Christianity. He states:

> Church growth has become one of the most noteworthy subjects in Christianity today. Before 1980, individual revival movements took place with such prominent figures as Billy Graham and Oral Roberts. More recently it appears that the individual revival movements have abated and revivals have burst forth in the local church. Every year has had its specific move of God. The healing movement in the 1960s; the charismatic movement in the 1970s; the church growth movement of the 1980s.[11]

Needless to say, church growth in Korea is completely based on Pentecostal and fundamental theology. Due to this miraculous church growth, about twenty-five percent of the entire population of South Korea are Christians, Catholics and Protestants. Christianity, a foreign religion, now exists as one of the main religions in Korea. In other words, "Christianity is now a Korean people's religion and no longer a foreign import."[12]

Bong-Rin Ro, a Korean scholar, attributes Korean church growth to circumstantial and spiritual factors. According to him, the use of native Korean characters by the church asserted the solidarity of Christianity and nationalism under Japanese colonial rule. In the rigid stratification of Korean society, the services, ceremonies, and activities of the church provided people with important opportunities for freedom, self-expression, and social contact. These made contributions to church growth. In addition, spiritual factors should be pointed to as reasons for church growth. Ro talks specifically about "A spiritual hunger among Koreans, arising from suffering through colonialism and civil war, the attractions of Christian ideas of salvation, the echoes in Christianity of other faiths such as Buddhism (heaven and hell) and shamanism (miracles, sacrifices and priesthood)."[13] On the contrary, this shows that the Korean church has developed a close relationship with other traditional religious cultures, although the main streams of Christianity are still opposed to other traditional religions.

David Martin, an expert in Pentecostalism, finds reasons for church growth in the unique historical experiences of Korean people. He claims:

> Korea is placed, like Judea, at a crossroad of peoples, and has been subject to many invasions and interventions. Above all, two invasions provided the psychic impetus to seek a new and messianic deliverance. One was the Japanese annexation in 1910, and the other was the invasion from the north after the Second World War which cut the country in two. The deliverance came from an American Protestantism, which in its first Korean incarnation was apolitical and pietistic, and reflected American ideas.[14]

Most Korean churches are still longing for church growth. So, they have developed a very conservative and fundamentalistic theology which functions only for individual salvation and church growth. Specifically speaking, these theological characteristics originated from the American missionaries. Arthur Judson Brown, the executive secretary of the Board of Foreign Missions of the Presbyterian Church of U.S.A. from 1895 to 1929, describes the faith and theology of early missionaries in Korea as follows:

> During the first twenty-five years, the average missionary was a man with a puritanical faith. Just as their New England ancestors of the previous century, these men faithfully kept the Sabbath, and regarded dancing, smoking and card playing as sin. Their theology was conservative, so they considered biblical higher criticism and liberal theology to be heretical.[15]

It is natural that early missionaries concentrated on missionary expansion with their conservative faith and theology. On the other hand, they did not have any concern for the theological development of anything other than their own conservative theology. David Kwangsun Suh thus claims:

> It was, at the early stage of evangelism work by the missionaries, too easy for them to impose on Korean Protestant churches the American brand of religious fundamentalism. This choked the development of Protestant theology by Korean theologians until the 1970's. Various schisms within the Protestant churches in Korea since 1950 have been deeply rooted in American Protestant fundamentalism and American religious anti-intellectualism. The non-intellectual, and indeed anti-intellectual approach of the missionaries in proselytizing the Korean masses became quite apparent when missionaries began to

reflect on the training of Korean church leaders.[16]

As Suh stated, a new theological movement, however, has developed in this ultra-conservative atmosphere. We can mention two schools: a theology of religions and a sociopolitical theology. First, some theologians such as Sung-Bum Yun, Dong-Shick Ryu, Sun-Hwan Pyun, and Ha-Tae Kim tried to reconcile Christianity and other traditional religions in Korea. They explored a meaning of Christianity in comparison with other religions: Buddhism, Confucianism, and Shamanism. Above all, those theologians actively took part in the so called "indigenization debates" in 1960s. As a result, they produced indigenized forms of theology such as "the theology of *sung'*"(誠, sincerity; Chinese *cheng*), "the theology of *kyung*" (敬, reverence; Chinese *jing*), and "the theology of other religions." Chul-Ha Han discusses these theological attempts:

> No one will dispute that the representatives of indigenization theology are Sung-Bum Yun and Tong-Shik Ryu. . . . They concentrate on the fact that Korean thoughts and the Korean religions are not '*tabula rasa*' but waiting for the Gospel. It is not the case that the Gospel is like a seal stamped on white paper; rather, it is received by the Korean's living 'heart character'(*shimsong*). They lay stress on both the Gospel and our Korean heritages.[17]

Jung-Young Lee also discusses Pyun's theological accomplishment in particular:

> He (Sun-Whan Pyun) approached the relationship between Christianity and other religions, especially Buddhism, from the perspective of *Missio Dei*. His pivotal message that 'there is salvation outside the church' aroused controversy. He sought not to convert Buddhists, but to engage in dialogue. Seeking the continuity between Christ and Buddha, Pyun found that self-giving love was the point where Christianity and Mahayana Buddhism.[18]

On the other hand, a few people and churches have been involved in sociopolitical issues such as justice, peace, human rights, democracy, and reunification from the beginning. And some churches have begun to participate in industrial missions and urban-rural missions since the 1960's. As the result of these, *minjung* theology emerged when a small group of Korean clergy and theologians began to interpret the meaning of Christian faith from the point of their solidarity with the *minjung*'s struggle for liberation and freedom in South Korea during the 1970's. *Minjung* theology and social praxis of the church are other dimensions of the Korean Church. Donald Clark explains well:

> Since the 1960s, dissenting elements within the church have been brewing a unique Korean theology which they call '*minjung* theology.' The word *minjung*

means 'masses,' and *minjung* theology is decidedly populist, even proletarian, in emphasis. Its association with the working class gives it a political ring, in contrast to the relatively apolitical theology of mainstream Korean Christians.[19]

David Martin mentions *minjung* theology in relation to Latin American liberation theology. He insists:

Political opposition is associated with students, intellectuals and some industrial workers, and it tends to come from the historic Protestant churches and from the Roman Catholic Church. Its distinctive ideological vehicle is '*minjung* theology' which is a variant of the Latin American 'option for the poor,' but drawing on Korean resources.[20]

Above all, the "Declaration of Korean Theologians" issued by members of the Korea Association of Accredited Theological Schools and of Christian Studies in the Centennial Theologians Conference which was held in Seoul in October of 1984 eloquently demonstrates this:

We are called to carry out our theological task while participating in the history of God . . . . The people of the Kingdom of God is the *Minjung*. . . . We shall participate in the pains and sufferings of the *Minjung*, and articulate the reality of suffering and of the structure of socio-political contradictions in theological terms. Furthermore, we shall dedicate ourselves to the struggle for the freedom and self-determination of the people in order to bring about a just democratic society.[21]

The Ancestor Worship as a Critical Issue in the Confucian-Christian Dialogue[22]

On June 26, 1998, Su-Jin Kim, a conservative Presbyterian, entered the Buddhist temple named *Wonmyungsonwon* on Cheju Island in Korea and destroyed seven hundred and fifty sitting figures of the Buddha. He did this out of his conservative militant faith. He thought that Buddhism should be removed from the earth because he considered it a false religion that worshipped false idols. He wished to destroy all religions other than Christianity in the name of God because for him Christianity was only true religion on earth.[23] This event shows a Korean Christian's typical attitude toward other religions. It is evident that most Korean Christians still regard other living religions as heresies, even though they have been existing as living religions longer than Christianity in Korea.

As shown in the event stated above, Korean Christianity still has major issues with traditional living religions, particularly Confucianism, Buddhism, Shamanism, and other new national religions. While conservative Christianity, particularly Protestantism, was introduced into Korea by American missionaries, traditionally Korea has been a religiously pluralistic society. In other words, the Christianity introduced from Western countries is still not fully indigenized or inculturized into the Korean soil in a true sense. Christians in Korea do not fully understand Korea's pluralistic religious culture, so they still regard non-Christian faiths as heretical.

Religious pluralism is not a strange phenomenon in Korea because Korean society consists of various living religions. Christianity is just one of those religions. Although Korean Christianity's history, Catholic and Protestant, is not long, it is practiced by a quarter of the entire population in the Republic of (South) Korea. So, it is equally true that Christianity, a foreign Western religion, now exists as one of the main religions in Korea. That is, "Christianity is now a Korean people's religion and no longer a foreign import."[24] Although the main streams of Christianity are conservative and still opposed to other traditional religions, it is clear that Christianity in Korea has been influenced by other traditional religious cultures. In particular, the Confucian influence on Christianity in Korea is extremely strong because the state religion of the Choson dynasty, which lasted until the Japanese occupation in the modern times of Korea, was Confucianism. Even though many people do not confess that Confucianism is their religion, it is inevitable that Confucianism functions as a core and basis for Korean life and culture.

Confucianism, which originated in China, served as a state religion for the Choson dynasty. As in other East Asian countries, the Choson dynasty maintained a traditional feudalistic society, which derived its ideologies from Confucianism. Above all, the Choson dynasty strengthened its foundation by emphasizing the rites of Confucianism rather than law and the political power. In other words, the four main rites of Confucianism, *kwan-hon-sang-jai* (冠婚喪祭; the ceremony of coming of age, marriage, funerals, and ancestral worship), were considered to be the basic standards of life. Ancestor worship was the most important among these. Therefore, ancestor worship has also been the most important issue in the encounter between Confucianism and Christianity in Korea.

Many Protestant Christians in Korea still regard ancestor worship as heresy or idolatry because early Western missionaries in Korea taught Korean Christians a conservative and fundamentalist faith. When new believers were baptized by missionaries, they had to swear, "Since God hates ancestor worship, I would not follow ancestor worship and, instead, I would only believe in and obey God."[25] Thus, there were many conflicts between the Christian faith and other religious cultures deriving from the conservative position of these missionaries. Ancestor worship was not the exception. In particular, this conflict between the Christian faith and Confucian culture became a social issue in 1920 because an event concerning Christian faith and ancestor worship was reported in the newspaper:

> There was a man named 'Kwon Sung-Wha,' who lived at Youngju, Kyongbuk. When his mother died, his wife, named 'Park Sung-Yo,' made an ancestral tablet and provided a meal in the morning and the evening as an expression of filial piety to her mother-in-law's ancestral tablet, as if her mother-in-law was alive. Her husband demanded that his wife stop her activity of providing a meal to the ancestral tablet because he had become a Christian. His wife entreated him to allow her to keep her activity in a traditional way. When her entreaty was refused by her husband, she threw her body into the river after she had buried the ancestral tablet at a clean place in the back yard, because she thought that she had to die in order for her husband's sin of impiety to his mother to be redeemed.[26]

This miserable event still continues for many pietistic Christians on different levels. This issue is not completely resolved yet. Ancestor worship is the issue with which most Korean Christians struggle. This means that it is one of key issues that we need to interpret in a new perspective for today.

Defining Spirituality in a Comparative Perspective

Before dealing with the theme of process and Confucian cosmological applications to the spirituality and spiritual practices of the Korean Church, we first need to narrow down the meaning of "spirituality" in a comparative perspective. Spirituality is one of the hot button issues in which contemporary people are interested. Spirituality is now explored in both religious institutions and secular places in numerous ways. For modern people, spirituality means something important beyond the boundary of institutionalized religions; it has become a very confusing topic. Robert Wuthnow thus makes the following claims:

> To be sure, the character of spirituality appears to be changing. Despite evidence that churches and synagogues are, on the surface, faring well, the deeper meaning of spirituality seems to be moving in a new direction in response to change in U.S. culture .... There are deeper reasons for how spirituality is changing. Consider the fact that growing numbers of Americans say they are spiritual but not religious, or that many say their spirituality is growing but the impact of religion on their lives is diminishing.[27]

John Berthrong also gives us a timely relevant comment on this problematic issue:

> Another term is inextricably linked to the popular modern use of meditation. This is spirituality. If ever there was a slippery, protean word in the general vocabulary of religious people, spirituality is now it. To those who favor spirituality, it means everything opposite to the deadening rigidities of all other forms of modern religious life. If you

are on the other side of the debate, spirituality simply means a mindless fascination with any religious fad that happens to wander down the pike from bioenergetics to yoga, deep ecology, and goddess worship. *Fuzzy* hardly begins to describe all the ways people define spirituality.[28]

Spirituality is now practiced in a much broader sense than ever before. Spirituality is defined in various ways by various people. To contemporary people, spirituality means much more than its original definition, which was "Christianity spirituality"; it refers to much broader beliefs, practices, and activities. Sandra Schneiders points out that: "the term spirituality, like psychology, is unavoidably ambiguous, referring to (1) a fundamental dimension of the human being, (2) the lived experience which actualizes that dimension, and (3) the academic discipline which studies that experience."[29]

Here, it is my basic position that, although spirituality can exist in various ways beyond the boundary of religions, it is the core element of all religions. It seems to me that spirituality basically refers to a human being's spiritual quest with regard to God, the divine mystery, the ultimate, and/or the absolute variously manifested within religious context by performing diverse forms of self-cultivation, prayer, meditation, study, and ritual in every religious tradition. Of course, spirituality is not limited to Christianity. Although the term "spirituality" has often been associated with the Christian church and theology, it can be used more generally in the context of world religions. As Julia Ching states, "Here, the meaning has to do with life of the spirit, including the ascetic and mystical life. More recently, the word is also being used in the study of the spiritual teachings of non-Christian religions."[30]

Therefore, we can first say that spirituality, in its broadest sense, refers to the humankind's spiritual experience with regard to what is absolute or ultimate or what defines the mystery of the divine or God.[31] In general, spirituality is the human attempt to be united with the ultimate or the divine reality by transcending oneself in a fundamentally normative or religious orientation.[32] "Spirituality" means the "inner dimension of the person called by certain traditions the spirit. This spiritual core is the deepest center of the person. It is here that the person is open to the transcendent dimension; it is here that the person experience ultimate reality."[33] In this respect, Margaret Mary Kelleher makes a pertinent comment:

> Spirituality refers to and is a reflection upon the experience of the dynamic interaction which occurs between the human spirit and the Holy Spirit in any given human life. The implicit anthropology, or theory of the nature of the human person which provides the foundations for such an understanding, is one which regards the human person as essentially open to transcendence and capable of the experience of self-transcendence.[34]

How do we understand spirituality in Christianity and Confucianism? What is meant by the term "interreligious spirituality" in the context of religious pluralism? First, spirituality is the starting point for Christians. It is called "walking according to the Spirit" (Rom.8:4), which is a theme throughout the New Testament. Specifically speaking, spirituality originated from the Pauline neologism "spiritual" (*pneumatikos*), the adjectival form of the Greek word for the Holy Spirit (*pneuma*). Paul uses this term in 1 Corinthians 2:14-15 to distinguish the spiritual person (*pneumatikos*) from the natural person (*psychkos anthropos*). Here, the spiritual person means "the one who lives under the influence and guidance of the Holy Spirit."[35]

The term "spirituality" has been used in various ways and developed throughout the history of the Church. Gustavo Gutierrez stated it in a historical perspective:

> The term 'spirituality' is a relatively recent one in the history of the church. It came into use around the beginning of the seventeenth century in French religious circles at a time that saw a wealth of contributions and works on the subject. Everything that had to do with Christian perfection fell under the heading of spiritual life, whereas reflection of the subject yielded a spiritual theology.[36]

Even though spirituality in Christianity has referred to the practice of inner life and the life of perfection in relationship with God or the Holy Spirit, it has now evolved into a broader and more general definition. Maria Harris provides some clarity to this term: "Spirituality is the touching and being touched of human, incarnate persons . . . . it is our need for the presence of God in the midst of our humanness."[37] Traditionally, spirituality has been concerned with "the personal life of prayer and asceticism."[38] Claire Wolfteich also provides a definition on spirituality: "I offer here a preliminary working definition of spirituality as the lived experience of faith, a seeking after self-transcendence, an openness to a comforting, challenging, and transforming Other."[39] On the basis of that working definition, Christian spirituality is specifically defined as "Life centered in God, who is both transcendent and immanent. Christian spirituality entails openness to and growth in this life, so that we are led into a deeper intimacy with God through Jesus Christ and sustained by the continuing grace of the Holy Spirit in loving community."[40]

Schneiders defines spirituality in a different way: "The experience of consciously striving to integrate one's life in terms not of isolation and self-absorption but of self-transcendence toward the ultimate value one perceives."[41] Following Walter Principe's thought, therefore, I believe that Christian spirituality is the striving for a radical union with God the Father through Jesus Christ the Son by living in the Holy Spirit.[42] This concept of spirituality is practiced in Christians' daily lives. In this respect, Segundo Galilea's definition of spirituality in historical Trinitarian terms is also very appropriate. He identified spirituality as "The process of following Christ, under the direction of the Spirit, and beneath the guidance of the Church. This process . . . . leads to identification with Christ, which in the life of the Christian takes the form of death to sin and selfishness to live for God and for others."[43]

Second, there are vigorous debates as to whether Confucianism is philosophy or religion. Even though many studies have been done about the religious dimension of Confucianism, many people are still opposed to defining Confucianism as religion. This is a very controversial issue because it is also related to the definition of religion. It is evident that Confucianism is not covered by the Western definition of religion. At the same time, it also true that Confucianism is not only a philosophy. I think that, in Korea, Confucianism in both a religion and a philosophy because Koreans had been influenced by Confucianism in all aspects of their lives and society. Confucianism exists as a living culture and moral life in Korea. John Berthrong explains this complicated identity of Confucianism:

> Confucianism is an internally complicated cultural artifact with different cultural manifestations, only some of which are clearly religious in nature. It is equally true to argue that Confucianism is also a philosophic tradition as well as a historical, poetic, artistic, economic and political set of related movements. There were clearly ancient, medieval, early modern and modern Confucians who were tone-deaf to the religious dimensions of their tradition although they define themselves as Confucians in terms of their scholarship as well as their political and cultural concerns . . . . Yet it is more and more clear, on the basis of modern understandings of religion, that there is a profound religious dimension to the tradition. If this religious dimension is ignored then a significant part of the historical and modern story of the Confucian Way is neglected to the detriment of true humane scholarship.[44]

I agree with Berthrong's understanding of Confucianism. It is thus my point that Confucianism as an expression of faith is one of the living religions, which has its own dimension of spirituality. Ha-Tae Kim also strongly believes in the religious dimension of Neo-Confucianism. He states:

> On the surface, Neo-Confucianism appears to be a philosophy that deals with the origin of the universe (cosmology) and the essence of the human nature (philosophy of human nature), but underneath all these discussions, one cannot help but detect a religious dimension of Neo-Confucianism, which is as profound and significant as any religion of the world.[45]

How do we understand Confucian spirituality? Wei-ming Tu, who considers Confucianism a religion, seeks Confucian spirituality as the question of "the Confucian religiousness." He claims as follows:

> We can define the Confucian way of being religious as *ultimate self-transformation as a communal act and as a faithful dialogical response to the transcendent* . . . . Confucian religiosity is expressed through the infinite potential and the inexhaustible strength of each human being for self-transcendence.

Three interrelated dimensions are involved here: the person, the community, and the transcendent.[46]

Julia Ching is also a scholar who insists on the spiritual dimension of Confucianism. She tries to "answer the question of Confucian spirituality by arguing that the quest for sagehood, which constitutes the heart of Confucianism, can only be understood with reference to the interior life, to the life of the spirit, to personal discipline, and sometimes to mystical experience."[47] On the basis of her understanding of Confucius as a great spiritual personality, Ching argues for spiritual dimensions of Confucianism in historical and theoretical ways: "It is a spirituality peculiarly Confucian, not dependent on belief in God, as is Christian or Jewish spirituality. And yet it does not deny God's existence. It is a spirituality which unites inner sageliness and outer kingliness, a life of contemplation and a life of activity." [48]

Therefore, on the basis of what we have discussed, if we undertake the interreligious dialogue between Christianity and Confucianism with special attention to the issue of spirituality, interreligious spirituality will emerge as one possible outcome. It is a new synthesized type of spirituality which can be applied to a certain context of religious pluralism. Especially, in the context of Korea, interreligious spirituality is developed by various dialogues or comparative studies among religions. It is unavoidable that such a new spirituality, based on dual or multiple religious identities, can and will emerge. Here we can find possibilities of a process-Confucian-Christian spirituality and spiritual practices in the Korean context.

Spiritual Formation in the Korean Church From the Process Confucian Cosmological Perspective

Christianity is not separated from its own community called "the church." As an integral part of Christian theology and discipline, spirituality should be taught and practiced in both churches and seminaries. This means that we need to undertake the task of spiritual formation and direction for Christians. Of course, this should be done in relation to other religions in Korea because all religions are interdependent and influence each other. Evidently, Korean Christianity, which exists as a living religion in the context of religious pluralism, should develop its own spirituality by encountering other religions for the purpose of mutual learning and transformation.

The purpose of this section is to focus specifically on the ways of enhancing Christian spirituality by applying process-Confucian cosmological insights to Korean Protestant churches. There will be six specific suggestions for the spiritual formation of the Korean church from the perspective of process-Confucian cosmology. Although they are not proven yet, they are based on my strong hypothesis that a process-Confucian cosmological thought can play positive roles in enhancing and enriching Korean Christians' spirituality in many ways and, furthermore, reforming Korean Christianity in a creative way. In addition, these suggestions will present certain ways and methods for those who are theoretically and practically committed to the spiritual direction of the Korean Church.

Process Cosmology as the Foundation of Christian Spirituality

As I stated earlier in this book, cosmology is a subject matter in the comparative study we are doing. We first need to define the term "cosmology." What does cosmology mean? Why do we need it as we study spirituality? Larry J. Alderink gives us a general definition of "cosmology":

> The most general sense of the term indicates a view of the world or universe, and particularly its order and arrangement. The Greek *kosmos* means 'world' and *logos* means 'speaking about a thing" as well as 'reason' or 'doctrine'. Since 'cosmology' in its larger sense is not a biblical term, but is to be traced back to Greek religious and philosophical roots, examination of the origins will help understand the large role cosmology has come to play in Christian theology.[49]

Cosmology has an important role in every world religion including Christianity and Confucianism, because cosmology presents worldviews on which religion is based. Whitehead also notes, "Whatever suggests a cosmology, suggests religion."[50] He continues to explicate the meaning of cosmology: "The theme of Cosmology, which is the basis of all religions, is the story of the dynamic effort of the World passing into everlasting unity, and of the static majesty of God's vision, accomplishing its purpose of completion by absorption of the World's multiplicity of effort."[51]

It is thus inevitable that cosmology has great impact on the formation of spirituality in religious traditions. More specifically, spirituality bespeaks an alternative worldview. In other words, spirituality is derived from certain types of cosmologies. Therefore, desirable spirituality should be based on a proper worldview, which is needed for today, because improper cosmology causes serious problems both in religion and society. Lynn White, Jr., argues how the traditional Christian worldview is closely associated with the ecological crisis. He wrote,

> Since the roots [of the ecological crisis] are so largely religious, the remedy must also be essentially religious, whether we call it that or not. We must rethink and refeel our nature and destiny. . . . Especially in its Western form,

> Christianity is the most anthropocentric religion that the world has seen. . . . Christianity, in absolute contrast to ancient paganism and Asia's religions . . . . not only established a dualism of man and nature but also insisted that it is God's will that man exploit nature for his proper ends.[52]

Christianity has been heavily influenced by various forms of cosmology: Greek cosmologies, in particular, Plato's and Aristotle's cosmologies, Ptolemaic cosmology, Copernican cosmology, and the Newtonian cosmology.[53] Now Christianity has the task of seeking a new cosmology which is required by a new era. Process cosmology should be considered as the new basis for Christian thought and spirituality because its processive, organismic, and relational view of reality would help to enhance Korean Christians' spirituality locally and globally. Paul L. Knitter's remark is pertinent to this point:

> Today a major movement in philosophy is articulating, in typically complex jargon, a vision of reality that many ordinary persons sense to be true of their individual lives: that the world and everything in it is *evolutionary* or *in process*, of *becoming*. Nothing in the world is simply given, or prefabricated, merely to be assembled according to a predetermined plan. Rather, we and everything around us are caught up in a process of constant change, of movement, of exploration into newness.[54]

In addition, process cosmology adequately expresses the insights of reality in the Judeo-Christian traditions. David Griffin states:

> The religious implication of reality as processive is in harmony with one of the chief consequences of the Judeo-Christian vision of reality. In this tradition, God has been viewed as active within the historical process. Accordingly, historical activity has had more importance than in traditions without a doctrine of the purposive providential presence of the sacred reality in history. Those cultures decisively affected by the Judeo-Christian view owe to it much of their vitality.[55]

Mary Evelyn Tucker, on the other hand, notes that we desperately need a process cosmology for this world in an ecological crisis. She actively advocates the Confucian tradition that contains a process cosmology.

> Confucianism, in particular, has significant intellectual and spiritual resources to offer in emerging discussions regarding attitudes toward nature, the role of humans, and environmental ethics. Its dynamic, organismic worldview, its vitalist understanding of *ch'i* (material force), its respect for the vast continuity of life, its sense of compassion for suffering, its desire to establish the grounds for just and sustainable societies, its emphasis on holistic, moral education, and its appreciation for the embeddedness of life in interconnected concentric circles are only some examples of the rich resources of the Confucian tradition in relation to ecological issues.[56]

Process-Confucian Way of Preaching and Bible Study

Preaching and the Bible Study from a Comparative Perspective

There are many ways of spiritual formation. Among them, preaching and Bible study are the most important elements for Korean Christians' religious lives because they firmly believe that "faith comes from what is heard, and what is heard comes through the word of Christ"(Romans 10:17).[57] Therefore, the Bible is an extremely significant source for spiritual formation. Reading and preaching the Bible are considered to be the central parts of worship in Korean Protestant churches. Undoubtedly, they have a great impact on Korean Christian spirituality.

The Korean Protestant Church has been stressing strictly the importance of the Bible for Christian faith from its inception. Despite the fact that the Bible has much in common with texts of other traditional religions, the early Korean Christians regarded it as only a text of Christian spirituality. It should be noted that the Bible shares many ethical values with the Confucian classics. So, it is necessary to preach this message in worship services and lead Bible study from a comparative perspective between Christianity and Confucianism. It would be a better way for Korean Christians to interpret the Bible with deep background of Confucianism. In addition, it would also be very meaningful to preach the gospel message and lead Bible study from the Confucian perspective because most Koreans are familiar with Confucian moral values. This could be an effective way of enhancing the spirituality of Korean Christians. For this, a comparative study of the two religious traditions should be done in advance. As Heup-Young Kim states:

> Confucianism and Christianity share a common interest in the issue of humanity. Furthermore, the special interest in both tradition lies in a practical, pedagogical question of 'how to be fully human' rather than the theoretical, philosophical apprehension of 'what is human being.' This central problematic for both traditions has produced distinctive, but comparable doctrines in each tradition; namely, self-cultivation and sanctification.[58]

First, if we accept sanctification as one goal of spiritual growth, Confucianism has many resources for achieving this goal. A typical example is "mind-and-heart"(Korean *shim*; Chinese *hsin*, 心), which is also a principal concept in Asian thought.[59] According to Confucian thought, mind-and-heart is the source and locus of the transcendent principle. To be a human being is possible only through self-cultivation of one's mind-and-heart. Mencius said: "He who exerts his mind to the utmost knows his nature. He who knows his nature knows Heaven. To preserve one's mind and to nourish one's nature is the way to serve Heaven."[60] Zhu Xi also claimed: "The mind embraces all principles and all principles are complete in this single entity, the mind. If one is not able to preserve the mind, he will be unable to investigate principle to the utmost. If he is unable to investigate principle to the utmost, he will be unable to exert his mind to the utmost."[61] Following Zhu's philosophy, Yulgok also emphasized the mind as the master of human nature, feeling, and will. He states:

> What the heavenly principle imparts to humanity is called 'the nature.' What is mastering over human body by combining the nature with material force is called the mind. What the mind operates outward as it reacts to things is called 'feeling.' The nature is the substance and the feeling is the operation of the mind. The mind includes both 'already operated' and 'not yet operated.' Therefore, the mind takes general control over nature and feeling.[62]

Of course, Christianity takes the Word of God as its most authentic source and foundation. However, we can find the emphasis of human mind-and-heart in the Bible: "I will give them a new heart, and put a new spirit within them"(Ezekiel 14:19); "Blessed are the pure in heart, for they will see God"(Matthew 5:8); "Let the same mind be in you that was in Christ Jesus"(Philippians 2:5); "But by your hard and impenitent heart you are storing up wrath for yourself on the day of wrath"(Romans 2:5); "Real circumcision is a matter of the heart"(Romans 2:29).

Second, in the Yulgok's Neo-Confucian thoughts, "*sung*" (*cheng,* 誠, sincerity) is another example of preaching in a comparative perspective. As Young-Chan Ro said, "Sincerity, thus, was not merely a moral concept, but took on, through the anthropocosomic assumption, a deep religious dimension as well."[63] *Sung* is the key concept in *Chung-yung* (the Doctrine of Mean) and plays a great role for fruitful development in theological thinking. It is possible for preachers to interpret the Christian term "*logos*" in terms of the Confucian term, '*sung*.' This presents us with "Confucian Christology" and develops a unique interelig- ious spirituality based on it in the Korean context. As Wei-ming Tu stated, this can be called "a distinctive Korean style of Confucian theologizing."[64]

Above all, the Confucian concept of *sung* is equivalent to the Christian concept of revelation. In particular, the transcendental and immanent natures of *sung* are compared to Karl Barth's two concepts of revelation, "the subjective revelation" and "the objective revelation."[65] This comparison was further developed by Sung Bum Yun. According to him, the most perfect theological expression of God is "*mal*" (word; sprache; logos). Karl Barth also demonstrated the Word (logos) of God on the basis of trinity, understanding it in its threefold form: "the Word of God as preached," "the written Word of God," and "the revealed Word of God."[66] The characteristic of "word" is expressed well in John 1:1: "In the beginning was the Word (*logos*), and the Word was with God, and the Word was God." In this phrase, it is evident that the Word is the essence of God, and the Word itself is "very God." Since the character '*sung*' (誠) consists of two Chinese characters, 言(*mal,* language, word, logos) and 成(*iruda,* accomplish), it literally means that "the word is accomplished."[67] This is the expression for God in Confucian traditions of Korea and is well applied to the preaching of Korean Christians.

This becomes even more evident when we consider that the ultimate dimension of *sung* is equivalent to the absolute or the ultimate in the *Zhongyong* (中庸). It is further justified by the transcendental and immanent characteristics of *sung*. Yulgok focused on two important concepts, "*sung-ja*"(誠者, the thing called sincerity) and "*sa-sung-ja*" (思誠者, thinking about sincerity), quoting one phrase from *Mencius*: "Sincerity is the Way of Heaven. To think about sincerity is the way of humanity."[68] Here, while "*sung-ja*" means "revelation, character of transcendence, and the Word of God," "*sa-sung-ja*" means "faith, immanent character of God's revelation, and the word of human beings." We can find the immanency of *sung-ja* in *sa-sung-ja*. In other words, "*sung*" has a transcendent and an immanent character, and an ability to connect human beings to God with the word of truth.[69]

Thirdly, certain dimensions of faith and salvation are similarly explained by both Christians and Confucians. That is, while in a Christian view one can be saved by one's faith, in a Confucian view one can reach "*sung*" (*cheng,* 誠, sincerity) by "*kyung*" (*jing,* 敬, reverence).[70] The important concept "*kyung*" as the way of achieving sincerity should be added here. Yulgok claims:

> Sincerity is a realistic principle of the heaven and the substance of the mind. The reason that human beings do not recover their original minds is because their original minds become filled with private ego and self-centeredness. Therefore, if one were to remove one's private ego and self-centeredness primarily by means of reverence, their original substance would be perfect. Reverence is the summary of effort and power. Sincerity is the collection of effort. Therefore, *one can reach sincerity through reverence.*[71]

As is well known, faith begins with believing in some object. Unlike other verifiable knowledge, faith becomes possible by believing in unverifiable knowledge. The definition found in Hebrews 11:1, "Faith is the assurance of things hoped for, the conviction of things not seen," indicates this kind of knowledge. Further, faith means to live out that knowledge; faith means to entrust ourselves to the object of faith. This faith also arises from the feeling of crisis and the boundary situation, where human beings are searching for the absolute with an attitude of humility.[72]

This kind of faith appears as the concept of *kyung* in Confucianism. Chang

Tsai first states this dimension in his "The Western Inscription":

> Heaven is my father and Earth is my mother, and even such a small creature as I finds an intimate place in their midst. Therefore that which fills the universe I regard as my body and that which directs the universe I consider as my nature. All people are my brothers and sisters, and all things are my companions.[73]

These ideas are also central to the Christian faith. Our self-understanding as small creatures enables us to have the faith to believe in objects like heaven or God. This kind of faith is described as 'reverence for Heaven' in Confucianism. In the above passage, the metaphor for heaven is "father." In the Confucian tradition, one should serve heaven as one serves one's father; one should revere heaven with the filial piety that one would show to a parent.[74] As Zhu Xi says, "Absolute sincerity in serving one's parents leads to the understanding of the way to serve Heaven."[75]

The practice of *kyung* (reverence, seriousness) is well connected with Confucian moral cultivation. The method of cultivation consists of *kyung*, which is the basis of everything. As Young-Chan Ro says, "The principle of things can be properly studied and investigated only when we reside in *kyung*."[76] *Kyung* is the foundation for searching for the truth. Yulgok thus claims:

> Reverence is the beginning and the end of the sage learning. Therefore, the master Zhu said, 'to reside in reverence is the fundamental of searching principle. Those who don't realize yet cannot know without reverence.' The master Chung also said, 'There is no other than reverence for reaching the Dao. In reaching the knowledge, there is nobody who does not reside in reverence.' This means reverence is the beginning of the sage learning. The master Zhu also said, 'those who already realized cannot keep it without reverence' and the master Chung said, 'If reverence and righteousness are completed, virtue will not be alone. The sage was the very case.' This means that reverence is the end of the sage learning.[77]

In addition, *Kyung* can be also the basic attitude of human beings for the Transcendental Being. In this sense, Ha Tae Kim states, "*kyung* or seriousness assumes a religious meaning and *kyung* can be interpreted as meaning reverence and fear. If *kyung* can be translated as Kierkegaardian 'purity of heart,' *kyung* definitely has religious implication."[78] This attitude is, of course, expressed as filial piety to parents, loyalty to kings, and awe of the Lord on High or heaven. This also reflects Biblical thought in a similar way. The Bible also says: "the fear of the Lord is the beginning of knowledge"(Proverbs 1:7); "You shall love the LORD your God with all your heart, and with all your soul, and with all your might"(Deuteronomy 6:5); and "Work out your own salvation with fear and trembling"(Philippians 2:12). Zhu Xi's explanation of *kyung* (*ching*) explains this way of thinking for the Confucian faith. He claims:

The task of seriousness is the first principle of the Confucian School. From the beginning to the end, it must not be interrupted for a single moment. Seriousness merely means the mind being its own master. If one succeeds in preserving seriousness, his mind will be tranquil and the Principle of Nature will be perfectly clear to him.[79]

Yulgok also maintains, "If we keep our mind in reverence and continue this cultivation, we will get power by ourselves. To cultivate our mind by dwelling in reverence is simply a method of ensuing that no worry rises just by staying quietly and no confuse or ambiguity exists by staying enlightened."[80] According to Ha-Tae Kim, "In as much as *kyung* or seriousness is the all important psychological prerequisite for the cultivation of the self in Neo-Confucianism, it becomes the essence of Sacred Learning. *Kyung* constitutes the beginning and the end of the Sacred Learning"[81] As stated above, *kyung* is obviously equivalent to the term "faith" in Christianity. In other words, *kyung* is the mind attitude of human beings arising from the fear of "*tien* (heaven), *shang-ti* (lord on high), Heavenly Lord, and God." This fearfulness or awfulness enables us to feel our creatureliness and experience the "*mysterium tremendum.*" This attitude is also the same as "the feeling of absolute dependence." Therefore, Christian faith and Confucian *kyung* are different expressions of the same situation. Even though the terms are different, the reality that both terms indicate is the same.[82]

What is the relationship between *kyung* and *sung*? According to Kim, *kyung* is the way of achieving *sung*. In other words, *sung* is the goal that human beings should reach through *kyung*. So the *Zhongyong* states this: "Sincerity is the way of Heaven. To think how to be sincere is the way of man."[83] Here, the dimension of *sung* is similar to the one of human salvation in a Christian sense.

In Christianity, the goal of the life of faith is to attain salvation. This is possible by faith in Jesus Christ. Believing in Jesus as Christ is possible by realizing how Jesus became a true human and God. In other words, Jesus is the one who realized the Godhood that human beings seek. The synthesizing of God and human being was realized in Jesus Christ because he overcame the gap between God and humanity. Therefore, we can call him "a Son of God, Human-God, and Sage." On the other hand, a human being can become a true human in Jesus Christ, while God realizes himself/herself in the human being. This is the act of believing. Believing in Jesus means that we become the children of God by imitating the characteristics of Jesus Christ. Becoming the children of God is the same reality as becoming a true human being. [84]

This truth is also expressed in Confucian terms that "one can reach *Sung* by *Kyung*." *Sung*, which is inevitably connected to *Kyung*, indicates to us the mind state of sagehood as the ultimate goal of self-cultivation.[85] Chang Tsai discusses out the meaning of *Sung*:

> What is meant by enlightenment resulting from sincerity is that in which there is no distinction between the Way of Heaven as being great and the nature of man as being small . . . . When humanity and wisdom are united in harmony, they will be preserved and abide in the sage. . . . And when the nature of man and the Way of Heaven are united in harmony, they will be preserved and abide in sincerity.[86]

Likewise, *sung* means the united state of the heavenly Way and human nature. To be a sage means to be a human being of sincerity, someone who has achieved the state of salvation or new being.[87] Namely, the attainment of *sung*, which is the essential quality of sagehood as the final goal of cultivation, is not different from being saved which is the final goal of the Christian faith. Hence, we can reach this state through *Kyung*, or faith in Jesus Christ. This is well applied to preaching and the Bible study.

Preaching and the Bible Study in a Process Perspective

In addition to the Confucian way of preaching and the Bible study discussed above, there is also a potential new way of enhancing preaching in places of worship or liturgical settings. In a process perspective, preaching and Bible study can be understood as invitations through conversation, rather than one-sided proclamations, because it is believed that God persistently invites humanity to the way of truth and salvation. More precisely, "God, then, neither exercises unilateral, brute force nor manipulates, but offers opportunities for creative advance that creatures are free to accept or to reject. In the optimum community, authority is exercised similarly."[88]

This concept of God is fully rooted in the Bible. I believe that preaching and Bible study based on this concept of God will be effective in strengthening Korean Christians' faith, deepening their spirituality, and reaching out to other peoples. It is well known that the Korean Protestant churches have been status quo since 1990's. The main reason is that the most churches are too authoritative and exclusive; they lack flexibility and inclusiveness and fail to reach out to people who are not Christians. These factors negatively affect the Christian mission. However, "A process approach to preaching offers the minister a lively, sensitive, reliable vessel with which to ride the crest of energy. Process perspective enriches all aspect of the preaching event: the notion of what a sermon is and what it can do, the preparation of the sermon, and its preaching."[89] A process approach presents a new concept of God: the God of conversation, invitation, and persuasion. Whitehead fully affirms this, saying: "The divine element in the world is to be conceived as a persuasive agency and not as a coercive agency."[90]

This perspective enables us to understand the Bible as the persuasive authority in the church and make it possible to activate dialogue between the Bible and humanity. This is also different from the traditional slogan, "only the Bible"(*sola scriptura*), on which the Korean Protestant Church is built. I believe a process approach makes the Bible more alive and appealing and enriches the "only Scripture centered spirituality." Most importantly, through the process perspective, conversation comes alive when we are reading, studying the Bible, and preaching the gospel message. David Tracy thus claims, "To understand is to interpret. To interpret is to converse. To converse with any classic text is to find oneself caught up in the questions and answers worthy of a free mind. Conversation in its primary form is an exploration of possibilities in the search for truth."[91] This is a main characteristic which leads us to a process hermeneutics applied to preaching and Bible study. Conversation can be useful in church, where the biblical texts are explored and messages are delivered. In this hermeneutics, we converse not only with biblical texts but also one another. David Tracy's remarks are appropriate to this point:

> If we read well, then we are conversing with the text. No human being is simply a passive recipient of texts. We inquire. We question. We converse. Just as there is no purely autonomous text, so too there is no purely passive reader. There is only interaction named conversation. . . . In conversation we find ourselves by losing ourselves in the questioning provoked by the text. We find ourselves by allowing claims upon our attention, by exploring possibilities suggested by others, including those others we call texts.[92]

Conversation basically involves questioning and inquiring about the meanings of the texts and the message. It is interaction between the text and the reader, the preacher and the audience. In the process of conversation with the Bible, Christians can gain richer spirituality and clearer Christian identities. This is possible because through conversation the Bible provides "images, concepts, principles, parables, etc. that serve to evoke, nurture and correct the identities of the members of the community and to the identity of the community itself."[93]

Prayer and Contemplation in the Process-Confucian Perspective

Prayer is found in every world religion. "Prayer is a universal religious phenomenon, because it stems from the natural human disposition to give verbal expression to thought and emotion."[94] Prayer is frequently mentioned as being synonymous with spirituality. It is true that prayer has a strong relationship with Christian spirituality. Urban T. Holmes states:

> Prayer is to spirituality as eating is to hunger. Spirituality is an inner disposition toward a relation with him who transcends the appearances and prayer is the action this begets. We pray because we are spiritual beings . . . In turn, the de-

sire for God is fed by the act of prayer. We become aware of our spiritual selves as we actively seek to enter into relationships with God. . . . Prayer awakens our spirituality.[95]

In particular, prayer plays a great role in forming Korean Christian spirituality. Prayer is a priority for Christian life. Specifically, a loud vocal prayer, which is called *"Tongsung Kido,"* is always emphasized at every Protestant church in Korea. *Gifts of Many Cultures,* published by the United Church Press, describes it,

> In Korean congregations, among others, *Tongsung Kido* is a popular and important part of prayer life. Usually the congregation is given a specific time period, with a common theme of petition or supplication. Then all pray aloud at the same time. The voices of others will not bother them when they concentrate on their own earnest prayers, longing for the empowerment of the Holy Spirit.[96]

Korean Christians believe that they can meet God and experience a number of God's miracles through loud prayers. So, they believe they should pray as much as possible. Thus, a Korean Christian's spirituality can be called "spirituality of loud vocal prayer." Yong-Gi Cho, a pastor of Youido Full Gospel church, confesses:

> My life as a new pastor was horrible and miserable. In fact, a couple times I almost gave up pastoring the church. The only thing I could do in that difficult situation was to pray. Prayer became my solution as I sought and found peace only through fervent prayer. Every night I prayed until the early hours of the morning for the congregation to increase.[97]

It is true that this kind of prayer made a large contribution to the active faith of Korean Christians. However, it is equally true that this kind of prayer does not provide the opportunity for deep self-reflection. It is one-sidedly related to seeking secular blessing and spiritual healing. So, it should be complemented by the other dimensions of prayer. I think that the Confucian way of contemplation will help to reform the meaning of prayer, especially if we understand prayer as a way of spiritual growth in relation with the Confucian project of self-cultivation.

According to Wei-ming Tu, "Learning to become a good person in the Confucian context is not only the primary concern but also the ultimate and comprehensive concern."[98] Therefore, he presents "the human project" to be fully human in terms of the Confucian way: true self, family, and community. First of all, he uses the term "true self" which is the central subject of creative transformation. The true self refers to the idea of self-cultivation (*hsiu-shen,* or *hsiu-chi*). It is in contrast to the idea of the private ego or self-centeredness (*ssu*). Only the true self can reach human fufillment. He argues: "The true self is an open system. Despite its embeddedness and rootedness, it draws spiritual resources from the common spring of humanity."[99] Here, he recommends the term

A Process Cosmological Application to Interreligious Spirituality 113

"vigilant solitariness"(愼獨, *shin-dok* in Korean, *shen-tu* in Chinese) as the method of self-cultivation and important ethical discipline. "*Shin-dok*," which means "watchful when one is alone," leads us to the true self. This is a Confucian way of contemplation, which is related to the notion of Christian prayer. The term "*shin-dok*" means that a person is sensitive to his/her inner feelings and, at the same time, perceptive of the surrounding world. Tu argues:

> The message, then, is that a person who watches over himself when alone is also likely to be sensitive to the external environment, to be aware of situations around him, and to be alert in confronting unexpected development. This sensitivity, awareness, and alertness enables him to apprehend with ready promptness that which 'he does not see and does not hear' under ordinary circumstances.[100]

He goes on to say: "If I am vigilant of my solitariness, I will hear my true self express the quality of my Heaven-ordained nature. Then I will know the great foundation (*ta-pen*) of the cosmos, because I will know what has made me really human."[101]

Tu's argument is of course firmly based on Neo-Confucian thoughts. Echoing Zhu's philosophy, Yulgok also claims:

> The master Zhu said, 'therefore the superior person should be watchful and afraid in his/her mind. Even when nobody watches or hears him/her, the superior person should not be negligent. This is why we keep the original nature of the heavenly principle in our minds and don't let it away from our mind even for a moment.' There is nothing more evident that what is hidden and nothing more manifest than what is minute. Therefore, the superior person should be watchful when he/she is alone with himself/herself.[102]

So, it is clear that vigilant solitariness is an important part of cultivating one's mind, meditating on the sage's teachings, and focusing on the heavenly way. It is similar to a dimension of contemplation and prayer in Christianity.

Julia Ching, on the other hand, presents the concrete method of Confucian contemplation called "*jong-jwa*"(靜坐; Chinese: *ching-tso*; *jingzuo*; quiet-sitting), which was influenced by Daoism and Buddhism and adapted by Neo-Confucians in China, Japan, and Korea. "*Jong-jwa*" is not about reading classics but about having time to be still and alone. According to Ching, Neo-Confucians practiced

> A simplified form of meditation, adapting freely from Ch'an practices of 'sitting in meditation'(*tso-ch'an* 坐禪; Japanese: *zazen*), 'pondering upon riddles' (*kung-an*, 公案; Japanese: *koan*) and awaiting illumination or enlightenment (*wu* 悟; Japanese: *satori*). The remote preparation for this exercise was, and is,

a morally upright life; the immediate preparation remains an attitude of stillness. An erect sitting posture, whether on the chair, or, like the Buddhist, on the rush-mat, and in a lotus position, is usually recommended. Attention is also given to the control and regulation of breathing during the exercise.[103]

This was exactly what Neo-Confucian scholars used to practice for during self-cultivation, reflecting deeply on themselves according to Confucian teachings. This is of course different from the Daoist or the Buddhist meditation. Zhu Xi clarifies:

> Quiet-sitting is not required to be like the sitting meditation practices [of the Buddhist], entering concentration and cutting off thought and cognition. It is just the gathering together of the mind. Without rambling activities and idle thought the mind naturally becomes focused and at one with unperturbed calm and no affairs. Even if it has affairs then it abides by those affairs, fulfills its duty and then returns to being unmoved and calm.[104]

Ching also makes the same claim:

> Confucians place greater emphasis upon the knowledge of the moral self—of one's own strengths and weaknesses—in view of achieving self-improvement, of becoming more perfect in the practice of virtues and the elimination of vices. Confucian speak of developing or realizing the Heavenly principle (*t'ien-li*) within and of removing passions or 'human desires' (*jen-yu* ; 人欲), even sometimes of achieving 'desirelessness' in stillness. But Confucian meditation is not just an exam of conscience. It is definitely oriented to a higher consciousness, through emptying of the self and its desires. Emotional harmony rather than dialogue remains its essence. As a form of inner concentration, Confucian meditation stands somewhere between two other forms: the intellectual concentration of discursive thought and the moral concentration of assuring that there is no thought. Confucian meditation seeks peace without doing violence to human nature.[105]

This is also how Whitehead basically understands religion. He focuses on internality and solitariness of humanity as the origin of religion. He wrote:

> 'Religion is force of belief cleansing the inward parts'; and again, that 'Religion is the art and theory of the internal life of man, so far as it depends on the man himself, and on what is permanent in the nature of things': and again, 'Religion is what the individual does with its own solitariness.' This point of the origin of rational religion in solitariness is fundamental.[106]

According to Marjorie H. Suchocki, a process theologian, a Whiteheadian understanding of religion has things in common with mysticism and enriches Christian spirituality by validating mystical experiences of God in one's solitariness and loneliness. She states:

> Mysticism offers a number of parallels to our usage of the phenomenon of loneliness, for the mystic tends to move into areas of inwardness in search of the divine presence. If loneliness is a leveling of finite relationality, constituting all finite relations as superficial, there is a parallel sense whereby the mystic at least initially tends to categorize finite relations as insufficient for the souls' needs. The mystic frequently experiences a place of loneliness, a 'dark night of the soul,' in the inwardness of experience; the mystic, too, speaks of alienation and isolation . . . . The mystic seeks the divine presence on the other side of loneliness, and indeed expects it, or at least hopes for it. The lonely individual is more apt to stumble upon the divine presence, or to sense it as an unnamed and haunting possibility at the boundary of loneliness.[107]

In Christian history, "The early monastic tradition stressed the need for purity of prayer: in prayer the mind must be fixed on God without distraction."[108] This is the dimension of contemplation, which is related to the one of Confucianism. This also helps Christians grow spiritually. Holmes points out: "As persons mature spiritually their prayers move from a more to less focused intentionality. Classically this has been described as a movement toward contemplation and union with God."[109] This is traditionally called "apophatic prayer," which indicates "the prayer whose purpose is to empty the mind of images."[110] Korean Protestant Christians are not familiar with "contemplation" and "apophatic prayer," but Confucian meditation as described above has many resources for developing such prayers.[111] Introducing apophatic prayers to Korean Protestants would be a way toward forming a mature Christian spirituality in Korea. In Confucian terms, it would also help people to become a truly human and, as Ching pointed out, would further present "essentially a lay spirituality."[112] In this respect Urban T. Holms argues adequately for the meaning of prayer:

> Prayer is a way of seeing. There are two components to an act of seeing. We look in a certain direction and we look through a lens, as in the lens of the eye. What we see depends on both these elements: our direction and our focus (the shape of our lens). In prayer we look in and through ourselves to God and through him the world."[113]

Process-Confucian Way of Reforming the Christian Liturgy

Korean Christians try to attend worship services as frequently as possible because they believe that public worship service is the best way to worship and praise God, experience God's grace, and grow their faith. For them, this is a meaningful way to form their religious spiritualities. Carolyn Gratton states the importance of liturgy for spiritual formation. She claims:

> Those in charge of preparing catechumens for baptism and commitment within the church in the early centuries were certainly aware of the need for an object approach to the mystery in its entirety. In their liturgical celebrations and liturgical life as a whole they recognized the church as a spiritual director who sets the foundation of the direction along which she will lead her people [and] in the word, sacraments, and liturgical year she realizes what she preaches and sustains her people in their direction toward the Lord.[114]

There are many types of worship services in the Korean Church. However, it is true that there are also many things that we should reconsider when regarding the liturgy used by the Korean Church. Most of Korean churches use the same style of liturgy that was introduced by the American missionaries. I think that they should reform the Christian liturgy into a significant means of spiritual growth, because liturgy has a strong impact on Korean Christian faith. In particular, I would like to focus on the communion of saints and the Eucharist, which should be revived and reemphasized in the Korean church, in relationship with the tradition of Confucian ancestor worship. On the other hand, this is closely related to the task of liturgical movement popular in this ecumenical age. Don E. Saliers states: "The liturgical reforms and renewal of Christian liturgical life, spearheaded by the reforms of the Second Vatican Council, emphasize the common action of the gathered community about the Scriptures, the meal of the Eucharist, and the baptismal font."[115]

Worship as the Experience of the Vision of God

According to Whitehead, the purpose of religion is closely related to the religious vision which is divine, transcendental, and mysterious. The Christian community usually experiences such a vision through worship. Whitehead states:

> Religion is the vision of something which stands beyond, behind, and within, the passing flux of immediate things; something which is real, and yet waiting to be realized; something which is a remote possibility, and yet the greatest of present facts; something that gives meaning to all, and yet eludes apprehension; something whose possession is the final good, and yet is beyond all reach; something which is the ultimate ideal, and the hopeless quest.[116]

This vision enables Christian believers to have faith in God and live out their faith on earth. According to Whitehead, with this vision Christians can experience the power of love inspired and lured by God. He goes on to say, "The vision claims nothing but worship; and worship is surrender to the claim for assimilation, urged with the motive force of mutual love. The vision never overrules. It is always there, and it has the power of love presenting the one purpose whose fulfillment is eternal harmony."[117]

Christian spirituality is formed by concentrating on this vision and on God who inspires it in worship. In other words, the focus of worship should be the vision of God; all other things are means of experiencing this vision. Through worship, Christian spirituality becomes more experiential and dynamic. Thus, Whitehead clearly states the purpose of worship,

> The power of God is worship. That religion is strong which in its ritual and its modes of thought evokes an apprehension of the commanding vision. The worship of God is not a rule of safety—it is an adventure of the spirit, a flight after the unattainable. The death of religion comes with the repression of the high hope of adventure.[118]

We vividly experience the vision of God whenever we truly worship God because worship is "an adventure of the spirit." As the scripture points out, "God is spirit, And those who worship him must worship in spirit and truth"(John 4: 24). Also, we experience an "anthropocosmic vision" with the help of Confucian thought: the vision of understanding heaven, earth, and humanity as a dynamically united and interactive whole.[119] This Confucian vision in particular will enrich Christian spirituality and make it ecologically healthy. To achieve this purpose, many effective means can be used for worship.

To place the focus of worship on the experience of religious vision is in harmony with the basic principle of process cosmology: individual actual entities are occasions of experiences. This leads the way to the enjoyment of worship and the embodiment of spirituality for Christians because all experience is basically enjoyment in a process perspective. In Whitehead's words, experience is the "self enjoyment of being one among many, and of being one arising out of the composition of many."[120] Hence, one can enjoy one's subjective immediacy in the moment of experiencing a religious vision through worship. There is no doubt that this will be a good way of enhancing Christian spirituality.

Positive Understanding of Ancestor Worship as an Expression of Filial Piety

Ancestor worship is the most important element of Confucian moral and religious values. It has been observed for hundreds of years in Korean society. Yulgok mentions the significance of ancestor worship in Confucianism as a living religion, focusing on the cardinal virtue of filial piety in particular:

> The filial person serves his/her parents by doing as follows: giving great reverence to one's parents while they are alive; attending to one's parents with happiness; taking care of one's parents with much concern when they are sick; ex-

pressing utmost sorrow when the parents die; and observing ancestor worship with seriousness. When one performs these five duties, one successfully serves one's parents.[121]

For Yulgok, it is clear that filial piety must be practiced on both living parents and dead parents and ancestor worship is considered a meaningful rite of continuously practicing filial piety to parents and ancestors. It is the first step toward the practice of humanity (Korean: *in* ; Chinese: *jen*, 仁) in the world. He states:

Those who love their parents do not hate other people. Those who respect their parents do not act arrogantly to other people. If one serves one's parents with love and respect, virtue and cultivation will grow among the people and he/ she will be a good example on earth. This is the filial piety that the heavenly one puts into practice.[122]

Even though most Korean Christians still consider ancestor worship idolatry, they cannot avoid participating in it on special occasions. In my opinion, Korean Christians should embrace ancestor worship with a more positive attitude, as it could help them significantly with spiritual formation and direction. In a process perspective, ancestor worship is not hard to accept because it can be understood as a meaningful awareness of the continuity of all actual entities in the process of transition and concrescence in the universe. According to Whitehead's philosophy, all entities are "momentary events which perish immediately upon coming into being. The perishing marks the transition to the succeeding events."[123] Human beings are no exception; the human being as an individual exists only in relationship with the past and the future. In other words, "One occasion succeeds another. The past is composed of those events that have occurred; the future is radically different, since it contains no occasions; and the presents is the occasion that is now occurring. The present is influenced by the past, and it will influence the future."[124] The memory of ancestors awakens us to our place in time and in history. Marjorie Suchocki also makes a good claim for this:

Every instant of becoming is a becoming through the dynamic convergence of past and future: the past, through many divergent influences demanding an accounting; the future, through a transforming decision concerning these many influences of the past might be unified. The present is the becoming of a new subject through this process of unifying the past and the future.[125]

Therefore, my basic point is that the nature of ancestor worship is different from the Christian notion of worshipping God, because it is an expression of filial piety. For this reason, it is urgently necessary to present a theological interpretation of ancestor worship as the basis of Confucian-Christian spirituality.

Conservative Christians' objection to ancestor worship is mainly based on the first and the second commandments in Exodus 20:3-4. These commandments emphasize the exclusiveness and uniqueness of the biblical concept of God and they present the largest obstacle to any positive interaction of Christianity with Confucian ancestor worship. However, it should be noted that the Judeo-Christian concept of God was developed in the Jewish tradition, which is quite different than the Confucian tradition. The spirit of the Ten Commandments is expressed in the preamble of Exodus 20:2: "I am the Lord your God, who brought you out of the land of Egypt, out of the house of slavery." Here, the Lord God is revealed as the great liberator who set free the oppressed slaves from Egypt. In this context, other gods in Exodus 20:2 were those who functioned as gods of oppression, i.e., ruling ideologies, in the ancient near Eastern countries. The Israelites were continually fighting against these false gods who oppressed human beings.[126] They finally established their own country called "Israel," which means, "'O, Lord (Yahweh), Rule us." This mono-Yahwism played an important role for Israel through the biblical traditions.[127] On the other hand, there is no such context in regard to the unique concept of god in Confucianism. Therefore, it is not possible to equate the biblical God in Christian tradition with gods in Confucian tradition. Also it is dangerous to select one verse of the Bible without regarding its contexts.

As we stated above, it is manifest that filial piety to ancestors is deeply and sincerely expressed in the tradition of Confucian ancestor worship. Likewise, there are also many verses of filial piety in the Bible: "Honor your father and your mother" (Exodus 20:12); "Children, obey your parents in the Lord, for this is right. Honor your father and mother—this is the first commandment with a promise"(Ephesians 6:1-2); "Hear, my child, your father's instruction, and do not reject your mother's teaching; for they are a fair garland for your head, and pendants for your neck" (Proverbs 1:8-9) and so forth. This thought was expressed well when the Israelites referred to their God as the "God of their ancestors." In Jewish tradition, Jesus also talked about "the Lord, the God of Abraham, the God of Isaac, and the God of Jacob"(Luke 20:37). Ideas of filial piety are also important in the biblical traditions. Therefore, I think that there is no problem in the acceptance of the ancestor worship for Christians in terms of filial piety and rather it would be beneficial for Christians to accept its positive meaning into their spiritual lives. Further, Christianity can be developed and enriched by Confucian values of filial piety, which have strongly influenced East Asian countries. In particular, Korean Christians can become more spiritually mature by actively accepting ancestor worship. In this sense, Wei-ming Tu's explanations of the significance of ancestor worship are helpful:

> Each ritual, no matter how trifling it appears to us today, symbolized a sacrificial tradition with generations of devoted observance. To sons who were filial in *Chung-yung*'s sense, repairing their ancestral temple, for example, must have

been a solemn occasion, observed year after year without any deviation from the prescribed methods.... The other ceremonial acts must also have been understood as significant parts of their impeccable record of filiality.... Ceremonial acts in this connection symbolize desirable patterns. To respect the old and to honor the dead is to show special concern for the common origin of all. The old are respected not only for their past service but also for the continual value of their wise guidance. The dead are honored because a loving memory of the forefathers brings forth communal identity and social solidarity. Society so conceived is not an adversary system consisting of pressure groups but a fiduciary community based on mutual trust.[128]

The Communion of Saints and Confucian Ancestor Worship

The community of the living and the dead is found in the Apostles' Creed as the communion of saints (*communio santorum*). This confession originally referred to the communion of the dead saints and the living Christians in the time of early Christianity. Gardiner M. Day comments on this: "This article (the communion of saints) is obviously an amplification of the previous one, the Holy Catholic Church, affirming our faith that the church, visible and invisible, is a fellowship of all believers, living or dead, who have become one with Christ and through him one with each other."[129] As an important factor in Christian faith, "The communion of the saints is one of those places where the love of God is embodied, and by implication Paul would have us believe that the promise of the Gospel is not only that death cannot separate the Christian from God, but that death cannot disrupt the communion of the saints."[130] This original meaning has been changed since the Reformation; the communion of saints now means only the Christian community (*congregatio fidelium*).[131]

There are, however, many examples of ceremonies for the dead. In the third century A.D, the Christian church performed the Eucharist at the buried place of the dead. This kind of thinking emphasized the communal life of both the living and the dead as members of Christian community who together received the body and blood of Jesus Christ. This was practiced for the sake of the martyrs. As Michael S. Driscoll says, "A link was thus established between the Eucharist and martyrdom: celebrating the Eucharist for those called upon to shed their blood or remembering in the Eucharist those who have already undergone martyrdom."[132] In addition, at the Eucharist on Sunday, the names of the dead were called out for the sake of their memory. This custom was practiced until the time of St. Augustine.[133]

The ceremony for the dead was developed broadly in the time of early Christianity in connection with the cult of the saints. According to *The New Dictionary of Sacramental Worship*,

> It initially took the form of praise and imitation of the deceased holy ones (Greek *hagioi*, Latin *sancti*), and involved as well, gatherings of celebration

and prayer at the places of burial. . . . In the ancient world, in which Christianity began, tombs were places of contact between humans and the gods. The tombs represented a home for the dead. . . . In like manner, the early Christians held the tomb to be the privileged places of the saint. And like the Greek hero, the saint was considered to an intercessor *(daemon)* who functioned as an intermediary between this world and the next. . . . Belief in the resurrection of Christ and its effects on all who fall asleep in Christ prompted the early Christians to ask the saints to intercede for those still living.[134]

There were many debates about the cult of the saints and the role of saintly intercessions in the history of the Christian Church. It was right for Martin Luther to strongly deny intercession by the saints for the sake of his Christocentrism; he prohibited the cult of the saints in his church because of the far-fetched legends about the saints which were negative influences on Christians at that time.[135] In this regard, Luther's reformation of the Catholic Church was a positive thing at that time.

However, Luther's reformation rejected many significant symbols and ceremonies of Christianity, which are important for Christian life. In particular, the Christian liturgy in the Protestant tradition has reached its most impoverished form since the Reformation. Hence, I think that there are many things which should be critically reaccepted by Korean Protestant churches. In particular, the communion of the saints between the dead and the living can help the Korean Church to meet and understand ancestor worship in a more positive way because Korean traditions emphasize the whole community of the living and the dead, the past and the present. For Protestant Christians, it can be acceptable on the basis of Christcentrism to consider all the saints in the history of Christianity the objects of veneration, and this can make their present Christian lives more rich and alive. Above all, the communion of the saints could become the common grounds in the encounter of Christianity with ancestor worship in Korea. In addition, ancestor worship could help Korean Christians revive the tradition of the communion of the saints. This would contribute to the development of Confucian-Christian spirituality in the Korean Church. Furthermore, this would enrich Christian faith. In this regard, Chin-Hong Chung, a Korean scholar of religion, correctly points out the problem of Protestant liturgy in Korea:

> Protestant liturgy could not contribute much to its secularization because it did not accept the community of 'the dead and living', 'the living and the dead'. If the community of the living does not combine with that of the dead, it is not a true human community. If we characterize ancestor worship in terms of the adoration or divinization of ancestors, it is the misguided and arbitrary which comes from theological prejudice. Ancestor worship should be an important moment understood in terms of rereading signs of human life. The community of the living in which the dead do not remain loses human dignity. All the

ceremonial activities, such as placing ancestral tablets, providing the meals on the ancestral table, asking spirits of ancestors to come, bowing, and making wishes, are not about idolatry, betrayal of God, or magical blessings. Rather, they represent the aspects of life of the human community in which its members have relationships with the dead, who continue to be with us, even after they die. The Protestant liturgy seriously destroys this community. [136]

I agree with Chung's criticism of Protestant liturgy in Korea. I think that the Protestant Church should consider Confucian ancestor worship more positively because it would be a meaningful way of contextualizing the Christian liturgy and enhancing Christian spirituality in the Korean context. As I indicated above, Confucian tradition still pulses strongly in the hearts of all Koreans. In many ways and forms, Korean Christians cannot avoid encountering the Confucian tradition, particularly ancestor worship. The communion of saints can provide the foundation for this encounter for Christians, because it can constitute the human community of love. In this sense, G. M. Day's comment on the communion of saints has much relevance to my position: "Participating in the communion of saints means being part of a great unseen society of those in the past, present and future who are joined together through sharing in the spirit and love of Christ. This is the most ecumenical society in the world."[137] Also, *Baptism, Eucharist And Ministry*, presented by the World Council of Churches, supports this position for contemporary churches in an ecumenical sense: "United to our Lord and in communion with all the saints and martyrs, we are renewed in the covenant sealed by the blood of Christ."[138]

Furthermore, the days of ancestor worship should be included in the Christian calendar as important rites, like the tradition of saints' days. As is well known, "The early Christians, like their pagan neighbors, kept the anniversaries of their dead, especially of the martyrs; for the martyrs had conquered in and for Christ and were now with Christ."[139] Many churches, such as the Catholic, Orthodox, and Anglican Churches, still celebrate the saints' day. It should be no problem for the Protestant Church to accept this tradition, because even the Bible witnesses the faith-life of ancestors in Hebrews 11. In a similar way, Korean Christians should celebrate the lives of their pre-Christian ancestors who sought the meaning of their life through ancestor worship by contacting the origin of their life in relationship with ancestors.

The Christian Eucharist and Ancestor Worship

As discussed above, it is certain that ancestor worship in Korea plays a significant role. It helps people to express filial piety and keeps a humanized society. If we understand ancestor worship not only as the cult of the dead but also as a practical norm for serving one's family and society, ancestor worship can have much in common with Christian Eucharist. Christians experience mystical unity with God through the Eucharist and are called to be apostles of peacemaking and reconciliation in the world.

The Eucharist has been central in the Christian liturgy and throughout Christian life. There have been many vigorous debates about the origin and meaning of Eucharist. In general, the Christian Church confesses that the Eucharist was instituted by the Lord Jesus. The Apostle Paul's statement is foundational for the Eucharist: "For I received from the Lord what I also handed on to you, that the Lord Jesus on the night when he was betrayed took a loaf of bread, and when he had given thanks, he broke it and said, 'This is my body that is for you. Do this in remembrance of me.' In the same way he took the cup also, after supper, saying, 'This cup is the new covenant in my blood. Do this, as often as you drink it, in remembrance of me."(I Corinthians 11:23-25).

Peter E. Fink attempts to define the Eucharist in a more strict way: "The Eucharist refers to the bread and wine consecrated during the eucharistic liturgy (e.g., holy Eucharist), received in communion and kept in reserve both for the sick and the sign of Christ's enduring presence in and to use the term in this restricted sense."[140] In a similar way, *Baptism, Eucharist And Ministry* defines: "The Eucharist is a sacramental meal which by visible signs communicates to us God's love in Jesus Christ, the love by which Jesus loved his own 'to the end' . . . . its celebration continues as the central act of the Church's worship."[141]

Even though the Eucharist is practiced as one complete act in the liturgy, it has many meanings. *Baptism, Eucharist and Ministry* explains five aspects of the Eucharist: "Thanksgiving to the Father, Memorial of Christ, Invocation of the Spirit, Communion of the Faithful, Meal of the Kingdom."[142] Among them, I would like to concentrate on the fourth aspect of the Eucharist for the sake of making a positive connection with ancestor worship. That is, the Eucharist demands that all participants be actively concerned about other fellow human beings. This is the social meaning of the Eucharist. In more detail,

> The eucharistic celebration demands reconciliation and sharing among all those regarded as brothers and sisters in the one family of God and is a constant challenge in the search for appropriate relationship in social, economic and political life. . . . Solidarity in the eucharistic communion of the body of Christ and responsible care of Christians for one another and the world find specific expressions in the liturgies: in the mutual forgiveness of sins; the sign of peace; intercession for all; the eating and drinking together; the taking of the elements to the sick and those in prison or the celebration of the Eucharist with them."[143]

This aspect of the Eucharist is derived directly from the ministry of the historical Jesus. In defining the Eucharist as the meal of the Kingdom, *Baptism, Eucharist And Ministry* emphasizes the characteristics of Jesus' ministry: "As Jesus went out to publicans and sinners and had table-fellowship with them during his earthly ministry, so Christians are called in the Eucharist to be in solidarity with the outcast and to become signs of the love of Christ who lived and sacrificed himself for all and now gives himself in the Eucharist."[144]

Korean *Minjung* theology declares this more emphatically. According to Jae-Soon Park, a Korean *Minjung* theologian, the Eucharist originated from "Jesus' Kingdom of God Movement," which is characterized as a table community movement.[145] He first takes a look at the Jesus movement: "Hungry and sick minjung always gathered around Jesus. Jesus ignored the Sabbath Law and the Purity Law to heal the maimed, the blind, the lame, the crippled, the paralyzed, and the lepers. He shared bread with hungry minjung, feeding five thousand people with five loaves of bread and two fish."[146] Therefore, he continues:

> The Jesus movement was not an ethical, religious movement based on an individual's personality. It was rather a collective, communal movement responding to the collective pains of the minjung who were sick, hungry and oppressed. Jesus' Kingdom of God movement bringing perfect, abundant life to the cripple, mentally ill and other sufferers was the life restoration movement. This movement that tried to share food with the starving minjung was the table community movement. This movement that proclaimed to the oppressed minjung the principle of serving was the movement of mutual service to one another."[147]

Interpreting the accounts regarding Jesus' movement in the perspective of minjung theology, Park connects the origin of the Eucharist with Jesus' movement. According to him, "The Eucharist initiated at the last supper was a witness to the table community movement, and it was permanently instituted to support this movement. At the Eucharist, God (the resurrected Christ) and food are holistically united. This unification is the unity of heaven (the Kingdom of God) and earth (reality), and it symbolizes the revolution against the unjust system that separates the heaven and the earth."[148]

Tissa Balasuriya, an Asian liberation theologian in Sri Lanka, also supports this kind of radical thinking about the Eucharist. Balasuriya explains how Jesus instituted the Eucharist:

> He (Jesus) knew that his enemies were planning to kill him. . . . It was at this stage of his life that Jesus established the Eucharist. He foresaw that he would soon leave his people and his community of followers. He wanted to leave to them a sign, a symbol, a memorial of his life work and a way of being present to them through their own identification with the poor and the suffering. For this he used the symbol and the ceremony for the Jewish *Pasch*. He gave the *Pasch* a new meaning and a wider relevance. The meaning of the Eucharist was fundamentally in his self-oblation for the cause of integral human liberation. As a meal it was also a symbol of the unity of the participants in the same cause (even though one of them was to betray him).[149]

As I have stated above, evidently, the Eucharist as a symbol of sharing, serving, sacrificing, and human liberation has much relevance to the encounter of Christianity with Confucian ancestor worship in the religiously pluralistic society of Korea. It is not surprising that some theologians in Asian countries attempt to understand ancestor worship from the perspective of the Eucharist for the sake of the indigenization of Christianity. Jong-Chun Park, a Methodist theologian in Korea, insists that, on the basis of his differentiation between ancestor worship as a patriarchal ideology and as an ethical expression of filial piety, the acceptance of ancestor worship is related to the task of rebuilding a community-oriented Christian ethic. In comparing the Christian memorial service to ancestor worship, he points out that the former differs from a community of the living and the dead because the spirits of the dead are not experienced by participants. Therefore, he suggests that the Korean Christian Church critically accept essential ceremonial acts of ancestor worship, such as meals on the table, bowing, and sharing of meals.[150]

Choan-Seng Song, a leading Asian theologian, also elucidates on the common denominators between ancestor worship and the Eucharist:

> There are positive factors in ancestor worship that can be shared by Christians as they sit at the Lord's Table in remembrance of Christ until he comes. In the experience of the living presence of Christ as we partake of his body through the bread and wine, we ought to be concerned not merely with our own personal relationship with him and our own life in him. We experience the living Christ as center of the family to which we belong, a family consisting also of those who have passed beyond this life into another life and of those who are to follow in the future. With Jesus Christ together with all the members of our family a communion is established on the foundation of the cross and the resurrection.[151]

This is of course harmonious with a process perspective because it basically puts faith in the interrelation and interdependence of all things in the world. As an important sacrament of the Church, the Eucharist in a process perspective can contribute to the forming of community of all people in the past, present, and future with its communal nature. Marjorie Suchocki states:

> First, there is the focus on the present community, ... Second, the sacraments relate us to the full community of the church, past and future. Third, they are an impetus to the societal witness of the church in the creation of communities of love and justice. The sacraments generate the power of community with the past and the future through the present creation of apostolicity and unity. Through apostolicity, the sacraments bespeak the community of the past, and of the many who have preceded the community of the present in this same act of participating in the sacrament. The very ritualized repetition of the sacrament

gives it a power in this process universe, for it strengthens the being-made-present quality of the past through prehension.[152]

Understanding the functions of ancestor worship is important for supporting a positive position on it. I would like to concentrate especially on the personal and social functions of ancestor worship. This can contribute to the creation of a Confucian-Christian spirituality. M. Odell and A. M. Schwartzbaum explain the functions of ancestor veneration (worship) in two ways. First, ancestor worship has the function of psychological adjustment. They say: "In societies with a strong unlineal descent principle, the brevity of a single human life is counteracted by the permanence of the lineage. Through the practice of venerating lineage ancestors, the individual can hope for continued existence as an ancestor as long as there are living descendants to conduct rituals." Second, ancestor worship reinforces social organization. Namely, "Ancestor veneration has an important role in preserving the continuity of the social order in spite of the death of individuals".[153]

I agree to two positive functions of ancestor worship in Korea. These can be easily accepted by Christians. In particular, all Koreans experience these when they gather to celebrate ancestral rituals on New Year's Day and the Full Moon's Day, regardless of their religions. The basic moral values of Confucianism are streaming in their blood. It is through ancestor worships and rituals that those who live in separated lonely societies can feel human love and brother/ sisterhood. It is true that Confucianism is not only a religion but also an essential part of Korean life today. In particular, ancestor worship functions as a bond of human love and sharing in family and society. It can enhance a spirit of humane community. This is the most important part of ancestor worship today in Korea. The presence of ancestors' gods and spirits, which is criticized by ultra conservative Christians, is now experienced only symbolically by modern generations. In many cases, young Koreans, including myself, do not believe literally that ancestors' gods and spirits descend to eat the meal on the table. Hence, I have no objection to ancestor worship as an ethical expression of filial piety, thanksgiving to ancestors, and to the origin of our lives. In this respect, it would be a natural phenomenon for Catholic churches in Korea to actively try to accept the essential elements of Confucian cultures, including ancestor worship, into Christian liturgies.

In regard to a positive understanding of ancestor worship in the context of family and society, Korean theologian Wi-Jo Kang's suggestion for ancestor worship as a means of Christian Eucharist for reforming the Christian family in Korea is a bold, advanced idea. This is related to the dimension of the spirituality of community. He first evaluates ancestor worship in a positive way:

> Ancestor worship became a powerful institution in Korean life and culture. It was a sacred symbol in which all Koreans found meaning and purpose for their lives and enhancement of their sense of belonging. Without both ancestor wor-

ship and family, Koreans lost the sense of meaning of their existence; but through the observance of these rites Koreans maintained the values of filial piety and loyalty, which in turn strengthened family life and solidified the fabric of Korean society.[154]

On the other hand, according to him, many Christians cannot experience the sacred in family life because "Traditional church life has not provided opportunities or support for the active participation of the laity in nurturing, strengthening, and preserving true Christian faith within the family."[155] Christians tend to separate their faith life from their daily life, including their family life, concentrating on the church as the only sacred institution. Therefore, it is necessary for Christians today in Korea to reform their faith life at home. Here, Kang proposes "the Eucharist at home." He says: "The purpose of 'the Eucharist at home' must be to strengthen the Christian family everywhere, thereby rendering corporate worship more meaningful. 'The Eucharist at home' is a call to a renewed Christian faith through enriched Christian family life and may be a means for the emergence of a ministerial role for the laity."[156] Of course, ancestor worship functions as an important means of building the Eucharist at home. It can make a spirituality of daily life possible for Christians.

Furthermore, the Eucharist can be practiced to offer "a cosmic vision of sacramentality,"[157] the idea that the world itself is a sacrament and reveals God's presence. Thus, to participate in the Eucharist becomes an important moment of new ecological awareness. The bread and wine as elements from the earth can be significantly visible and tangible signs of God's presence. This new understanding opens a way for developing ecological spirituality by enabling more frequent practices of the Eucharist. The Ecumenical Patriarch Dimitrios makes an interesting comment in the following statement:

> *Thine Own of Thine own we offer unto thee* . . . . In the form of bread and wine, material from creation moulded into new form by human hands is offered to God with the acknowledgement that all of creation is God's and that we are returning to God that which is His. In the sense that this captures the primordial relationship of Adam to both God and Creation, it is a sight of the restoration of that relationship and even more than that, a foretaste of the eschatological state of creation. When we partake of the body and blood of Christ, God meets us in the very substance of our relationship with creation and truly enters into the very being of our biological existence.[158]

Process-Confucian Spirituality as Eco-Spirituality

Ecological problems are the emergent issues the global community faces now. Nobody on earth is excepted from these issues. We all live in the midst of an ecological crisis. It is well known that human beings have been destroying nature and the environment with science and technology. Without overcoming the ecological crisis we cannot exist any longer. The ecological crisis is fundamental and complicated in its character and scope. James Nash claims:

> Whether or not ecological angst is a fad, whether or not ecological concerns will be 'definitely in' a few years or decades hence, the fact remains that the ecological crisis is definitely dangerous. The scale and scope of the problems are severe, and if present trends continue without sufficient human changes and constraints, the crisis and the difficulties of ameliorating it will again intensify, just as they did following the early seventies.[159]

So, at the beginning of the third millennium the cardinal question for the global community is raised all the more urgently. On what basic ecological conditions can we survive on a habitable earth? On what presuppositions can the whole global community be rescued? On what basis can a human being achieve a happy and peaceful life in coexistence with his/ her environment? In this respect, our spirituality must include an ecological perspective, which means that we need to see our environment, the earth, and nature in a new perspective. In other words, our spirituality should be an eco-spirituality which is fully responsible for ecological crisis. This is because the ecological crisis is closely related to the spirituality of a wrong theological-ethical viewpoint. James Nash thus points out:

> The crisis is partly rooted in philosophical, theological, and ethical convictions about the rights and powers of humankind in relation to the rest of the biophysical world. According to one popular conception—actually, a misconception and stereotype—of 'dominion,' humankind is a distinctive creation designed for domination. We are a species segregated from nature and possessed with an ultimately sanctioned and unrestricted right to exploit the bountiful supply of nature's 'raw materials' provided for human benefit. Nature is simply matter, resources waiting to be re-formed for human utility. This viewpoint embodies the fundamental failures at the roots of the ecological crisis: the failure to adapt to the limiting conditions (the carrying and recuperative capacities) of our earthly habitat, the failure humankind and the rest of the ecosphere, and the failure to respond benevolently and justly to the theological and biological fact of human kinship with all creation. Without doubt, Christian traditions bear some responsibility for propagating these failed perspective.[160]

More specifically, this is because in the past we lacked an ecological worldview. As Ralph Metzner claims:

> A growing chorus of voices is pointing out that the fundamental roots of the environmental disaster lie in the attitude, values, perceptions, and basic worldview that we humans of the industrial-technological global society have come to hold. The worldview and associated attitudes and values of the industrial age

have permitted and driven us to pursue exploitative, destructive, and wasteful applications of technology. I suggest that we are in the midst of a transition phase to an ecological age, characterized by an ecological worldview, the outlines of which are being articulated in the natural sciences, the social sciences, and in philosophy and religious thought.[161]

Fortunately, process-Confucian cosmology can contribute to the making of the eco-spirituality by providing an ecological worldview for us. As we have discussed, process thought presents an organic, relational, interdependent, and processive worldview, which has true ecological relevance. The process cosmology of Whitehead and Yulgok basically understands the world and the universe as a living organism. This cosmology is called "an organismic worldview" which sees the universe as a becoming process. According to Mary Evelyn Tucker, it is the worldview shared by Confucianism and Daoism that can be described "as organic, vitalistic, and holistic. They see the universe as a dynamic, ongoing process of continual transformation."[162] "It is this organic, vitalistic worldview which has special relevance for developing a contemporary ecological perspective."[163] This worldview replaces a mechanistic worldview which sees the universe merely as tools and machinery. Ralph Metzner adequately describes this change:

> The 'mechanical philosophy' of Newton, Galileo, and Descartes, which began by devising quantitative, mechanical models of physical processes, developed in the course of three centuries into a *mechanomorphic* worldview, in which the universe is erroneously identified with the analogical models originally designed to explain it. This mechanistic worldview is giving way in many circles to an *organismic* view, which sees the universe as an evolving process, a 'story' in Berry's terms. Instead of seeing life as biochemical machinery somehow derived from random molecular combinations, the new biology defines life as self-generating (*autopoietic*), genetically coded process adaptively coupled with the environment. The Earth, instead of an inert body of dead matter, is seen in the Gaia theory of James Lovelock and Lynn Margulis as a kind of superorganism, evolving in homeostatic reciprocal interaction between living organisms and the physicochemical environment.[164]

Therefore, in the process cosmology of Whitehead and Yulgok, all things including humanity are interdependent and interrelated in the process of becoming; they are all comprised of actual entities and eternal objects, and principle and material forces in the midst of the processes of concrescence and ingression, and the movement and quiescence of yin-yang forces. There is no such concept that nature is considered merely matter and resources or machinery because humanity is also a part of nature, and humanity exists in interaction with nature and the earth in the universe.

It is well known that Whitehead explored this new worldview and a new religion based on it, criticizing traditional western worldviews which played a great role in causing the ecological crisis. David Griffin summarized Whitehead's worldview as follows:

> (1) it portrays all individuals as having intrinsic value; (2) it portrays all things as internally related to their environments; (3) it portrays the self in particular as an ecological self; (4) it portrays the divine reality as ecologically interconnected with the world and shows that the support given to an ecological consciousness by this portrayal of the divine reality is not undermined by the problem of evil; and (5) it shows how a special concern for human beings and other higher animals is not inconsistent with concern for the biosphere as a whole and with the intuition that, in some sense, all forms of life have (roughly) equal inherent value.[165]

To him, even the concept of God has an ecological relevance. That is, God is considered to be a co-creator who continues to work for a better world along with humanity. In this sense, creation is not an act committed once by the creator; it is still in process by God and humanity and all other things, which makes an active ecological movement possible. For Whitehead, God is transcendent as well as immanent; God not only gives all things a subjective aim to move forward; he is a new creation of the world and also is involved in all process of creation. Whitehead expresses his unique view on God and the world in his metaphoric languages. He states:

> It is as true to say that God is permanent and the World fluent, as that the World is permanent and God is fluent. It is as true to say that God is one and the World many, as that the World is one and God many. It is as true to say that, in comparison with the World, God is actual eminently, as that, in comparison with God, the World is actual eminently. It is as true to say that the World is immanent is God, as that God is immanent in the World. It is as true to say that God transcends the World, as that the World transcends God. It is as true to say that God creates the World, as that the World creates God.[166]

According to Tucker, "Cosmologically, early Confucianism, like Daoism, understood the world to be part of a changing, dynamic, and unfolding universe. The ongoing and unfolding process of nature was affirmed by the Confucians and seasonal harmony was highly valued."[167] Following this cosmological thought, Yulgok also beautifully expresses his viewpoint on heaven and earth. To him, the human mind is the central force bringing nature and the environment into proper order. Undoubtedly, his cosmological thought has numerous ecological implications. He writes:

> The great substance of all the changes in all things is only one material force. When principle and material force move, they become yang. When principle and material force stay restful, they become yin. Once activity in movement

and once quiescence is material force. The reason of moving and quiescence is principle. In heaven and earth, among all things that have forms, some are comprised of right material forces of five phases; some are comprised of twisted material force of heaven and earth; some come out of fights between yin and yang; some come out of issuance of both yin and yang forces. The sun, the moon, and the stars are hung in the sky; rain, snow, frost, and dew come down to the earth; and wind, clouds, thunder, and the sharp strokes of lightning are caused. All these are nothing but material forces. The reason why these are hung in the sky, come down to the earth, and caused is nothing but principle. When yin has harmony with yang, the sun and the moon will not lose the proper cycles of their rotation, the rain and the snow that come down to the earth will be subject to the proper seasons, and the wind, clouds, thunder, and sharp strokes of lightning will be in harmonized material forces. This is normality of principle. If principle does not have harmony with material force, the sun and the moon will lose the right cycles of their rotation, the rain and the snow that come down to the earth will not be subject to the proper seasons, and the wind, clouds, thunder, and sharp strokes of lightning will come out of distorted material force. This is distortion and break of principle. However, humanity is the mind of heaven and earth. If one's mind is right, the mind of heaven and earth will be right. If the material force of humanity is meek, the material force of heaven and earth will be meek.[168]

As seen in the above phrases, Yulgok's cosmological thought can be termed as "a form of social ecology because a key component is the relationship of the human order to the natural order. A profound sense of the interconnectedness of humanities with one another and with nature is central to Confucian thinking."[169] For Yulgok, humanity is understood in unity with heaven and earth. According to Young Chan Ro, this can be called a "cosmoanthropic" vision of unity between the cosmos and human beings. Yulgok's cosmology fully implies the significance of a cosmoantropic vision in his Neo-Confucian studies.[170] Moreover, "For Yulgok, the cosmos was not just an object of human analysis but a subject to be appreciated, observed, or even encountered by humans. Yulgok thus developed a comprehensive way of understanding, and a proper way to relate, the universe."[171]

This ecological vision of Confucianism is realized by the "profound person" (*kunja, chun-tzu,* 君子) as an example of the ideal human being. According to Wei-ming Tu, "The profound person recognizes that the possibility of a complete realization of the ideal of the unity of man and Heaven is inherent in each human nature."[172] That is, the profound person, with a faith in humanity, is fully aware of the Way. Every human being can become a profound person by the ordinary process of self-cultivation, which leads to an ecological peace and justice on earth. Thus, *Chung-yung* says: "The Way of the profound person functions everywhere and yet is hidden. Men and women of simple intelligence can share its knowledge."[173]

Therefore, in sum, process cosmology can significantly help Christians striving for ecological spirituality, which focuses on the interrelationship of all things in the universe. David Griffin's comment is very pertinent to this point: "The relations one has with one's body, one's larger natural environment, one's family, and one's culture are instead are constitutive of one's very identity."[174] This spirituality resonates with the biblical vision of shalom. Clark M. Williamson and Ronald J. Allen make an appropriate claim:

> This spirituality articulates the biblical vision of shalom, according to which all creation is one, every creature is related to every other creature, and all should live in security and harmony and in a way that is supportive of the well being and joy of each other. An appropriate spirituality must be concerned not only with justice toward other people (committed to their equality, dignity and participatory rights) but with what is called "sustainability." Sustainability has to do with a just relationship between human beings and our natural environment.[175]

Process-Confucian Spirituality as Socio-Political Spirituality

Feminist Critical Consideration of Confucianism

Before exploring the subject of the development of socio-political spirituality from a process cosmological perspective, we need to address the recent feminist critiques on Confucianism, which are arising as one of the powerful legacies these days. Confucianism has been criticized because it served as a ruling ideology over a long period in the Korean society and, in particular, had functioned as a patriarchal system, oppressing women. A Korean feminist theologian, Hyun-Kyung Chung, described this problem in her writing, reflecting on her life experience:

> In Korean society, which is strongly influenced by Confucian law, women who give birth out of wedlock are ostracized. No law, custom, or community structure protects them. They are treated as outcasts. The social message is that these women should feel ashamed of themselves. The social ostracism they go through does not stop in their generation. It passes on to their children. In the Yi dynasty, which lasted until the dawn of the twentieth century in Korea, children of a surrogate mother could not take an exam to hold governmental offices. This tradition still thrives in Korean society today, although in a subtle way.[176]

The Chinese feminist theologian, Pui-lan Kwok, also presents critical argument regarding Confucianism from a feminist perspective, differentiating between classical Confucianism and Neo-Confucianism. She claims:

The study of the influence of Asian religions on women should also be cross-cultural. For example, classical Confucian teaching, originating with Confucius (551-479 BCE), may not have included extremely restrictive and derogatory views of women. But Neo-Confucianism, which emerged between the tenth and the twelfth centuries, promulgated a stricter code of sexual conduct for women. Chastity became an utmost virtue for women, and widows were discouraged from remarriage. It was Neo-Confucianism that was introduced to Korea during the Yi Dynasty (1392-1910), and which soon became political ideology to control Korean people and to subdue women. . . . the Confucian ideology in Korea has not gone through such in-depth and wholesale criticism and its grip on the Korean people is still strong. Today, Korean women may feel the impact of Confucianism more than women in socialist China, Westernized Hong Kong and a politically transformed Taiwan.[177]

I agree with these feminist criticisms of Confucianism. Confucianism still advocates unequal gender construction, the religious and cultural validation of patriarchy, and political conservatism in Korean society. This is why young modern Koreans often eschew Confucianism as their religious preference. However, it is equally true that such criticism should be made about all other religious traditions in Korea, such as Buddhism, Daoism, Shamanism, and Christianity. This issue is not related only to Confucianism. All world religions have historically been male-dominated. Hence, they are not free from these feminist criticisms in history. More specifically, most Christian churches, Protestant and Catholic, contributed greatly to the development and preservation of patriarchy in Korea. Therefore, to be sure, if we want to enhance Korean Christians' spirituality from a process cosmological perspective, we need to reevaluate and reconstruct both Confucian and Christian traditions by means of "feminist critical hermeneutics."[178] This means that we need to rediscover insights and traditions of human liberation concealed by a patriarchic ideology and a male oriented perspective in these traditions. In other words, our task is to continuously develop new reformed interpretations of Christianity and Confucianism. Doing this will surely pave a way to develop a socio-political spirituality from a process cosmological perspective. This will keep all living religions vital, so that they may remain valuable cultural, spiritual resources for humanity. As an advocate of Confucianism who insists on a critical reassessment of the Confucian heritage, Julia Ching appropriately states:

> It is to be hoped that, humbled and made powerless politically, Confucianism will survive and become transformed, not as an ideology but as a spiritual influence, both in China and outside . . . . Confucianism may need to die, in order to live again, as a new synthesis, to serve a new age—an age of pluralism with an increasing recognition of Eastern and Western heritages as heritages of all mankind.[179]

Process Spirituality as Socio-Political Spirituality

Most Korean churches have been focusing on a personal pietism rather than socio-political issues. In other words, they have been teaching mainly the practice of interior life and the life of perfection in relationship with God or the Holy Spirit. This type of faith, forming out of such a focus, often gives rise to a one sided, narrow, and limited spirituality. It is true that most Korean Christians have been unaware of socio-political issues; instead they have focused on indulging in their own pietism and spiritual growth. They are not interested in action in the secular world. In this respect, it is an urgent task to develop a spirituality which lays its focus equally on both personal faith and socio-political issues. In other words, it is necessary for Korean Churches to combine spiritual contemplation and action in order to formulate a spirituality that is both traditionally pietistic and socio-politically progressive. According to Karl Rahner, this will be the desirable future of contemplative Christians and theologians who seek to embrace action in their lives. He made the following comments: "The Christian of the future will be a mystic or he or she will not exist at all. . . . Only a theology that is rooted in the spiritual commitment of the theologian and oriented toward praxis will be meaningful in the church of the future."[180]

Donal Door attempts to clarify this by suggesting the so-called "balanced spirituality." In pointing out three dimensions of a balanced spirituality, he refers to the biblical passage: "What does the Lord require of you but to do justice, and to love kindness, and to walk humbly with your God" (Micah 6:8). Spirituality here begins by walking with God, which refers to the personal relationship with God. Spirituality then demands us to love other people, which refers to the interpersonal aspect. Spirituality also should be practiced in a public, social life, which focuses on the issue of social justice.[181]

The spirituality of liberation, a theme developed by Latin American liberation theology, can greatly help us enhance spirituality with special attention to the socio-political liberation of the poor and oppressed in Latin America. The spirituality of liberation is concerned about poor neighbors and their situation. Gutierrez defines it:

> A spirituality of liberation will center on a conversion to the neighbor, the oppressed person, the exploited social class, the despised ethnic group, the dominated country. Our conversion to the Lord implies this conversion to the Lord. . . . To be converted is to commit oneself to the process of liberation of the poor and oppressed, to commit oneself lucidly, realistically and concretely.[182]

How do we use process and Confucianism traditions as meaningful resources for making Christian spirituality more keenly aware of socio-political issues? Julia Ching makes an interesting comment on this issue, affirming Confucius' vision and attitude toward society and politics:

Instead of speculating upon life after death, Confucius kept his eyes fixed firmly on this life and this world, especially the social and political. Active political service was, according to him, an inherent human responsibility, and any departure from this norm could be tolerated only when undertaken itself as a form of social protest—as with the sage-hermits of legendary antiquity. Confucian involvement in society was intended as a mission of self-transcendence, both for the individual so engaged, and for the "salvation" of the social order. But the very political concern of Confucian philosophy led to the risk of its becoming subservient to political authority and its being transformed into political ideology.[183]

Wei-Ming Tu attempts to interpret Confucian classics in a new perspective.[184] According to Tu, Confucianism is basically an inclusive humanism which embraces all human beings, men and women. He is trying to realize a so-called "a third epoch of Confucian humanism." For Tu, what is important is "how a revived Confucian humanism might answer questions that science and democracy have raised."[185] In other words, he considers humanity to be his central concern.

According to Tu, the point of departure is a living human being, "the person living here and now."[186] In particular, he believes that the *Zhongyong* (*Chung-yung*, 中庸, The Doctrine of Mean), an important Confucian text, clearly demonstrates a holist humanist vision of humanity. He says:

> As *Chung-yung* demonstrates, the concrete, living human being is the point of departure for an overall reflection on the human condition. As living persons, we are inevitably embedded in this earth. Furthermore, each one of us is fated to be a particular person in a particular time and place. To reflect on the things at hand, as the Confucians are fond of recommending, is to take our embeddedness as the primary datum for our self-education.[187]

This embeddedness of humanity reminds us that as living humans, we live here and now in the politically socially interwound complex context, which should be also our point of departure for a socio-political spirituality. He clearly presents his humanist vision by stating, "I felt that, without imposing an alien structure upon the text, we could clearly see, in *Chung-yung*, the unfolding of a holistic human vision, a vision that takes the ultimate realization of the human project as the fulfillment of an anthropocosmic promise."[188] Therefore, his purpose is to unfold a humanistic vision by doing persistent self-cultivation through study of Confucian texts, and by exploring the human being with regard to family, society, and Heaven. This provides us with useful insights into developing desirable spirituality in a socio-political context.

For Tu, the humanist vision is concretely accomplished by the project of

"Learning to be Fully Human."[189] He suggests that in order to be fully human, one should start with one's true self as the central subject of creative transformation by which one can reach human fulfillment. In Confucian tradition, then, the family is considered the natural home for nourishing and helping the self to build a dyadic relationship and fruitful communion with other members of the family, which enables the self to understand the surrounding world and transcend the private ego. In the family there are important virtues such as filial piety (孝, Korean *hyo*) and brotherly love (兄弟愛, Korean *hyong-jae-ai*), which are the roots of humanity.[190] As an open system, the true self is not an isolated individual, but a person living in the family with an attitude of filial piety and brotherly love. In the words of Tu, therefore, "When we cultivate the art of embodying the family in our mind-and-heart, we enable ourselves to move beyond egocentrism and transform the enclosed private ego into an open self."[191] This principle is applied to the community, the state, and the world. In this sense, Confucian learning to be a true human being can be characterized as altruistic, for its primary purpose is for the sake of others, family, community, and society.[192] This is very significant insight which can be used to complement Christian spirituality of socio-political implication.

It is well known that Yulgok not only explored his own philosophical thoughts in Neo-Confucian tradition, but vigorously involved himself in politics as a politician. He was extremely concerned with the application of his philosophical thought to the political realm. Yulgok, as a politician, attempted to apply Confucian thought to the reality of his times. He regarded fields such as politics, economics, education, and national defense as *yong* (用; use) on the basis of Zhu Xi Studies as *che* (體; substance). He had much concern for people's situations. The noble unity (妙融) of principle (理) as a theoretical dimension and material force(氣) as a practical dimension is a unique characteristics of his philosophy.[193] In this sense, his thought has much relevance on the enhancement of a socio-political spirituality.

Yulgok expressed his great concern for the people's situation, making critiques on wrong politics in his time. He wrote:

> Oh, there have never been such days; the country is facing miserable disaster and the people are poor and weak. In the time of such hardship, keeping the weak and thin people at work like slaves, oppressing the righteous spirits of scholars, obstructing the way of public opinion, damaging the pulse of the country, and pushing the people into more miserable situations will bring us immeasurable trouble and indescribable disaster. The *Book of Odes* says, "It seems that we don't know where the boat floating in the water is heading. Oh! Worry of the mind. There is no moment to sleep at all." This really expresses well what I worry about.[194]

In 1567, at the age of 32, Yulgok shared his worries and concerns about the country with T'oegye and he lamented:

It has been twenty years since the country became seriously sick. But it is not possible to cure the sickness because the people in both high and low positions are all conventional. Now the power of the people is exhausted and the savings of the country are squandered. If we do not reform, the country will not play the role of the country. Isn't the learned person in a government post at risk, like the swallow whose nest is on the roof? Thinking of this in the middle of tonight, I immediately wake up and remain seated even without recognizing myself.[195]

Yulgok not only pointed out socio-political problems in his critical understanding of the historical reality, but did his best to reform in the real political world. It is certainly here that, like a prophet in the Hebrew Bible, Yulgok expressed his deep love for the people and, at the same time, presented sharp criticism on the politics, and advocated a new reform. Thus, the prophet Micah also declares:

Alas for those who devise wickedness and evil deeds on their beds! When the morning dawns, they perform it, because it is in their power. They covet fields, and seize them; houses, and take them away; they oppress householder and house, people and their inheritance (Micah 2:1-2); "Listen, you heads of Jacob and rulers of the house of Israel! Should you not know justice?-You who hate the good and love the evil, who tear the skin off my people, and the flesh off their bones; who eat the flesh of my people, flay their skin off them, break their bones in pieces, and chop them up like meat in a kettle, like flesh in a caldron (Micah 3:1-3).

In one of his famous petitions to the king entitled *"man-on-bong-sa"* (萬言封事, the sealed ten thousand word petition submitted to the king,). Yulgok maintains:

The reason that the present ruling is not effective is because there is no real effort. There are seven things to worry about. First, there is no real effort to make the king and the subjects trust each other. Second, there is no real effort to get the subjects to take responsibility. Third, there is no real effort to achieve anything at the royal symposium. Fourth, there is no real effort to invite a wise man into certain position. Fifth, there is no real effort to respond to the heaven when facing disaster. Sixth, there is no real effort to save the people in all policies. Seventh, there is no real effort to move toward the good in the people's minds.[196]

Yulgok here shows us his profound concern for the welfare of the people, even for the situation of the lowly and slaves in the society, and the country as a whole with his critical political awareness. Above all, he diagnosed that the ways of heaven, the king, and the sage were not properly practiced in this world. Yulgok basically believed that people are at the root of politics. According to him, "in order to effectively rule and govern over the people, the king should first cultivate virtue in himself"; in other words, the king should be a profoundly moral person.[197] This moral king also should learn from the politics of the former wise kings and reflect on the signs and warnings of heaven. In other words, kings should have an attitude of reverence for the way of the heaven. He applied the master Zhu's comment on reverence (*kyung,* seriousness) by quoting, "To have reverence means to be apprehensive and careful and dare not give free rein to oneself. Only then it can be called seriousness."[198]

Yulgok believed that the country governed by the sage is an idealist concept in Confucian tradition. This ideal is described as a time when the Great Unity is realized and the world belongs to all. In order to put this Confucian ideal into practice, Yulgok submitted special petitions and reports to the king. The "Great Summary of the Sage Learning," which was written for and dedicated to the king Sunjo in 1575 is an example. He expressed his Confucian vision of *daedong-sa-hoe* (大同社會, the Society of the Great Unity) by quoting the passage from the *Book of Rites.*

> When the Great Way was practiced, the world was shared by all alike. The worthy and the able were promoted to office and men practiced good faith and lived in affection. Therefore, they did not regard as parents only their own parents, or as sons only their own sons. The aged found a fitting close to their lives, the robust their proper employment; the young were provided with an upbringing and the widow and widower, the orphaned and the sick, with proper care. Men had their tasks and women their hearths . . . . This was the age of Great Unity.[199]

This means, as described in the *Zhongyong,* an age "when equilibrium and harmony are realized to the highest degree, heaven and earth will attain their proper order and all things will flourish."[200] For Yulgok, this refers to the world in which the human mind is in harmony with the dao mind, principle as the great ultimate pervades in the world as a whole, while material force delimits and hence individual characters are perceived.[201] Yulgok himself tried to put this great vision into practice as a scholar and politician. A similar vision is declared by the Jewish prophets in the Hebrew Bible:

> On this mountain the LORD of hosts will make for all peoples a feast of rich food, a feast of well-aged wines, of rich food filled with marrow, of well-aged wines strained clear. And he will destroy on this mountain the shroud that is cast over all peoples, the sheet that is spread over all nations; he will swallow up death forever (Isaiah 25:6-8).
>
> The wilderness and the dry land shall be glad, the desert shall rejoice and blossom; like the crocus it shall blossom abundantly, and rejoice with joy and sing-

ing. . . . Then the eyes of the blind shall be opened, and the ears of the deaf unstopped; then the lame shall leap like deer, and the tongues of the speechless sing for joy. For waters shall break forth in the wilderness, and the streams in the desert; the burning sand shall become a pool, and the thirsty ground springs of water; the haunt of jackals shall become a swamp, the grass shall become reeds and rushes(Isaiah 35:1-6).

On the other hand, Whitehead's concept of God likewise has a profound socio-political implication. According to Karen Armstrong, "Whitehead had been able to make no sense of God as another Being, self-contained and impassible, but had formulated a twentieth-century version of the prophetic idea of God's pathos."[202] For Whitehead, "God is the great companion—the fellow-sufferer who understands."[203] This is the God who sides with the poor, the weak, and the oppressed. This is the God who is present in the midst of all creatures' suffering including humanity. Compassion and love are ways of fulfilling the Kingdom of God. This is a way of embodying the Galilean origin of Christianity initiated by Jesus. Whitehead states this Christianity:

It dwells upon the tender elements in the world, which slowly and in quietness operate by love; and it finds purpose in the present immediacy of a kingdom not of this world. Love neither rules, nor is it unmoved; also it is a little oblivious as to morals. It does not look to the future; for it finds its own reward in the immediate present.[204]

Therefore, it is true to say that the spirituality derived from Whitehead's thought is a socio-political spirituality, which is inspired by love for other human beings in the society. In another place, Whitehead expressed his vision of a new world, which is in adventure toward truth, beauty, and peace despite human suffering and tragedy:

At the heart of the nature of things, there are always the dream of youth and the harvest of tragedy.

The Adventure of the Universe starts with the dream of Zest with Peace: —that the suffering attains its end in a Harmony of Harmonies. The immediate experience of this Final Fact, with its union of Youth and Tragedy, is the sense of Peace. In this way the World receives its persuasion towards such perfections as are possible for its diverse individual occasions.[205]

Conclusion

In conclusion, it is quite evident that the process cosmologies presented by both Whitehead and Yulgok, along with their processive, organismic, relational characteristics, provide many meaningful implications for reflecting upon Christian spirituality and spiritual practices in the Korean Church. In other words, not only do these cosmologies propose creative suggestions for spiritual formation with regard to other traditional religions, but they also give way to the emergence of a new type of interreligious spirituality as a possible result of the Confucian-Christian dialogue in the global context of religious pluralism. After all, process cosmology can make a significant contribution to Christians making efforts to reform, enhance, and enrich their spiritualities and spiritual practices.

CONCLUSION

Various religions have interacted with one another and deeply penetrated peoples' lives in Korea. Conflicts among religions were not critical until modern times when Christianity was introduced from Western countries. This means that Christianity has been taking a major role in creating conflicts among religions in the modern history of Korea. This was due largely to Christianity's conservative theology and exclusivistic attitude toward other religions. In this respect, it is an unavoidable task for Korean Christianity to become actively engaged in an interreligious dialogue, in order to truly indiginize Christianity in the Korean soil and facilitate its own spirituality and spiritual practices demanded in the context of religious pluralism.

It seems quite certain that, among various religious traditions, Confucianism is an important counterpart in the Christian encounter with traditional religions in Korea. Precisely speaking, however, modern Koreans are estranged from traditional Confucian moral values because they consider Confucianism to be outdated and preventing modernization in Korea. Nevertheless, nobody can deny the reality of Confucianism as a valuable historical heritage in Korea. In particular, the cosmology or worldviews of all modern Koreans, religious and non-religious, are still greatly influenced by Confucianism. Without regard to Confucianism, therefore, it is not possible to consider the various characteristics of Korean spirituality. In this book, I have declared a Confucian-Christian dialogue to be an urgent mission because the two religions have together existed as influential forms of culture and moral values in Korean society for an extended period of time.

With special attention paid to such situations, I have made a theoretical comparative study of process cosmology and a practical integration of these comparative studies in terms of spirituality and spiritual practices in Korea. In regard to a hypothetical Confucian-Christian dialogue as a practical model of comparative religious studies in the Korean context, I have deliberately chosen Whitehead's process philosophy and Yulgok's Neo-Confucian philosophy as two poles. This choice was based on two fundamental convictions: 1) Process theology based on Whitehead's process metaphysics can be a possible alternative to traditional Western Christianity and its processive, organic, and relational characteristics have more affinity with Oriental thought than Western substance thought; 2) Yulgok's Neo-Confucian thought is considered to be a good partner in Confucian-Christian dialogue in the Korean context because as a diligent student of Zhu's Neo-Confucianism, Yulgok also tried to develop a Neo-Confucian cosmology in a distinctive way through his own creative interpretation of the Confucian canons.

Broadly speaking, both Whitehead and Yulgok revealed very similar modes of process cosmology, understanding the universe as changing and becoming, rather than static and separated substances. Although they have different philosophical and cultural backgrounds, the strong resemblance between the two thinkers' versions of cosmology enables us to effectively pursue such dialogue and comparative study in this book.

Specifically, this study has focused on a set of key concepts in the process cosmologies of both two thinkers and, at the same time, their practical applications to the Christians' spiritual praxis in the Korean Church. This study is derived from two primary assumptions: 1) Cosmology can significantly influence the creation of religion and spirituality by presenting a world view on which religion and spirituality is based; 2) Process and Neo-Confucian cosmologies can offer some practical implications for enhancing the Korean Christians' spirituality. For the purpose of this dialogue, this book has theoretically investigated the major cosmological articulations surrounding the related key terms and motifs before conducting a comparative study of them.

First, this book has examined the processive, organismic, relational, and dynamic cosmology of Alfred N. Whitehead, focusing on some key concepts and categories for understanding his metaphysical system. Whitehead understood the universe as the interplay of two fundamental components: actual entities and eternal objects. In other words, an actual entity and an eternal object are concretized in the process of creativity by means of transition and concrescence. An actual entity also becomes subject to experience by a seizing and grasping process called "prehension," in which an initial subjective aim is offered by an eternal object. Whitehead completed his process metaphysics by explicating the concept of God with regard to his role and meaning in process cosmology. His concept of God was developed in terms of his unique panentheism, which equally emphasized both the transcendence and the immanence of God and regarded God as a co-creator along with all other things. This balance was advocated via the dipolarity of God: God of consequent nature as well as of primordial nature.

In the same way, this book has uncovered the general structure of the Neo-Confucian cosmology of Yi Yulgok. Yulgok basically understands that the world consists of *li* (principle) and *qi* (material force) and functions due to the constant interaction of these two components. Principle and material force are interrelated with and interdependent upon each other, although they have different roles. Namely, material force produces all things by operating through them, whereas principle functions as the source of the movement of material force. Yulgok organized his unique position on the philosophical system of principle-material force by presenting his famous rubrics. These were *ki-bal-yi-seung* (material force issues and principle mounts it), *i-il-bun-su* (principle is one but its manifestations are many), *i-tong-ki-kuk* (principle pervades and material force delimits), and *i-ki-ji-myo* (the marvel of principle and material force). He laid equal emphasis both on principle and material force. In addition, Yulgok investigated his cosmology by means of exploring a neo-Confucian *taiji* (the Great Ultimate), another expression of principle, by showing its cosmological significance in the creative mutual rotation of the yin-yang forces. For him, the Great Ultimate was considered to be an ultimate truth, the Way, the origin of all things in the cosmos, but it also caused yin-yang forces to move. Finally, Yulgok applied his cosmological thought to the doctrine of human nature in the famous philosophical debate called *Sa-Dan-Chi-Jong-Non* (the Debate on the Four Beginnings and Seven Feelings). Yulgok was convinced that both the Four Beginnings and the Seven Feelings have one origin and the Seven Feelings included the Four Beginnings. He firmly believed that, as human nature is one, human feeling is one and human feeling is nothing other than the issuance of human nature.

As indicated in chapters one and two, there were many similarities between the two thinkers' cosmological system, providing even more theoretical comparisons. First of all, the dynamic interrelation between principle and material force compares to the eternal objects present in actual entities as the form of the entities. I have examined, in great detail, the interdependent relationship between eternal objects and principle as potentiality and between actual entities and material force as actuality. Finally, I have compared Whitehead's concept of God with Neo-Confucian concept of *taiji* (the Great Ultimate). I have shown that the Great Ultimate has a very similar place to God in terms of process cosmology.

As a result of theoretical comparison in this study, I have suggested certain implications drawn from the process and Confucian cosmologies and their applications to the study of spirituality. More specifically, I have suggested using the process cosmologies of Whitehead and Yulgok to enhance Korean Christians' spirituality and spiritual practices in a creative way. For this purpose, the definition of spirituality was based on a comparative perspective and the range and context of its use in this study was explained. Then, in order to show how this Confucian-Christian dialogue can help Christians form a mature spirituality in harmony with other religions, how process cosmologies can play a great role in the formation of new type of Christian spirituality in a religiously pluralistic culture, and how all of this paves the way for a new possibility of making a 'Confucian Christianity' (a model of indigenized Christianity, in the Korean context), I have applied some useful implications derived from Whitehead's and Yulgok's cosmological thoughts to the issues of the contemporary praxis of Christian spirituality within the pluralistic context of Korea.

Specifically, I have proposed six practical suggestions for reforming Korean Christians' spirituality and enhancing their spiritual practices: (1) process cosmology as the foundation of Christian spirituality; (2) a process-Confucian way of preaching and Bible study; (3) prayer and contemplation in the process-Confucian perspective; (4) process-Confucian way of reforming the Christian liturgy; (5) process spirituality as eco-spirituality; (6) process spirituality as socio-political spirituality. Although they are hypothetical, these may be good components for forming a new Christian spirituality necessary for Korean society as it faces the issue of religious pluralism as well as increasing socio-political and ecological problems.

In regard to the significance of this comparative religious study focused both on theoretical and practical dimensions, I firmly believe that it is of pioneering significance in building bridges between Western Christian tradition and Korean Confucian tradition, process philosophical tradition and Korean Confucian-Christian tradition. In particular, the comparative study and the interreligious dialogue of Confucianism and Christianity, the subject matter explored in this book, makes a contribution in three ways: first, it will create way of peaceful coexistence and mutual learning between religions; second, it will enhance and enrich Christians' spirituality and spiritual practices in the Korean Context; third, it will influence other Christians in similar contexts all over the world as a meaningful reference of indigenized Christianity and Christian spirituality in relationship with neighboring religions. In other words, this Confucian-Christian dialogue within the pluralist context of Korea can function as a good model for prompting interreligious dialogue in other places as well.

Despite the significance and validity of this study, however, there remain some issues that must be further studied. In order to facilitate the continuing Confucian-Christian dialogue and spiritual studies or comparative theology and religion in a more effective and vigorous way, those issues are presented in the following ways.

First, we need to keep in mind a fundamental principle in performing interreligious dialogue and comparative theology: we should not view other religions from our own perspective; rather, we should try to understand a religion on its own terms and from its own perspective. Then a true mutual learning becomes possible. This principle is often disregarded when similarities among religious traditions are too heavily emphasized. Such a phenomenon is easily found in the position of inclusivism. A typical example is the so-called "anonymous Christian" discussed by Karl Rahner (1904-1984), who tries to embrace certain values of non-Christian traditions in the inclusivist model.[1] An inclusivistic position on other religions, however advantageous, can weaken other religions' distinctiveness. For this reason, this study might be criticized for its Christian orientation and perspective. Francis X. Clooney's remark is very pertinent to this point:

> Good comparative study, including good comparative theology, of course depends heavily on the ability of the comparative to articulate a viable understanding of the "other," in which the encountered "other" is not manufactured to fit the comparativist's prejudices and expectations. The comparative theologian must achieve a certain distance from her or his own starting point, in order to be able to learn from another tradition by understanding it on its terms, and in a way that can never be entirely predicated on the expectations of one's home tradition, because it reformulates those expectations regarding the home tradition.[2]

Thus, in the case of Christianity and Confucianism, both can learn from each other through good comparative study guided by this fundamental principle; after good comparative study, mutual transformation can occur. In this book, we have obviously not fully dealt with the case of Confucianism; rather, we have started from a very Christian context and concentrated on the enhancement of Christian spirituality. This is, of course, a weakness of this study. Therefore, for a better and well-balanced comparative work, it is our task to focus equally both on Confucianism and Christianity and carefully consider the terms and motifs in these two traditions.

This issue, on the other hand, requires a thorough examination of our own as well as the other's religious situations. In particular, the religious context which comparative theology explores is important. For instance, it is necessary to concretely and carefully understand the Confucian tradition in general and its present distinctive condition in Korean society, where it is still streaming in the blood of Koreans, not only as a specification of prominent worldviews and moral values, but also as a patriarchal, conservative ideology of society. Hence, for Korean Christians, there is a responsibility to create a Confucian Christianity, which can be a future model of genuinely indigenized Christianity in the Korean context, to continuously facilitate reformed interpretations of both Christianity and Confucianism. In regard to Confucianism, it is also true that a critical reassessment of the Confucian heritage is necessary to make Confucianism alive and valid today. This will be a task of renewing and updating the Confucian tradition through the vigorous dialogue with other religions and contemporary sciences. This task has not been dealt with in this book. As the master Zhu did in his time, it is necessary to once again synthesize Confucian traditions with other critical modern ideas, in order to make it relevant to the modern people. Julia Ching appropriately states:

> It is to be hoped that, humbled and made powerless politically, Confucianism

will survive and become transformed, not as an ideology but as a spiritual influence, both in China and outside.... Confucianism may need to die, in order to live again, as a new synthesis, to serve a new age—an age of pluralism with an increasing recognition of Eastern and Western heritages as heritages of all mankind.[3]

Secondly, we must more carefully articulate the problem of translation in a cross-cultural and religious linguistics for comparative study between Christianity and Confucianism. For instance, there is a great deal of controversy about the many essential terms for constructing Confucian Christianity or Christian Confucianism: *"ti"* (帝, Korean *jae*), *"shang-ti"* (上帝, Korean *sangjae*), *"tien"* (天, Korean *chon*), and *"shen"* (神, Korean *shin*) in Chinese, and *"hanunim"* or *"hananim"* in Korean for the Christian term God; *"tien-t'ang"* (天堂, Korean *chondang*) for the kingdom of God; *"hun"* (魂, Korean *hon*) or *"lunghun"* (靈魂, Korean *yonghon*) for the soul; and *"sheng-shen"* (聖神, Korean *sungrshin*) or *"sheng-lung"* (聖靈, Korean *sungryong*) for the Holy Spirit. The deep and careful study of the technical terms appropriate for both groups is an important task for the Confucian-Christian dialogue and comparative studies. In Sung-BumYun's Confucianized Christianity, for instance, his finding that the term *"sung"* (誠, sincerity) is composed of two Chinese words (言+成) is significant, but his theory can be criticized on the grounds that his interpretation of Confucianism goes beyond the central meaning of Confucianism. This is because there are other key terms in Confucianism, such as *"in"*(humanity; benevolence, 仁), a foundation of other Confucian virtues, and *"hyo"*(filial piety, 孝), a cardinal moral value of Confucianism. In addition, he is often criticized by Korean Confucians not only for disregarding the Confucian traditions as whole and Confucian terms on their own, but also of his Christian-oriented interpretation of Confucianism.[4] Therefore, we need to carefully and thoroughly study specific terms in particular with the deep understanding of each religious tradition when we perform interreligious dialogue and comparative theology.

Third, on the issue of Korean spirituality, it is necessary to deeply and broadly research the various roots and characteristics of spirituality in the history of Korean Christianity. Confucianism is just one religion which influenced the forming of Christian spirituality. Other religions, such as Buddhism, Shamanism, Daoism, and other religious faiths in Korean history have also been mutually influenced. Tong-Shick Ryu, a Korean theologian, appropriately points out that Korea is characterized by various religions during different times.[5] These religions contributed remarkably to the development of Korean spirituality and determined the heart-mind nature (心性, Korean *shimsung*) and religious ground of Korean people before they received Christianity. We need to pay much attention to all of these other religions and their influences on Christian spirituality.

Pentecostalism, which was uniquely formulated through influence and interaction with other traditional religions, must be taken into deep consideration. Pentecostalism greatly contributed to a remarkable growth of Christianity and the emergence of a unique Christian spirituality in Korea. According to Walter Hollenweger, "Korean Pentecostalism is not presented as a product of Western Pentecostal missionaries. . . . All other founding pioneers are Koreans, who are deeply rooted in Korean popular culture and integrate this culture selectively into their spirituality."[6] Evidently, Korean Christians are still living under its powerful influence, especially in the matter of their spirituality. In this regard, it is important to study comparatively Pentecostalism and process Confucian cosmology in order to create a type of spirituality fully indigenized for Korean Christians. Basically, Korean Christians focus on the dimension of experience, which can be an important factor of both process cosmology and Christian spirituality. Furthermore, it will be very significant to present a new understanding of the Holy Spirit as the basis for spiritual formation in the Korean context, because for Korean Christians, spirituality usually refers to the dominion of the Holy Spirit. This will make it possible to understand the Holy Spirit as the source of life in comparison with the Neo-Confucian concept "*qi*"(*ki*, material force). That is, the Hebrew word "*ruah*" and Greek word "*pneuma*" indicate the source of life that makes human beings and the world alive. It is interesting that this understanding of the Holy Spirit is similar to the Neo-Confucian concept *qi* that also refers to the fundamental energy flowing in human beings and the universe. This might be an important topic for formulating Confucian pneumatology in a religiously plural context in Korea. This is another future task which should be undertaken in order to facilitate the continuing dialogue between Confucianism and Christianity.

Notes

Introduction

1. Diana L. Eck, *Encountering God* (Boston: Beacon Press, 1993), ix.
2. The ruling and guiding principle of the Choson Dynasty was Confucian ideals. More precisely speaking, "the nature of the Yi (Choson) society is the extent of ramification into every aspect of the dynastic life of the Confucian political ideal and moral doctrines." Wanne J. Joe, *Traditional Korea: A Cultural History* (Seoul: Chung'ang University Press, 1981), 298. For the great details, see Ki-baek Lee's *A New History of Korea*, trans. Edward W. Wagner and Edward J. Shultz (Seoul: Ilchokak Publishers, 1986), chapter 9 (173-200).
3. Kyoung Jae Kim, *Christianity and the Encounter of Asian Religions* (Zoetermeer: Uitgeverij Boekencentrum, 1994), 181.
4. Ibid., 87-95.
5. Robert C. Neville, ed., *Ultimate Realities* (Albany: State University of New York Press, 2002), 238.
6. Robert C. Neville, ed., *Human Condition* (Albany: State University of New York Press, 2002), 10.
7. Ewert Cousins, "Preface to the Series," in *Christian Spirituality I: Origins to the Twelfth Century*, eds. Bernard McGinn and John Meyendorff, vol. 16 of *World Spirituality: An Encyclopedic History of the Religious Quest* (New York: Crossroad, 1985), xiii.
8. Walter Principe, "Toward defining Spirituality," *Studies in Religion / Sciences Religieuses* 12, no. 2 (Spring 1983): 139

Chapter 1: The Process Cosmology of Alfred North Whitehead

1. John Cobb and David Griffin, *Process Theology: An Introductory Exposition* (Philadelphia: The Westminster Press, 1987), 7.
2. Marjori H. Suchocki, *God Christ Church A Practical Guide to Process Theology* (New York: The Crossroad Publishing Company, 1989), 108.
3. Cf. Paul Edward, ed., *The Encyclopedia of Philosophy* (New York: The Macmillan Company & The Free Press, 1967), vol.2 498-505, vol.5 52-56; Robert Audi, ed., *The Cambridge Dictionary of Philosophy* (Cambridge: Cambridge University Press, 1995), 224-225, 437-440, 445-446.
4. Alfred North Whitehead, *Process and Reality: An Essay in Cosmology*, eds. David Ray Griffin and Donald W. Sherburne, Corrected edition, (New York: The Free Press, 1978), xiv. (Hereafter *Process and Reality*).
5. Ibid., 3.

Notes

6. Ibid., 5.

7. Thomas E. Hosinski, *Stubborn Fact and Creative Advance: An Introduction to the Metaphysics of Alfred North Whitehead* (Lanham, MD: Rowman & Littlefield Publishers, Inc., 1993), 12.

8. *Process and Reality*, 157.

9. Ibid.

10. Ibid., 6.

11. Ibid., 157.

12. Ibid., 13.

13. Alfred North Whitehead, *Science and the Modern World* (New York: The Free Press, 1925), 72.

14. Ibid., 58.

15. Ibid., 36.

16. Ibid., 70.

17. *Process and Reality*, 153.

18. Thomas E. Hosinski, *Stubborn Fact and Creative Advance*, 1.

19. Lucien Price, *Dialogues of Alfred Whitehead* (New York: New American Library, 1964), 9; "Alfred North Whitehead," in *The Encyclopedia of Philosophy*, ed. Paul Edwards (London: Macmillan, 1972), vol. 8, 291.

20. Norman Pittenger, *Alfred North Whitehead* (Richmond: John Knox Press 1969), 3.

21. Victor Lowe, *Alfred North Whitehead: The Man and His Work vol.1* (Baltimore, MD: The Johns Hopkins Press, 1985), 176.

22. Bertrand Russell, *Portrait from Memory* (New York: Simon and Schuster, 1956), 93.

23. Lucien Price, *Dialogues of Alfred Whitehead*, 14.

24. According to Bertrand Russell, Whitehead moved forward from the period of philosophy of science in England to the period of new metaphysics in the United States. Bertrand Russell, *My Philosophical Development* (London: Unwin Books, 1975), 57-58.

25. *Process and Reality*, 167.

26. Ibid., xiv.

27. Ibid., 349.

28. Ibid., 25.

29. Thomas E. Hosinski, *Stubborn Fact and Creative Advance*, 22.

30. Ibid.

31. Ibid., 26.

32. Ivor Leclerc, *Whitehead's Metaphysics* (Bloomington: Indiana University Press, 1975), 88.

33. Donald W. Musser and Joseph L. Price, eds., *A New Handbook of Christian Theologians* (Nashville: Abingdon Press, 1996), 108-109.

34. Ivor Leclerc, *Whitehead's Metaphysics* (New York: Indiana University Press, 1975), 53.

35. Whitehead, *Process and Reality*, 18.

36. Ibid., 73.

37. Ibid., 19.

38. Ivor Leclerc, *Whitehead's Metaphysics*, 55.

39. *Process and Reality*, 6.

40. Ivor Leclerc, *Whitehead's Metaphysics*, 54-55.

42. Ibid., 58.

42. *Process and Reality*, 18.

43. Ibid., 75.
44. Ibid., 48.
45. Ibid., 73.
46. Ivor Leclerc, *Whitehead's Metaphysics*, 60-61.
47. *Process and Reality*, 18.
48. William A. Christian, *An Interpretation of Whitehead's Metaphysics* (New Haven: Yale University Press, 1967), 12.
49. *Process and Reality*, 29.
50. Ibid., 20.
51. Ibid., 154.
52. Ibid., 214.
53. Ibid., 215.
54. Ibid., 50.
55. Alfred North Whitehead, *Adventures of Ideas* (New York: The Free Press, 1967), 219.
56. *Process and Reality*, 211.
57. Ibid., 44.
58. William A. Christian, *An Interpretation of Whitehead's Metaphysics* (New Haven: Yale University Press, 1967), 13.
59. Donald W. Sherburne, *A Key to Whitehead's Process and Reality* (Bloomington: Indiana University Press, 1966), 220.
60. *Process and Reality*, 23.
61. Ibid., 43-44.
62. Ibid., 39-40.
63. William A. Christian, *An Interpretation of Whitehead's Metaphysics*, 202.
64. Alfred North Whitehead, *Modes of Thought* (New York: The Free Press, 1968), 93.
65. *Process and Reality*, 17.
66. Ivor Leclerc, *Whitehead's Metaphysics*, 93-94.
67. Ibid., 94.
68. Ibid., 94-95; Sang-Il Kim, *Whitehead wa Dongyangchollhak* [Whitehead and the Oriental Philosophy] (Seoul: Sokwangsa, 1993), 134-135.
69. Alfred N. Whitehead, *The Concept of Nature* (Cambridge: The Cambridge University Press, 1964), 169.
70. *Process and Reality*, 56-57.
71. *Adventures of Ideas*, 233-234.
72. *Process and Reality*, 56.
73. Ibid., 52.
74. Ivor Leclerc, *Whitehead's Metaphysics*, 145.
75. *Process and Reality*, 22.
76. Ibid., 23.
77. Robert B. Mellert, *What Is Process Theology?* (New York: Paulist Press, 1975), 24.
78. William Christian, *An Interpretation of Whitehead's Metaphysics*, 235.
79. *Process and Reality*, 41.
80. Charles Hartshorne, "The Formally Possible Doctrine of God," in *Process Philosophy and Christian Thought*, eds. D. Brown, R. James, and G. Reeves (New York: The Bobbs-Merill Co, 1971), 213-214.
81. *Process and Reality*, 164.
81. Ibid., 40-41.

83. Ibid., 221.
84. Ibid., 222.
85. Ibid., 45.
86. Ibid., 231.
87. Ibid., 232.
88. Ibid., 233.
89. Ibid.
90. Ibid., 41-42.
91. Ibid., 23-24.
92. Ibid., 41.
93. Ibid., 41.
94. Ivor Leclerc, *Whitehead's Metaphysics*, 88.
95. Whitehead, *Adventures of Ideas*, 236.
96. *Process and Reality*, 19.
97. Ibid., 211.
98. This is Ivor Leclerc's position. See Ivor Leclerc, *Whitehead's Metaphysics*, 89.
99. *Process and Reality*, 21.
100. Ibid., 210.
101. Whitehead, *Modes of Thought*, 120.
102. *Process and Reality*, 149-150.
103. Ibid., 21.
104. Ibid., 26.
105. Ibid., 29.
106. Although some scholars such as Donald Sherburne attempt to explore Whitehead philosophy without God, I believe Whitehead's philosophy cannot be understood without his concepts of God and religion. As John Berthrong rightly comments: "It still remains the case that most Whiteheadians continue to be fascinated by the religious dimensions of his work." John Berthrong, *Concerning Creativity: A Comparison of Chu Hsi, Whitehead, and Neville* (Albany: State University of New York Press, 1998), 56 (chapter two endnote 1).
107. Thomas Hosinski, *Stubborn Fact and Creative Advance*, 25.
108. Alfred North Whitehead, *Religion in the Making* (New York: Macmillan Company, 1926); Reprint, (New York: Fordham University Press, 1996), 68-69 (page citations are to the reprint edition).
109. John Berthrong, *Concerning Creativity: A Comparison of Chu Hsi, Whitehead, and Neville*, 35.
110. John W. Lansing, "The Nature of Whitehead's God," *Process Studies* 3 (Fall 1973): 143.
111. It is true that there have been many controversies regarding the necessity of Whitehead's concept of God in his metaphysical system. Was he a theist or did he remain agnostic? I am firmly convinced that he made a significant change in his philosophical religious views after experiencing the loss of his youngest son. He then gradually developed his idea of God in terms of a panentheism as an essential component of his process metaphysics, emerging from his earlier agnosticism. Whitehead gradually developed the concept of God, which was glimpsed in his early writings, as his metaphysics was formulated. See Lewis S. Ford, *The Lure of God: A Biblical Background for Process Theism* (Philadelphia: Fortress Press, 1978), 8-10; Bertrand Russell, *Portraits from Memory* (New York: Simon and Schuster, 1956), 93.
112. *Religion in the Making*, 74.

113. *Process and Reality*, 342-343.
114. Ibid., 343.
115. *Religion in the Making*, 68-69.
116. Many process scholars agree that Whitehead developed his ideas of God in several phases. According to Lewis Ford, there are four phases of development of Whitehead's concept of God: first in chapter XI of *Science and the Modern Word*; second in *Religion in the Making*; third in *Process and Reality*; fourth in *Adventures of Ideas* and *Modes of Thoughts*. See Lewis Ford, *The Emergence of Whitehead's Metaphysics: 1925-1929* (Albany: State University of New York Press, 1984).
117. Alan Richardson and John Bowden, eds., *The Westminster Dictionary of Christian Theology* (Philadelphia: The Westminster Press, 1983), 423.
118. *Process and Reality*, 108.
119. Chares Hartshorne revises Whitehead's idea of God as an actual entity to "a personally ordered society of accessions" because he thinks Whitehead's concept of God is inconsistent and incoherent in the whole scheme of his metaphysics. But Thomas Hosinski simply considers this revision to be the "Hartshornian wing of process philosophy," which is far from Whitehead's philosophy. Hosinski says, "For Whithead the world is temporal and God is nontemporal. This is one of the ways in which Whitehead captures God's transcendence." But Hartshorne does not fully understand or explain God's transcendence. Here, I agree with Hosinski's position. Thomas Hosinski, *Stubborn Fact and Creative Advance*, 220-221.
120. *Process and Reality*, 348.
121. *Religion in the Making*, 92-93.
122. Kenneth F. Thomson, Jr., *Whitehead's Philosophy of Religion* (The Hague: Mouton Publishers, 1971), 57.
123. *Process and Reality*, 244.
124. Ibid., 345.
125. Ibid., 93-94.
126. Ibid., 343.
127. Ibid., 244.
128. Ibid., 224.
129. Ibid., 225.
130. John W. Lansing, "The Nature of Whitehead's God," *Process Studies* 3 (Fall 1973): 144.
131. Daniel Day Williams, "How Does God Act?", in *Process and Divinity*, eds. W. Reese and E. Freeman (Lasalle: Open Court, 1964), 175.
132. Robert B. Mellert, *What is Process Theology?* (New York: Paulist Press, 1975), 46.
133. *Process and Reality*, 349.
134. Ibid., 348-349.
135. Ibid., 351.
136. Ibid., 349.
137. *Religion in the Making*, 156.
138. *Process and Reality*, 31.
139. See Ibid., 31-32.
140. Ibid., 31.
141. *Process and Reality*, 21.
142. *Religion in the Making*, 154.
143. *Process and Reality*, 225.
144. Ibid., 348.

145. Ibid., 346.
146. Ibid., 349.
147. Ibid., 348.
148. Lewis S. Ford, *The Lure of God* (Philadelphia: Fortress Press, 1978), 11.

Chapter 2: The Neo-Confucian Cosmology of Yi Yulgok

1. Spencer J. Palmer, *Confucian Rituals in Korea* (Berkeley, Cal.: Asian Humanities Press, 1984), 14.
2. Jang-Tae Keum, *Hanguk yukyo ui ihae* [Understanding of Korean Confucianism](Seoul: Minjokmunwhasa, 1989), 103-104.
3. Ki-baik Lee, *A New History of Korea*, trans. Edward W. Wagner with Edward J. Shultz (Seoul: Ilchokak Publishers, 1984), 58.
4. Ibid.
5. Ibid., 129.
6. Quoted in Spencer J. Palmer, *Confucian Rituals in Korea* (Berkeley, Cal.: Asian Humanities Press, 1984), 18.
7. Sang-Yun Hyun, *Choson Yuhak Sa* [A History of Choson Confucianism] (Seoul: Minjung Sokwan, 1974), 25.
8. Wanne J. Joe, *Traditional Korea: A Cultural History* (Seoul: Chung'ang University Press, 1981), 299; Ki-bak Lee, *A New History of Korea*, 172.
9. Two schools were located in two different provinces. While "Yongnam" means "Kyongsang" province, "Kiho" means Chola province in the Southern part of Korea. Schools are often named according to their provinces.
10. Edward Y. J. Chung, *The Korean Neo-Confucianism of Yi T'oegye and Yi Yulgok* (Albany: State University of New York Press, 1995), 26-27
11. Yulgok's biography will be described on the basis of the appendixes attached on the vols. 33 and 34 of *Yulgok Chonso* and Yulgok's life in *Park Sai-Chai Munjip* (Writings of Park Sai-Chai). For his life in more details, see Byong-Do Lee's *Yulgok ui saengae wa sasang* [Yulgo's Thoughts and Life] (Seoul: Suhmundang, 1984); Jong-Ho Lee's *Yulgok: Inkan gwa sasang* [Yulgok: Man and Thoughts] (Seoul: Hyunamsa, 1984); Joon-Yon Hwang's *Yi Yulgok: Geu Salm Eui Moseup* [Yi Yulgok: The Image of His Life] (Seoul: Seoul National University Press, 2000).
12. Yi, Yulgok. *Yulgok Chonso* [Complete Works of Yulgok] (Seoul: Sungkyunkwan University Press, 1971), 20:2. (hereafter *Yulgok Chonso*).
13. Ibid., 10:12 b.(All quotations in *Yulgok Chonso*, unless otherwise noted, are taken from the author's translation.)
14. Yu-lan Fung, *A History of Chinese Philosophy*, trans. Derk Bodde (Princeton: Princeton University Press, 1953), vol. II, 533 (parenthesis is mine).
15. Wei-ming Tu, "Confucianism", in *Our Religions*, ed. Arvindo Sharma (New York: Harper Collins Publisher, 1993), 174.
16. Wing –Tsit Chan, *A Source Book in Chinese Philosophy* (Princeton, NJ: Princeton University Press, 1953), 589-590.
17. John H. Berthrong, *Transformations of the Confucian Way* (Boulder, CO: West-

Notes

view Press, 1998), 109.

18. According to Fung, Neo-Confucianism has three main sources: the classical Confucian tradition; the Zen of Buddhism, (for Neo-Confucianism, Buddhism, and Zen have the same meaning); and the yin-yang of Daoism. See Yu-lan Fung, *A Short History of Chinese Philosophy*, trans. Derk Bodde (New York: Macmillian Company, 1948), 232-235.

19. Chung-Ryul Kim, *Koryo Yuhaksa* [A History of Koryo Dynasty Confucianism] (Seoul: Korea University Press, 1987), 158-160.

20. Min-Hong Choi, *A Modern History of Korean Philosophy* (Seoul: Seong Moon Sa, 1980), 17.

21. Wing Tsit-chan, *A Source Book in Chinese Philosophy*, 588.

22. Julia Ching, *The Religious Thought of Chu Hsi* (Oxford: Oxford University Press, 2000), 36-38.

23. Yung Sik Kim, *The Natural Philosophy of Chu Hsi (1130-1200)* (Philadelphia: American Philosophical Society, 2000), 19 (parenthesis is mine).

24. Quoted in Yung Sik Kim, *The Natural Philosophy of Chu Hsi (1130-1200)*, 38.

25. Ha-Tai Kim, *Tongso Cholhak Ui Mannam* [An Encounter of Philosophy East and West] (Seoul: Chongno Book Publisher, 1988), 179.

26. Wing-tsit Chan, *A Source Book in Chinese Philosophy*, 636 (parenthesis is mine).

27. Ibid., 590.

28. Quoted in Yung-Sik Kim, *The Natural Philosophy of Chu Hsi (1130-1200)*, 20.

29. This is Fung's opinion. *A History of Chinese Philosophy*, vol. II, 533.

30. Quoted in Yu-lan Fung's *A History of Chinese Philosophy* (Princeton, NJ: Princeton University, 1953), vol. II, 535.

31. Wm. Theodore de Bary, ed., *Sources of Chinese Tradition* (New York: Columbia University Press, 1960), vol. 1, 483.

32. Ha-Tae Kim, *Tongso Cholhak Ui Mannam* [An Encounter of Philosophy East and West], 171.

33. Yu-lan Fung, *A History of Chinese Philosophy*, vol. II, 537.

34. Ibid.

35. Ha-Tai Kim, *Tongso Cholhak Ui Mannam* [An Encounter of Philosophy East and West], 179.

36. Robert C. Neville, *Behind The Masks of God* (Albany: State University of New York Press, 1991), 80.

37. Wm. Theodore de Bary, ed., *Sources of Chinese Tradition* (New York: Columbia University Press, 1960), vol. 1, 481 (with slight modification).

38. Ha-Tae Kim, *Tongso Cholhak Ui Mannam* [An Encounter of Philosophy East and West], 173.

39. Ibid., 180.

40. Quoted in Yu-lan Fung, *A History of Chinese Philosophy*, vol. II, 542 (parenthesis is mine).

41. John H. Berthrong, *Transformations of the Confucian Way*, 110-111.

42. Quoted in Yu-lan Fung, *A History of Chinese Philosophy*, vol. II, 546-548.

43. John. H. Berthrong, *Transformations of the Confucian Way*, 111.
44. Young-Jo Han, *Zhu Xi aeso Chung Yak-Yong uro* [From Zhu Xi To Chung Yak-Yong] (Seoul: Segyesa, 2000), 41-42.
45. Zhu Xi, *Zhuzi yulei* [朱子語類, Conversations of Master Zhu, Arranged Topically] (Beijing: Zhonghua, 1986), 65:1(translation is mine).
46. Young Chan Ro, *The Korean Neo-Confucianism of Yi Yulgok* (Albany, NY: State University of New York Press, 1989), 6.
47. *T'oegye Chonso* [The Complet Works of Yi T'oegye], vol. 35 (Seoul: Songgyungwan University Press, 1958).
48. Ibid., vol. 8.
49. Ibid., vol.13.
50. The original statement is '太極動而生陽'.
51. Quoted in Ha-Tai Kim, "The Difference Between T'oegye And Yulgok on the Doctrine of *Li* and *Qi*" in *Traditional Thoughts and Practices in Korea*, ed. Eui-Young Yu and Earl Philips (Los Angeles, CA : California State University, 1983), 14. *T'oegye Chonso*, vol 39, 161,
52. Ibid., vol 18.
53. Quoted in Ha-Tai Kim, "The Difference Between T'oegye And Yulgok on the Doctrine of *Li* and *Qi*" in *Traditional Thoughts and Practices in Korea*, ed. Eui-Young Yu and Earl Philips (Los Angeles, CA : California State University, 1983), 14.
54. Michael C. Kalton, Ibid., 167
55. Ibid., 182.
56. Suh Hwadam, *Hwadamjip* [Complete Works of Hwadam] , vol.2, "Original Principle and material Force" (Seoul: Saegye-sa, 1992).
57. Ibid.
58. Byong-Do Lee, *Hanguk yuhaksa* [A History of Korean Confucianism] (Seoul: Asia Munhwasa, 1987), 181.
59. *Hwadamjip*, Ibid.
60. Ibid.
61. Ki-Rak Ha, "Jurironui jonmang"[Perspective of Li-Monism], *Cholhakyonku* [Philosophical Studies],vol.32, 10.
62. *Yulgok Chonso*, 10:37b.
63. Tsai-chun Chung, *The Development of the Concepts of Heaven and of Man in the Philosophy of Chu Hsi* (Taiwan: Institute of Chinese Literature and Philosophy, 1993), 39.
64. Kyoung-Jae Kim, *Christianity and the Encounter of Asian Religions*, 87.
65. Young-Bae Song and others, eds., *Hanguk yuhak qwa iki cholhak* [Korean Confucianism and the Philosophy of Principle and Material Force] (Seoul, Korea: Yaemoonsowon, 2000), 7.
66. *Li* (Korean *i*) can be translated as principle, form, reason, law, and so on. In the same way, *Qi* (*ch'i*; Korean *ki*) can be translated as material force, vital energy, vital force, breath, ether, strong and moving power, and so on. There is no single word in English that best translates these terms. Here I will choose 'principle' for *Li* and 'material force' for *Qi*. On the possible translations for the terms, see Chu Hsi and Lu Tsu-chi'en, *Reflections on Things at hand: The Neo-Confucian Anthology*, trans. Wing-tsit Chan (New York: Columbia University Press, 1967), 360; 367.
67. Young-Kyung Lee, *Yulgok Yulrisasang ui Insongnonjok Tamsaik* [A Study of

Yulgok's Ethical Thoughts from a Perspective of Human Nature] (Pusan, Korea: Saejong Publishing Company, 2001), 214.

68. A. C. Graham, *Disputers of the Tao: Philosophical Argument in Ancient China* (La Salle, Ill: Open Court Publishing Company, 1989), 335-340.

69. Ha-Tae Kim, *Tongso Cholhak Ui Mannam* [Encounter of Philosophy East and West], 188.

70. Quoted in Young-Chan Ro, *The Korean Neo-Confucianism of Yi Yulgok* (Albany: State of New York University Press, 1989), 66 (with slight modification).

71. Some scholar insists that while T'oegye's School tends to focus on the unmixibility of principle and material force, Yulgok's School focuses on the inseparability of two. But I think Yulgok lays focus on both. This will be discussed later. He further develops two points in his unique way. See Young-Bae Song and others, eds., *Hanguk yuhak qwa iki cholhak* [Korean Confucianism and the Philosophy of Principle and Material Force], 125.

72. Michael C. Kalton et al., *The Four-Seven Debate*, 152.

73. Sa-Soon Yun, *Critical Issues In Neo-Confucian Thought: The Philosophy of Yi T'oegye* (Seoul: Korea University Press, 1990), 51, 60.

74. Quoted in Ha-Tai Kim, "The Difference Between T'oegye And Yulgok on the Doctrine of *Li* and *Qi*" in *Traditional Thoughts and Practices in Korea*, ed. Eui-Young Yu and Earl Philips (Los Angeles: California State University, 1983), 20.

75. *Yulgok Chonso,* 14:48b-49a.

76. Ibid., 10:5a.

77. Michael C. Kalton et al., *The Four-Seven Debate*, 115.

78. *Yulgok Chonso,* 10:2a.

79. Ibid., 10:25b-10:26a.

80. For this reason, Yulgok is often called an advocate for material force. But, in my opinion, it is more accurate to define him as an advocate of both principle and material force in a harmonious relationship.

81. Ha-Tai Kim, "The Difference Between T'oegye and Yulgok on the Doctrine of *Li* and *Qi*," 21.

82. Wing-tsit Chan, *A Source Book in Chinese Philosophy*, 639.

83. Ibid., 638.

84. *Yulgok Chonso*, 9:39a.

85. Ibid.,, 12:19b-20a.

86. The original statement is "萬物統體一太極." *Explanation of the Diagram of the Great Ultimate, Hsing-li ta-ch'üan,* 1.31a-b.

87. *Yulgok Chonso*, 10:2-3.

88. Michael Kalton et al., *The Four-Seven Debate*, 120.

89. Ibid., 126.

90. Suk-Gu Song, *Yulgok ui cholhak sasang yonku* [Study of Yulgok's Philosophical Thought] (Seoul: Hyungsol Publishing Company,1994), 56.

91. Michael Kalton et al, *The Four Seven-Debate*, 119.

92. *Yulgok Chonso,* 10:38a.

93. Jong-Ho Bae, *Hankuk Yuhak Ui Cholhakjok Chonkai* [Philosophical Survey of Korean Confucianism] (Seoul: Yonsei University Press, 1985), Vol. II, 151.

94. *Yulgok Chonso,* 10:25a.

95. Michael Kalton et al, *The Four Seven-Debate*, 173.

96. *Yulgok Chonso*, 10:26a.
97. Ibid., 10:26a-b.
98. Mu-Song Chai, *Toe Yul Songrihak Bigyo Yonku* [A Comparative Study of T'oegye and Yulgok's Confucian Stidies] (Seoul: Sungkyunkwan University, 1972), 111.
99. *Yulgok Chonso*, 10:40a.
100. Ibid., vol. 14:4a-b.
101. Ibid., 10:17b-18a.
102. Ibid., 20:59b.
103. Ibid., 10:17b-10:18b.
104. Ibid., 10:22a.
105. Jun-Yon Hwhang, *Yulgok Cholhak Ui Ihae* [Understading of Yulgok's Philosophy] (Seoul: Sokwangsa, 1995), 95.
106. *Yulgok Chonso*, 14:4a.
107. Ibid., 12:20a.
108. Ibid., 31:2a.
109. Ibid., 10:2a.
110. Ibid., 10:2a-10:2b (emphasis is mine).
111. Ibid., 20:59b.
112. *Tai-ji* (太極) can be translated both as the "Great Ultimate" and the "Supreme Ultimate."
113. Wing-tsit Chan, *A Source Book in Chinese Philosophy*, 267.
114. Ibid., 501.
115. Wm. Theodore de Bary, ed., *Sources of Chinese Tradition* (New York: Columbia University Press, 1960), vol. 1, 484.
116. *Yulgok Chonso*, 20:43b.
117. *Yulgok Chonso*, 10:5b.
118. The full quotation is as follows: "The beginning and ending of all things are nothing but integration and disintegration. Positive and negative spiritual forces are the function of creation. If viewed from the causes of what is hidden and what is manifest, from the principle of life and death, and from the features of positive and negative spiritual forces, the Way of Heaven and Earth can be understood . . . Activity and tranquility have no beginning and yin and yang have no starting point. Unless one knows the Way, how can he understood this?" Wing-tsit Chan, *A Source Book in Chinese Philosophy*, 571.
119. *Yulgok Chonso*, 9:17a.
120. Ibid., 9:18b-19a.
121. Ibid., 10:21b.
122. Michael Kalton, *The Four-Seven Debate*, xv.
123. *Mencius*, 2A:6; Wm. Theodore de Bary, ed., *Sources of Chinese Tradition* (New York: Columbia University Press, 1960), vol. 1, 91.
124. *Book of Rites*, Chapter 9.
125. *The Doctrine of Mean*, 1; Patrick Edwin Moran, *Three Smaller Wisdom Books* (Lanham: University Press of America, 1993), 202.
126. Wing-Tsit Chan, *A Sourcebook in Chinese Philosophy*, 131.
127. *Yulgok Chonso*, 14:32b.
128. Ibid., 10:7b-10:8a.
129. Ibid., 10:15a.
130. Ibid., 10:5a.
131. Ibid., 10:6b-10:7a.
132. Kyoung-Jae Kim, *Christianity and the Encounter of Asian Religions*, 90 (Li

Whang is the real name of T'oegye and Li Yi is of Yulgok and parenthesis is mine).

Chapter 3: A Comparison of Whitehead And Yulgok on Cosmology

1. According to Hyong-Jo Han, a Korean Philosophy, "the *li-ch'i* (*qi*) scheme is a unique theory which interprets the substance and function of human energy in the framework of cosmic patterns. This is especially the case for Yulgok." Hyon-Jo Han, "Yulgok's Plan of Self-Cultivation," in *Confucian Philosophy in Korea,* eds. Haechang Choung and Han Hyong-Jo (Seongnam: The Academy of Korean Studies, 1996), 97.

2. Joseph Needham, *Science and Civilization in China,* Corrected Reprinted ed., (Cambridge: Cambridge University Press, 1954), vol.2, 458.

3. Chung-ying Cheng, *New Dimension of Confucian and Neo-Confucian Philosophy* (Albany: State University of New York, 1991), 537.

4. Quoted in Joseph Needham, *Science and Civilization in China,* Corrected Reprinted ed., (Cambridge: Cambridge University Press, 1954), vol.2, 489.

5. Alfred North Whitehead, *Process and Reality,* 7.

6. Julia Ching, *The Religious Thought of Chu Hsi* (Oxford: Oxford University Press, 2000), 53. Furthermore, Ching more explicitly expresses her belief of a comparative study between Zhu Xi (Chu Hsi) and Whitehead: "A comparative study of Chu Hsi and Whitehead is especially appropriate and useful for several reasons. Whitehead was personally conscious of possible resemblances between his philosophy and that of China or East Asia—of which Chu remains an important representative. Chu Hsi and Whitehead shared a common interest in the world of nature—the starting point in their respective philosophies." Ibid., 244.

7. Alfred North Whitehead, *Adventures of Ideas* (New York: The Free Press, 1967), 172.

8. John B. Cobb Jr., *Transforming Christianity and the World* (New York: Orbis Books, 1999), 180.

9. Julia Ching, *The Religious Thought of Chu Hsi,* 243.

10. *Process and Reality,* 18.

11. Ibid., 19.

12. Quoted in Yung-Sik Kim, *The Natural Philosophy of Chu Hsi (1130-1200),*36.

13. Quoted in Ha-Tai Kim, "The Difference Between T'oegye And Yulgok on the Doctrine of *Li* and *Qi*" in *Traditional Thoughts and Practices in Korea,* eds. Eui-Young Yu and Earl Philips (Los Angeles: California State University, 1983), 20.

14. *Yulgok Chonso,* vol.14, 48-49.

15. Zhu Xi, *Zhuzi yulei* [朱子語類, Conversations of Master Zhu, Arranged Topically], (Beijing: Zhonghua, 1986), 65:1.(Translation is mine).

16. Julia Ching calls *li* the formal principle and *qi* the material principle respectively. Cf, Julia Ching, *The Religious Thought of Chu Hsi* (Oxford: Oxford University Press, 2000), 248.

17. Quoted in Ha-Tai Kim, "The Difference Between T'oegye And Yulgok on the Doctrine of *Li* and *Qi*" in *Traditional Thoughts and Practices in Korea,* Eui-Young Yu and Earl Philips, eds., (Los Angeles: California State University, 1983), 20.

18. A. C. Graham, *Disputers of the Dao: Philosophical Argument in Ancient China* (Chicago, Il: Open Court, 1997), 335-340.

19. Ha-Tae Kim, "The Difference Between T'oegye and Yulgok on the Doctrine of *Li* and *Qi,*" 188.

20. Wanne J. Joe, *Traditional Korea: A Cultural History* (Seoul: Chung'ang University Press, 1972), 337 (parenthesis is mine).

21. *Process and Reality*, 211.

22. Ibid., 21.

23. Michael Kalton et al., *The Four-Seven Debate,* 175-177.

24. Ibid., 126.

25. *Process and Reality*, 25.

26. Ibid., 351.

27. Lewis S. Ford, *The Lure of God A Biblical Background for Process Theism* (Philadelphia: Fortress Press, 1978), 12.

28. Whitehead, *Process and Reality*, 348-349.

29. Julia Ching, *The Religious Thought of Chu Hsi*, 45.

30. The original statement is "無極而太極."

31. Whitehead, *Process and Reality,* 348.

32. Wing-Tsit Chan, *A Source Book In Chinese Philosophy* (Princeton: Princeton University Press, 1963), 638.

33. With regard to the creativity between "the one" and "the many", it is necessary to note some major differences. That is, Whitehead's concept of God and the world make a creative advance into novelty, while the Great Ultimate and the yin-yang forces are in the cyclical movement.

34. Julia Ching, *The Religious Thought of Chu Hsi*, 53.

35. Whitehead, *Process and Reality*, 211.

36. Young Chan Ro, "Ecological implications of Yi Yugok's Cosmology", in *Confucianism and Ecology*, eds. Mary Evelyn Tucker and John Berthrong (Cambridge, Mass.: Harvard University Press,1998), 178.

37. Julia Ching, *Confucianism and Christianity* (Tokyo: Kodansha International, 1978), 164. Of course, it is not possible to say that Neo-Confucianism explores the concept of absolutes such as the Great Ultimate in the same context as Western theistic tradition. It is also true that there are great differences between God and the Great Ultimate in their historical and cultural traditions.

38. Julia Ching, *The Religious Thought of Chu Hsi*, 252 (parenthesis is mine).

Chapter 4: A Process Cosmological Application to Interreligions Spirituality in Korea

1. Ki-baik Lee, *A New History of Korea* (Seoul: Ilchokak Publishers, 1984), 239.

2. McGrath, Alister E., ed. *The Blackwell Encyclopedia of Modern Christian Thought* (Malden, MA: Blackwell Publishers, 1993), 309.

3. David Chung, *Syncretism The Religious Context of Christian Beginnings in Korea* (Albany: State University of New York, 2001), 3.

4. Ki-baik Lee, *A New History of Korea,* 334.

5. Ibid., 335.

6. Duk-Whang Kim, *A History of Religions in Korea* (Seoul: Daeji Moonhwa-sa, 1988), 329.

Notes

7. Alister E. McGrath, ed., *The Blackwell Encyclopedia of Modern Christian Thought*, 310.

8. Donald N. Clark, *Christianity in Modern Korea* (Lanham, MD: University Press of America, 1986), 21.

9. Harvey Cox, *Fire From Heaven* (Reading, MA: Addison-Wesley Publishing Company, 1995), 222.

10. These statistics, presented by the National Statistics Department of Korea, were obtained from the website of Korean statistics (http:// 203.240.190.33/ statistics/5/ s004.html). It is very important to note Korean theologian Kyoung-Jae Kim's comment on these statistics: "This survey is based on the method of self-identification which asks 'what is your religion?' People who do not attend regular religious meetings or participate in religious groups like that of Confucianism or Shamanism tend to answer that they have no religion. Therefore, in this respect, the statistics do not show the true picture." Kyoung-Jae Kim, *Christianity and the Encounter of Asian Religions* (Zoetermeer, Netherlands: Uitgeverij, 1994), 61.

11. Yong-Gi Cho, "The Secrete Behind the World's Biggest Church," in L. Grant McClung, *Azusa Street and Beyond* (New Jersey: Bridge Publishing INC., 1986), 99.

12. Donald N. Clark, *Christianity in Modern Korea*, 36.

13. Ibid.

14. David Martin, *Tongues of Fire* (Oxford: Basil Blackwell Ltd, 1990), 138.

15. Quoted in Tong-Shik Ryu, "Rough Road to Theological Maturity," in Gerald H. Anderson, ed., *Asian Voices in Christian Theology* (New York: Orbis Books, 1976), 163.

16. David Kwangsun Suh, "American Missionaries and A Hundred Years of Korean Protestantism," *International Review of Mission* 74 (January 1985): 12.

17. Chul-Ha Han, "Hankuk Shinhakgye Ui Donghyang" [Trends of Korean Theologies] in *Kidokgyo Yonkam* [A Yearbook of Christianity] (Seoul : National Council of Churches in Korea, 1970), 44.

18. Alister E. McGrath, ed., *The Blackwell Encyclopedia of Modern Christian Thought*, 311.

19. Donald N. Clark, *Christianity in Modern Korea*, 44.

20. David Martin, 141.

21. "Declaration of Korean Theologians," in *East Asia Journal of Theology* 3, no. 2 (1985): 30.

22. Ancestor worship (祖上祭祀, Korean *jo-sang-jae-sa*) can be also replaced by as 'ancestor veneration' or ancestor ritual.' In this book, I use the term 'ancestor worship.'

23. This event became a social issue in Korean society. So, the dialogue between Buddhist leaders and Christian leaders was held by the Department of Culture and Tourism in the Korean government for discussing this event and resolving conflicts among religions in Korea, but an official apology was not expressed by Christian church. *The Hankyoreh Newspaper* (Seoul), 27 June, 1998; 28 August, 1998.

24. Donald N. Clark, *Christianity in Modern Korea*, 36.

25. Samuel Hugh Moffett, *The Christians of Korea* (New York: Friendship Press, 1962), 41.

26. This event titled "An Innocent Sacrifice of Christianity" was reported in *Dong-A-Il-Bo* (Sep. 1, 1920). Translated by myself and quoted from Sai-jong Oh, "An Essay for the Making of Theology of Rites" (in Korean), *Theology and Context* 5 (September 1995): 301.

27. Robert Wuthnow, *After Heaven Spirituality in America Since the 1950* (Berkeley: University of California Press, 1998), 1-2.

28. John H. Berthrong, *The Divine Deli: Religious Identity in the North American Cultural Mosaic* (New York: Orbis Books, 1999), 99.

29. Sandra M. Schneiders, I.H.M. "Spirituality in the Academy", in *Modern Christian Spirituality,* ed. Bradley C. Hanson (Atlanta, Georgia: Scholar Press, 1990), 17.

30. Julia Ching, "What is Confucian Spirituality?" in *Confucianism: The Dynamics of Tradition,* ed. Irene Eber (New York: Macmillan Publishing Company, 1986), 64.

31. I owe this idea to Ann Carr. She defines spirituality as "the whole of one's spiritual or religious experience, one's beliefs, convictions, and patterns of thought, one's emotions and behavior in respect to what is ultimate, or to God." Anne Carr, *Transforming Grace: Christian Tradition and Women's Experience* (San Francisco: Harper & Row, 1988), 201.

32. This is my position. I am aware that some might disagree with my broad view of spirituality that describes spirituality as the union with the ultimate or the divine reality. This still remains as a controversial issue in the study of spirituality and theological anthropology.

33. Ewert Cousins, "Preface to the Series," in *Christian Spirituality I: Origins to the Twelfth Century,* eds. Bernard McGinn and John Meyendorff, vol. 16 of *World Spirituality: An Encyclopedic History of the Religions Quest* (New York: Crossroad, 1985), xiii.

34. Margaret Mary Kelleher, "The Meaning of Christian Spirituality," in *Spirituality and Prayer Jewish and Christian understandings,* eds., Leon Klenicki and Gabe Huck (New York: Paulist Press, 1983), 19.

35. Sandra M. Scheiders, "Spirituality in the Academy," 20.

36. Gustavo Gutierrez, *We Drink from Our Own Wells: The Spiritual Journey of a People* (New York: Orbis Books, 1984), 54.

37. Maria Harris, "The Religious Educator as Spiritual Director," *Pace 8* (1977): 3.

38. Donal Dorr, *Spirituality and Justice* (New York: Orbis Books, 1984), 19.

39. Claire Wolfteich, "Graceful Work: Practical Theological Study of Spirituality," *Horizons* 27 (Spring 2000): 14.

40. Ibid.

41. Sandra M. Schneiders, "Spirituality in the Academy," 22.

42. Walter Principe, "Toward defining Spirituality," *Studies in Religion/ Sciences Religieuses* 12, no. 2 (Spring 1983): 139.

43. Segundo Galilea, *The Way of Living Faith: A Spirituality of Liberation* (San Francisco: Harper & Row, 1985), 4.

44. John H. Berthrong, *All Under Heaven: Transforming Paradigms in Confucian-Christian Dialogue* (Albany: State University of New York Press, 1994), 70-71.

45. Ha-Tae Kim, *Dong-so-cholhak-ui-mannam* [An Encounter of Philosophy East and West], 325.

46. Wei-ming Tu, *Centrality and Commonality: An Essay on Confucian Religiousness* (Albany: State University of New York Press, 1989), 94.

47. Julia Ching, "What is Confucian Spirituality?", in *Confucianism The Dynamics of Tradition,* ed. Irene Eber (New York: Macmillan Publishing Company, 1986), 79.

48. Ibid., 80.

49. Larry J. Alderink, "Cosmology," in *The Westminster Dictionary of Christian Theology,* eds. Alan Richardson and John Bowden (Philadelphia: The Westminster Press, 1983), 125.

50. Whitehead, *Religion in the Making,* 141.

51. Whitehead, *Process and Reality,* 349.

52. Lynn White, Jr., "The Historical Roots of Our Ecologic Crisis," in *Machina Ex Deo* (Cambridge, MA: MIT Press, 1968), 93, 86.

53. Larry J. Alderink, "Cosmology," 126-127.
54. Paul F. Knitter, *No Other Names: A Critical Survey of Christian Attitudes Toward the World Religions* (New York: Orbis Books, 1985), 7.
55. John B. Cobb, Jr. and David Ray Griffin, *Process Theology an Introductory Exposition* (Philadelphia: The Westminster Press, 1976), 14.
56. Mary Evelyn Tucker, "World Religions and Global Ecological Ethics: Contributions from Confucianism and Buddhism," in *Earth Ethics* 7, 3-4 (Spring-Summer), 151. This will be discussed in great detail in the section entitled "Process spirituality as Ecological-Spirituality."
57. All scripture quotations, unless otherwise noted, are taken from the *New Revised Standard Version of the Bible* (New York: The National Council of the Churches of Christ in the U.S.A., 1989).
58. Heup-Young Kim, *Wang Yang-Ming and Karl Barth: A Confucian-Christian Dialogue* (Lanham, MD: University Press of America, 1996), 8.
59. 'Mind,' 'heart,' and 'heart-and-mind'(Chinese character 心) are translated into the same Korean word *'maum'* or *'shim'*.
60. Wing-Tsit Chan, *A Source Book in Chinese Philosophy* (Princeton, NJ: Princeton university Press, 1973), 606.
61. Ibid., 628.
62. Yulgok, *Yulgok Chonso*, vol. 14.
63. Young-Chan Ro, *The Korean Neo-Confucianism of Yi Yulgok* (Albany: State University of New York Press, 1989), 3.
64. Ibid., xii.
65. In other words, Karl Barth maintains that Jesus Christ is the objective reality of revelation and the Holy Spirit is the subjective reality of revelation. See Karl Barth, *Church Dogmatics* (New York: Charles Scribner's Sons, 1956), Vol. I/ 2, 1-25.
66. Karl Barth, *Church Dogmatics*, Vol. I/ 2, 98-135.
67. Sung-Bum Yun, *Han-guk-chok Sinhak - Sung ui Hae-sok-hak* [Korean Theology - Hermeneutics of *Sung*] (Seoul: Sonmyung Munwhasa, 1972), 14-18.
68. This is my translation from Yun's quotation in Chinese ("誠者天之道也, 思誠者人之道也"). Ibid., 20.
69. Ibid., 18-20.
70. Ha-Tae Kim, *Maum-momul-gok-ul-chajaso* [Looking For the Shelter of My Mind] (Seoul: Chongnosojok, 1991), 181.
71. Yulgok, *Yulgok Chonso,* 21:35b-36a. (translation and emphasis are mine). The original expression of the last sentence is "由敬而至於誠矣."
72. Ibid., 183.
73. Wing-Tsit Chan, *A Source Book in Chinese Philosophy* (Princeton: Princeton University Press, 1969), 497.
74. Ha-Tae Kim, *Maum-momul-gok-ul-chajaso* [Looking For the Shelter of My Mind], 185.
75. Wing-Tsit Chan, *A Source Book in Chinese Philosophy*, 500.
76. Young-Chan Ro, *The Korean Neo-Confucianism of Yi Yulgok* (Albany: State of New York University Press, 1989), 87.
77. *Yulgok Chonso,* 20:9b.
78. Ha-Tae Kim, *Dong-so-cholhak-ui-mannam* [The Encounter of Philosophy East and West] (Seoul, Korea: Chongnosojok, 1988), 319.
79. The term *'kyung'* (*ching*) is here translated as "seriousness." Wing-Tsit Chan, *A Source Book in Chinese Philosophy,* 606.

80. *Yulgok Chonso,* 21:21b.
81. Ha-Tae Kim, *Dong-so-cholhak-ui-mannam,* 310.
82. Ha-Tae Kim, *Maum-momul-gok-ul-chajaso* [Looking For the Shelter of My Mind], 187.
83. Wing-Tsit Chan, *A Source Book in Chinese Philosophy,* 107.
84. Ha-Tae Kim, *Dong-so-cholhak-ui-mannam,* 193-194.
85. Ibid., 194.
86. Wing-Tsit Chan, *A Source Book in Chinese Philosophy,* 507.
87. Ha-Tae Kim, *Maum-momul-gok-ul-chajaso* [Looking For the Shelter of My Mind], 194.
88. Clark M. Williamson and Ronald J. Allen, *Adventures of the Spirit A Guide to Worship from the Perspective of Process Theology* (Lanham, MD: University Press of America, Inc., 1997), 118-119; See also Alfred North Whitehead, *Modes of Thought* (New York: The Free Press, 1968), 1-27.
89. Clark M. Williamson and Ronald J. Allen, *Adventures of the Spirit A Guide to Worship from the Perspective of Process Theology,* 138.
90. Alfred North Whitehead, *Adventures of Ideas* (New York: The Macmillan Co., 1935), 213.
91. David Tracy, *Plurality and Ambiguity* (San Francisco: Harper and Row Publishers, 1987), 20.
92. Ibid., 19.
93. Charles Wood, *The Formation of Christian Understanding* (Philadelphia: Westminster Press, 1981), 84.
94. S.G. F. Brandon, ed., *A Dictionary of Comparative Religion* (New York: Charles Scribner's Sons, 1970), 507.
95. Urban T. Holmes, *Spirituality for Ministry* (San Francisco: Harper & Row Publishers, 1982), 19.
96. Maren C. Tirabassi and Kathy Wonson Eddy, eds., *Gifts of Many Cultures* (Cleveland: United Church Press, 1995), 71.
97. Yon-Gi Cho, "The Secrete Behind the World's Biggest Church," in *Azusa Street and Beyond,* ed. L. Grant McClung (New Jersey: Bridge Publishing INC: 1986), 100.
98. Wei-ming Tu, *Confucian Thought: Selfhood as Creative Transformation* (Albany: State University of New York Press, 1985), 52.
99. Wei-ming Tu, *Centrality and Commonality,* 108.
100. Ibid., 26.
101. Ibid., 109.
102. *Yulgok Chonso,* 19:13b.
103. Julia Ching, *Confucianism and Christianity,* 163.
104. Quoted in Rodney L. Taylor, *The Confucian Way of Contemplation* (Columbia: University of South Carolina Press, 1988), 40.
105. Julia Ching, *Confucianism and Christianity,* 164.
106. Whitehead, *Religion in the Making,* 58.
107. Marjorie Hewitt Suchocki, *God Christ Church: A Practical Guide to Process Theology* (New York: Crossroad, 1989), 58-59.
108. *The Oxford Dictionary of the Christian Church* (London: Oxford University Press, 1997), 1316.
109. Urban T. Holmes, *Spirituality for Ministry,* 21.
110. Ibid., 22.
111. It is here my basic point that Confucian meditation is in common with contemplation and apopatic prayers of Christian monastic traditions.

Notes

112. Julia Ching, *Confucianism and Christianity*, 164.
113. Urban T. Holmes, *Spirituality for Ministry*, 132.
114. Carolyn Gratton, *The Art of Spiritual Guidance* (New York: The Crossroad Publishing Company, 1995), 115.
115. Don E. Saliers, "Christian Spirituality in an Ecumenical Age," in *Christian Spirituality Post-Reformation and Modern,* eds. Louis Dupre and Don E. Saliers (New York: The Crossroad Publishing Company, 1989), 529.
116. Alfred North Whitehead, *Science and the Modern World* (New York: The Free Press, 1953), 191-192.
117. Ibid., 192.
118. Ibid.
119. This is a term used by Wei-ming Tu in his writings. See Wei-ming Tu, *Centrality and Commonality* (Albany: State University of New York, 1989).
120. Whitehead, *Process and Reality,* 220.
121. Yulgok, *Yulgok Chonso,* 23:4a.
122. Ibid.
123. John B. Cobb and David Ray Griffin, *Process Theology,* 14.
124. Ibid., 15-16.
125. Marjorie Hewitt Suchocki, *God Christ Church A Practical Guide to Process Theology,* 57.
126. Jose Severino Croatto, *Exodus: A Hermeneutics of Freedom* (New York: Orbis Books, 1981), 16.
127. Byung-Mu Ahn, *Minjungshinhak Iyaki* [Stories of Minjung Theology] (Chonan: Korea Theological Study Institute, 1990), 50.
128. Wei-Ming Tu, *Centrality and Commonality: An Essay on Confucian Religiousness* (Albany: State University of New York Press, 1989), 47-48.
129. Gardiner M. Day, *The Apostles' Creed* (New York: Charles Scribner's Sons, 1963), 134.
130. George W. Stroup, "Death, Resurrection, and the Communion of the Saints" in *Reformed Liturgy and Music,* XX/4, Fall, 1986, 192.
131. Sung-Soo Choi, "A Theological Questions of Ancestor Worship" in *Christian thought* 478 (October 1998): 128.
132. Peter E. Fink, ed., *The New Dictionary of Sacramental Worship* (Minnesota: The Liturgical Press, 1990), 109.
133. Sang-Bum Lee, "Ancestor Worship in the light of the Gospel" in *Kidogkyo wa kwan-hon-sang-jae,* ed.Keun-won Park (Seoul: Chonmangsa, 1984), 95.
134. Peter E. Fink, ed., *The New Dictionary of Sacramental Worship,* 110.
135. Ibid., 113.
136. Chin-Hong Chung, "the Ceremonies of Coming of Age, Marriage, Funeral, and Ancestral Worship" in *Kidogkyo wa Kwan-hon-sang-jae* [Christianity and the Ceremonies of coming of age, marriage, funeral and ancestral worship], ed. Keun-won Park, (Seoul: Chonmangsa, 1984), 74-75. (translation is mine.)
137. Gardiner M. Day, *The Apostles' Creed,* 140.
138. World Council of Churches, *Baptism, Eucharist And Ministry* (Geneva: World Council of Churches, 1982), 12.
139. J. G. Davis, ed., *The New Westminster Dictionary of Liturgy and Worship* (Philadelphia: The Westminster, 1986), 471.
140. Peter E. Fink, ed. *The New Dictionary of Sacramental Worship* (Minnesota: The liturgical Press, 1990), 431.
141. World Council of Churches, *Baptism, Eucharist And Ministry* (Geneva: World

Council of Churches, 1982), 10.

142. Ibid.
143. Ibid., 14.
144. Ibid., 15.
145. The term, *minjung*, in Korean means people who are politically oppressed, economically exploited, and culturally alienated.
146. Jae-Soon Park, "Jesus Table Community Movement and the Church," *Asian Journal of Theology* 7 (April 1993): 65.
147. Ibid., 67.
148. Ibid., 73.
149. Tissa Balasuriya, *The Eucharist and Human Liberation* (New York: Orbis Books, 1979), 16.
150. Jong-Chun Park, *Ki-o-ga-si-nun Hananim* [The Crawling God] (Seoul: The Methodist Theological Seminary Press, 1995), 521-523.
151. Choan-Seng Song, *Third-Eye Theology: Theology in Formation in Asian Setting* (New York: Orbis Books, 1979),174-175.
152. Marjorie Hewitt Suchocki, *God Christ Church A Practical Guide to Process Theology* (New York: Crossroad, 1989), 161.
153. Keith Crim, ed., *Abingdon Dictionary of Living Religions* (Nashville: Abingdon Press, 1981), 32.
154. Wi-Jo Kang, "Ancestor Worship: From the Perspective of Family Life" in *Ancestor Worship*, ed. Jung-Young Lee (New York: The Edwin Mellen Press, 1988), 74.
155. Ibid., 76.
156. Ibid., 78.
157. Kisimita P. Pederson, "Environmental Ethics", in *Explorations in Global Ethics*, eds. Summer B. Twis and Bruce Grelle (Boulder, Col.: Westview Press, 1998), 267. This will be discussed in more details in the section entitled "Process Spirituality as Eco-Spirituality."
158. The Ecumenical Patriarchate, assisted by the Worldview Fund for Nature, "Orthodoxy and the Ecological Crisis" (Istanbul: The Ecumenical Patriarchate, 1990), 7-8.
159. James Nash, *Loving Nature Ecological Integrity and Christian Responsibility* (Nashville: Abingdon Press, 1991), 18.
160. Ibid., 19.
161. Ralph Metzner, "Emerging Ecological Worldview" in *Worldviews and Ecology Religion, Philosophy, and the Environment*, eds. Mary Evelyn Tucker and John A. Grim (New York: Orbis Books, 1994), 163-164.
162. Mary Evelyn Tucker, "Ecological Themes in Taoism and Confucianism" in *Worldviews and Ecology Religion, Philosophy, and the Environment*, eds. Mary Evelyn Tucker and John A. Grim (New York: Orbis Books, 1994), 151.
163. Ibid., 152.
164. Ralph Metzner, "Emerging Ecological Worldview," 165.
165. David Ray Griffin, "Whitehead's Deeply Ecological Worldview," in *Worldviews and Ecology Religion, Philosophy, and the Environment*, eds. Mary Evelyn Tucker and John A. Grim (New York: Orbis Books, 1994), 192.
166. Whitehead, *Process and Reality*, 348.
167. Mary Evelyn Tucker, "Ecological Themes in Taoism and Confucianism," 156.
168. *Yulgok Chonso*, 14:54b-55a.
169. Mary Evelyn Tucker, "Ecological Themes in Taoism and Confucianism," 157.

170. Young Chan Ro, "Ecological implications of Yi Yugok's Cosmology", in *Confucianism and Ecology*, eds. Mary Evelyn Tucker and John Berthrong (Cambridge, Mass.: Harvard University Press,1998), 171-172.

171. Ibid., 177.

172. Wei-ming Tu, *Centrality and Commonality: An Essay on Confucian Religiousness* (Albany: State University of New York Press, 1989), 23.

173. Wing-Tsit Chan, *A Source Book in Chinese Philosophy,* 100.

174. David Ray Griffin, "Introduction: Postmodern Spirituality and Society," in *Spirituality and Society,* ed. David Ray Griffin (Albany: State University of New York Press, 1988), 14.

175. Clark M. Williamson and Ronald J. Allen, *Adventure of the Spirit A Guide to Worship from the Perspective of Process Theology* (Lanham, MD: University Press of America, Inc., 1997), 31.

176. Hyun Kyung Chung, *Struggle To Be The Sun Again: Introducing Asian Women's Theology* (New York: Orbis Books, 1990), 4.

177. Pui-lan Kwok, *Introducing Asian Feminist Theology* (Cleveland: The Pilgrim Press, 2000), 48-49.

178. This is a term used by E. S. Fiorenza. See E. S. Fiorenza, *In Memory of Her A Feminist Theological Reconstruction of Christian Origins* (New York: Crossroad, 1984).

179. Julia Ching, *Confucianism and Christianity* (Tokyo: Kodansha International, 1978), 64.

180. Karl Rahner, *The Practice of Faith: A Handbook of Contemporary Spirituality* (New York: Crossroads, 1983), 17-22.

181. Donal Door, *Spirituality and Justice* (New York: Orbis Books, 1984), 19.

182. Gustavo Gutierrez, *A Theology of Liberation* (New York: Orbis Books, 1988), 118.

183. Julia Ching, *Confucianism and Christianity* (Tokyo: Kodansha International, 1977), 185.

184. John Berthrong calls Wei-Ming Tu's position 'a reformed modern Confucianism.' See John Berthrong, *All Under Heaven* (New York: SUNY Press, 1994), 2.

185. Wei-ming Tu, "Toward a Third Epoch of Confucian humanism" in *Confucianism: The Dynamics of Tradition,* ed. Irene Eber (New York: Macmillan Publishing Company, 1986), 20.

186. Wei-ming Tu, *Confucian Thought: Selfhood as Creative Transformation,* 51.

187. Wei-ming Tu, *Centrality and Commonality,* 98.

188. Ibid., ix.

189. Wei-ming Tu, "Confucianism" in *Our Religions,* ed. Arvind Sharma (New York: HarperCollins Publisher, 1993), 141.

190. Ibid., 100.

191. Ibid., 114.

192. Tu, *Confucian Thought: Selfhood as Creative Transformation,* 55.

193. Sang-Un Lee, *Hankuk-ui-yuhak-sasang* [Confucian Thoughts in Korea] (Seoul: Samsung Publishing Company, 1988), 36.

194. *Yulgok Chonso,* 3:5a-b.

195. Ibid., 9:6b-7a.

196. Ibid., 5:16b.

197. Ibid., 24:9a. "臣按 人君修德 是爲政之根本."

198. Ibid., 25:19b.

199. Yulgok, *Yulgok Chonso,* 25:62a-b. This is W. T. de Bary's translation. See W. T.

deBary, ed., *Sources of Chinese Tradition* (New York: Columbia University Press, 1960), vol.1, 176.
   200. Wing-tsit Chan, *A Source Book in Chinese Philosophy,* 98.
   201. Jun-Yon Whang, *Yulgok Cholhak us Ihae* [*Understanding of Yulgok's Philosophy*] (Seoul: Sokwangsa, 1995), 194.
   202. Karen Armstrong, *A History of God* (New York: Ballantine Books, 1994), 384.
   203. Whitehead, *Process and Reality,* 351.
   204. Ibid., 343.
   205. Whitehead, *Adventures of Ideas,* 296.

Conclusion

   1. Karl Rahner, *Foundations of the Christian Faith,* trans. William V. Dych (New York: The Seabury Press, 1978), 311-321
   2. Francis X. Clooney, *Theology After Vedanta* (Albany: State University of New York Press, 1993), 7.
   3. Julia Ching, *Confucianism and Christianity* (Tokyo: Kodansha International, 1978), 64.
   4. Theologians also criticize Sung-Bum Yun's theology as being too heavily based on Karl Barth's neo-Orthodox theology, which is very famous for its exclusivism on other religions. They wonder how the Barthian theology is the basis of interpreting of Neo-Confucian term "sincerity" and constructing Confucian-Christianity in Korea.
   5. Tong-Shik Ryu, *The Christian faith Encounters the Religions of Korea* (Seoul: The Christian Literature Society of Korea, 1962), 13.
   6. Walter J. Hollenweger, *Pentecostalism* (Peabody, MA: Hendrickson Publishers, 1997), 103.

GLOSSARY OF KOREAN AND CHINESE TERMS

che, t'i	體
chljong	七情
chil-jong-po-sa-dan	七精包四端
chon li, t'ien li	天理
ch'ondo ch'aek	天道策
do, dao, tao	道
doshim, dao hsin	道心
hyo (filial piety)	孝
hyong-jae-ai	兄弟愛
i-bal-ki-su	理發氣隨
i-il-bun-su	理一分殊
i-ki-ho-bal	理氣互發
i-ki-ji-myo	理氣之妙
in, jen,	仁
i-tong-ki-kuk	理通氣局
jayon (thus-so of things)	自然
jongjwa, ching-tso	靜坐
ki, qi, ch'i	氣
ki-bal-yi-seung	氣發理乘
kun-ja, chün-tzu	君子
kyung, ching	敬
man-on-bong-sa	萬言封事
minjung	民衆
mu-geuk, wu-ch	無極
sa-sung-ja	思誠者
shim, hsin	心
shin-dok, shen-tu	愼獨
shimsong	心性
songhak chipyo	聖學輯要
song, hsing	性
Suh Hwadam	徐花潭
sung, ch'eng,	誠
sung-ja	誠者
tae-gek, t'ai-chi	太極

um-yang, yin-yang	陰陽
yi, li	理
Yi T'oegye	李退溪
Yi Yulgok	李栗谷
Yulgok Chonso	栗谷全書
yong, yung	用
Zhongyong, chung-yung	中庸
Zhu Xi, Chu Hsi, Ju Hee	朱熹
Zhuzi yulei, Juja O Ryu	朱子語類
Zhuzi Chia-li, Juja Karye	朱子家禮

Bibliography

Primary Sources

Whitehead, Alfred North. *Adventures of Ideas*. New York: The Free Press, 1961.

———. *Process and Reality: An Essay in Cosmology*. Edited by David Ray Griffin and Donald W. Sherburne. Corrected ed. New York: The Free Press, 1978.

———. *Modes of Thought*. New York: The Free Press, 1968.

———. *Science and the Modern World*. New York: The Free Press, 1953.

———. *Religion in the Making*. New York: Macmillan Company, 1926. Reprint, New York: Fordham University Press, 1996.

———. *The Concept of Nature*. Cambridge: Cambridge University Press, 1964.

———. *The Function of Reason*. 1929. Reprint, Boston: Beacon Press, 1958.

———. *Symbolism: Its Meaning and Effect*. 1927. Reprint, New York: G.P. Putnam's Sons, Capricorn Books, 1959.

Yi, Yulgok. *Yulgok Chonso* [Complete Works of Yulgok]. Seoul: Sungkyunkwan University Press, 1971.

———. *Yulgokjip* [Selected Korean Translation of Yulkok's Works]. Seoul: Minjokmunhwachujinhoe, 1985

Secondary Sources

Ahn, Sang Jin. *Continuity and Transformation: Religious Synthesis in East Asia*.

New York: Peter Lang, 2001.

Ariarajah, S. Wesley. *The Bible and People of Other Faith*. Geneva: World Council of Churches, 1991.

Armstrong, Karen. *A History of God*. New York: Ballantine Books, 1994.

Audi, Robert, ed. *The Cambridge Dictionary of Philosophy*. Cambridge: Cambridge University Press, 1995.

Aumann, Jordan. *Christian Spirituality in Catholic Tradition*. San Francisco: Ignatius Press, 1986.

Bae, Jong-Ho. *Hankuk Yuhak Ui Cholhakjok Chonkai*. [Philosophical Survey of Korean Confucianism]. Seoul: Yonsae University Press, 1985.

Balasuriya, Tissa. *The Eucharist and Human Liberation*. New York: Orbis Books, 1979.

Barry, William A. *The Practice of Spiritual Direction*. San Francisco: New York: HarperCollins Publishers, 1995.

Barth, Karl. *Church Dogmatics*. Vol.1., New York: Charles Scribner's Sons, 1956.

Berger, Peter. *A Far Glory The Quest for Faith in an Age of Credulity*. New York: The Free Press, 1992.

Berthrong, John H. *All Under Heaven: Transforming Paradigms in Confucian-Christian Dialogue*. Albany: State University of New York Press, 1991.

―――. *Concerning Creativity A Comparison of Chu Hsi, Whitehead, and Neville*. Albany: State University of New York Press, 1998.

―――. *The Divine Deli: Religious Identity in the North American Cultural Mosaic*. New York: Orbis Books, 1999.

―――. *Transformations of the Confucian Way*. Boulder, Colorado: Westview Press, 1998.

Berthrong, John and Evelyn Nagai Berthrong. *Confucianism: A Short Introdction*. Oxford: Oneworld Publications, 2000.

Bibliography

Black, Alison Harley. *Man and Nature in the Philosophical Thought of Wang Fu-Chi.* Seattle: University of Washington Press, 1989.

Bouyer, Louis. *A History of Christian Spirituality.* 3 vols. New York: Seabury, 1969.

———. *Introduction to Spirituality.* New York: Desclee, 1961.

Bradley, P. Holt. *Thirsty For God: A Brief History of Christian Spirituality.* Minneapolis, MN: Augsburg Fortress, 1993.

Brandon, S.G.F., ed. *A Dictionary of Comparative Religion.* New York: Charles Scribner's Sons, 1970.

Brown, Delwin, ed. *Process Philosophy and Christian Theology.* New York: The Bobbs-Merill Company, Inc., 1971.

Brown, Robert M. *Spirituality and Liberation.* Philadelphia: Fortress Press, 1989.

Caraway, James E. *God as Dynamic Actuality.* Washington, D.C.: University Press of America, 1978.

Carr, Anne. *Transforming Grace: Christian Tradition and Women's Experience.* San Francisco: Harper & Row, 1988.

Chai, Mu-Song. *Toe Yul Songrihak Bigyo Yonku* [A Comparative Study of T'oegye and Yulgok's Confucian Stidies]. Seoul: Sungkyunkwan University Press, 1972.

Chan, Wing-tsit. *Chu Hsi: New Studies.* Honolulu: University of Hawaii Press, 1989.

———, ed. *Chu Hsi and Neo-Confucianism.* Honolulu: University of Hawaii Press, 1986.

———. *Neo-Confucianism, Etc.: Essays by Wing-tsit Chan.* Hanover, NH: Oriental Society, 1969.

———. *A Source Book in Chinese Philosophy.* Princeton: Princeton University Press, 1963.

Chase, Randall. "Spiritual Direction: An Integrating Function for Ministry in the Parish." D.Min Thesis, Boston University School of Theology, 1979.

Cheng, Cung-ying. *New Dimensions of Confucian and Neo-Confucian Philosophy.* Albany: State University of New York Press, 1991.

Ching, Julia. *Chinese Religions.* New York: Orbis Books, 1993.

———. *Confucianism and Christianity.* Tokyo: Kodansha International, 1978.

———. *The Religious Thought of Chu Hsi.* London: Oxford University Press, 2000.

Choi, Min-Hong. *A Modern History of Korean Philosophy.* Seoul: Seongmoonsa, 1980.

Chon, Mok. *Chujahak ui saekye* [Lectures on Chu Hsi Studies]. Translated by Wan-Jae Yi and To-Kun Paek. Taeku: Eemun Publishing Company, 1996.

Chong, Haechang, and Hyung-jo Han, eds. *Confucian Philosophy in Korea.* Kyonggi-do: The Academy of Korean Studies, 1996.

Christian, William A. *An Interpretation of Whitehead's Metaphysics.* New Haven: Yale University Press, 1967.

Christian Conference of Asia, ed. *Minjung Theology.* Singapore: Christian Conference of Asia, 1981.

Chu, Hsi. *Chujaoryu* [Works of Chu Hsi, 朱子語類]. Translated by Hur Tak and Lee Yo-Sung. Seoul: Chong Gye Publishing Company, 1998.

———. *The Philosophy of Human Nature.* Translated by J. Percy Bruce. London: Probsthain; New York: AMS Press, 1973 (reprint).

Chu, Hsi and Lu Tsu-Ch'ien. *Reflections on Things at Hand* [近思錄]. Translated y Wing-Tsit Chan. New York: Columbia University Press, 1967.

Chung, David. *Syncretism: The Religious Context of Christian Begginnings in Korea.* Albany: State University of New York Press, 2001.

Chung, Edward Y.J. *The Neo-Confucianism of Yi T'oegye and Yi Yulgok: A Re-*

appraisal of the 'Four-Seven Thesis' and Its practical Implication for Self-Cultivation. Albany: State University of New York Press, 1995.

Chung, Tsai-chun. *The Development of the Concepts of Heaven and of Man in the Philosophy of Chu His*. Taiwan: Institute of Chinese Literature and Philosophy, 1993.

Clark, Donald N., *Christianity in Modern Korea*. Lanham: University Press of America, 1986.

Clooney, Francis X. *Theology After Vedanta*. Albany: State University of New York Press, 1993.

Cobb, John B. Jr., and David R. Griffin. *Process Theology: An Introductory Exposition*. Philadelphia: The Westminster Press, 1976.

Cobb, John B., Jr. *A Christian Natural Theology*. Philadelphia: The Westminster Press, 1965.

———. *Transforming Christianity and the World*. New York: Orbis Books, 1999.

Commission on Theological Concerns of the Christian Conference of Asia (CTC-CCA.), ed. *Minjung Theology: People as the Subjects of History*. London: Zed Press, 1983; New York: Orbis Books, 1983; Singapore: Christian Conference of Asia, 1983.

Confucius. *Confucius: The Analects*. Translated by D. C. Lau. Hong Kong: Chinese University Press, 1992.

Conn, Joann Wolski. *Spirituality and Personal Maturity*. New York: Paulist Press, 1989.

Cousins, Ewert, ed. *World Spirituality: An Encyclopedic History of the Religious Quest*. New York: Crossroad, 1985.

Coward, Harold. *Pluralism: Challenge to World Religions*. New York: Orbis Books, 1985.

Cox, Harvey. *Fire From Heaven*. Reading, MA: Addison-Wesley Publishing Company, 1995.

Cratton, Carolyn, *The Art of Spiritual Guidance.* New York: Crossroad, 1992.

Crim, Keith, ed. *Abingdon Dictionary of Living Religions.* Nashville: Abingdon Press, 1981.

Croatto, Jose-Severino. *Exodus: A Hermeneutics of Freedom.* New York: Orbis Books, 1981.

Culligan, Kevin G. *Spiritual Direction: Contemporary Readings.* Covent Valley, N.Y.: Living Flame Press, 1983.

Cummings, Charles. *Eco-Spirituality: Toward a Reverent Life.* New York: Paulist Press, 1991.

Day, M. Gardiner. *The Apostle's Creed.* New York: Charles Scribner's Sons, 1963.

Dayton, Donald W. *Theological Roots of Pentecostalism.* Metuchen, NJ: The Scarecrow Press, 1987.

De Barry, William T. ed. *Sources of Chinese Tradition.* Vol.1. New York: Columbia University Press, 1960.

De Barry, William T. and Haboush, Jahyun Kim, eds. *The Rise of Neo-Confucianism in Korea.* New York: Columbia University Press, 1985.

Deuchler, Martina. *The Confucian Transformation of Korea: A Study of Society and Ideology.* Cambridge: Harvard University Press, 1992.

Downey, Michael, ed. *The New Dictionary of Catholic Spirituality.* Minnesota: The Liturgical Press, 1993.

Dorr, Donal. *Spirituality and Justice.* New York: Orbis Books,1984.

Eck, Diana L. *Encountering God: A Spiritual Journey from Bozeman to Banaras.* Boston, MA: Beacon Press, 1993.

Edwards, Paul, ed. *The Encyclopedia of Philosophy.* New York: The Macmillan Company & The Free Press, 1967.

Eigo, Francis, ed. *Contemporary Spirituality: Responding to the Divine Initiative.* Villanova: Villanova University Press, 1983.

Eliade, Mircea, ed. *The Encyclopedia of Religion.* New York: Macmillan Publishing Company, 1987.

Fink, Peter E. ed. *The New Dictionary of Sacramental Worship.* Minnesota: The Liturgical Press, 1990.

Fiorenza, E. S. *In Memory of Her A Feminist Theological Reconstruction of Christian Origins.* New York: Crossroad, 1984.

Ford, Lewis S. *The Emergence of Whitehead's Metaphysics: 1925-1929.* Albany: State University of New York Press, 1984.

———. *The Lure of God: A Biblical Background for Process Theism.* Philadelphia: Fortress Press, 1978.

———. *Transforming Process Theism.* Albany: State University of New York, 2000.

Fremantle, Anne, ed. *The Protestant Mystics: An Anthology of Spiritual Experience.* New York: New American Library, 1964.

Fuller, Robert C. *Spiritual, but Not Religion.* New York: Oxford University Press, 2001.

Fung, Yu-Lan. *A Short History of Chinese Philosophy.* New York: Macmillan Company, 1948.

———. *A History of Chinese Philosophy.* Vol.2. Princeton: Princeton University Press, 1953.

Genji, Simada. *Chu Hsi Studies and Yang Ming Studies.* Translated by Sok-Kun Kim and Kun-Woo Yi. The Korean eds. Seoul: Kachi Publishing Company, 1996.

Graham, A. C. *Disputers of the Dao: Philosophical Argument in Ancient China.* La Salle, Il: Open Court Publishing Company, 1997.

Gray, James R. *Modern Process Thought: A Brief Ideological History.* Lanham, MD: University Press of America, 1982.

Gutierrez, Gustavo. *A Theology of Liberation.* New York: Orbis Books, 1981.

———. *We Drink From Our Own Well: The Spiritual Journey of a People.* New York: Orbis Books, 1985.

Hall, David L., and Roger T. Ames. *Thinking Through Confucius.* Albany: State University of New York Press, 1987.

Han, Young-Jo. *Zhu Xi aeso Chung Yak-Yong uro* [From Zhu Xi To Chung Yak-Yong]. Seoul: Segye-sa, 2000.

Hanson, Bradley C., ed. *Modern Christian Spirituality.* Atlanta: Scholar Press, 1990.

Harris, Maria. "The Religious Educator as Spiritual Director." *Peace* 8 (1977): 3.

Hartshorne, Charles. *A Natural Theology for Our Time.* La Salle, Ill: Open Court, 1967.

———. *Whitehead's Philosophy: Selected Essays, 1935-1970.* Lincoln: University of Nebraska Press, 1972.

———. *Omnipotence and Other Theological Mistakes.* Albany: State University of New York Press, 1984.

Heim, S. Mark. *Salvation: Truth and Difference in Religion.* New York: Orbis Books, 1995.

Hessel, Dieter T. *Social Ministry.* Philadelphia: The Westminster Press, 1982.

———, and Rosemary Radford Ruether, eds. *Christianity and Ecology.* Cambridge, Mass: Harvard University Press, 2000.

Hick, John. *God Has Many Names.* Philadelphia: Westminster Press, 1982.

———. *Philosophy of Religion.* Englewood Cliffs: Prentice-Hall, INC., 1973.

Hollenweger, Walter J. *Pentecostalism.* Peabody, MA: Hendrickson Publishers, 1997.

Holmes III, Urban T. *Spirituality for Ministry.* New York: Harper & Row Publishers, 1982.

Bibliography

Hosinski, Thomas E. *Stubborn Fact and Creative Advance*. Maryland: Rowman & Little Field Publisher, 1993.

Hwang Joon-Yon. *Yi Yulgok: Geu Salm Eui Moseup* [Yi Yulgok: The Image of His Life]. Seoul: Seoul National University Press, 2000.

Hwang, Ui-Dong. *Hankug ui Yuhak Sasang* [Confucian Thoughts of Korea]. Seoul: Suhkwangsa, 1995.

———. *Yulgok Sasang ui Chaegyejok Ihae* [Systematic Understanding of Yulgok's Thoughts]. 2 vols. Seoul: Suhkwangsa, 1998.

Hyun, Sang-Yun. *Choson Yuhak Sa*. [History of Choson Confucianism]. Seoul: Minjung Sokwan, 1974.

Isabell, Damien. *The Spiritual Director: A Practical Guide*. Chicago: Franciscan Herald Press, 1976.

Jang, Sook-Pil. Yiyi Yulgok Junsu [Yiyi and Complete Works of Yulgok]. Ulsan: Ulsan University Press, 1999.

Joe, Wanne J. *Traditional Korea: A Cultural History.* Seoul: Chung'ang University Press, 1981.

Jorgensen, Jorgen. *The Development of Logical Empiricism*. Chicago: University of Chicago Press, 1951.

Kalton, Michael C., et al. *The Four-Seven Debate: An Annotated Translation of the Most Famous Controversy in Korean Neo-Confucian Thought*. Albany: State University of New York Press, 1994.

Kang, Jae-Eun. *Sonbi ui Nara Hankuk Yuhak Echon Nyon* [The Korean Confucianism 2000 Years]. Seoul: Hangilsa Publishing Co., 2001.

Keum, Jang-Tae Keum. *Hanguk yukyo ui ihae* [Understanding of Korean Confucianism]. Seoul: Minjokmunwhasa, 1989.

Kim, Chongsuh., ed. *Reader in Korean Religion.* Kyonggi-Do: The Academy of Korean Studies, 1993.

Kim, Chung-Ryul. *Koryo Yuhaksa* [History of Confucianism in Koryo Dynasty]. Seoul: Korea University press, 1963.

Kim, Duk-Whang. *A History of Religions in Korea.* Seoul: Daeji Moonhwa-sa, 2000.

Kim, Ha-Tai. "Chu Hsi Studies and the Tasks of Korean Theology." In *Bogum Kwa Munhwa,* ed. Korean Christian Academic Society. Seoul: Christian Literature Society, 1991.

———. *Maum-momul-gok-ul-chajaso* [Looking For the Hometown of My Mind]. Seoul: Chongnosojok,1991.

———. *Tongso Cholhak Ui Mannam* [Encounter of Philosophy East and West]. Seoul: Chongno Book Publisher, 1988.

Kim, Heup-Young. *Wang Yang-Ming and Karl Barth.* Lanham, Maryland: University Press of America,1996.

Kim, Kyung-Jae. *Christianity and the Encounter of Asian Religions.* Zoetermeer, The Netherlands: Boekencentrum Publishing House, 1994.

———. *Haesokhak kwa Jongkyosinhak* [Hermeneutics and Theology of Religions]. Chonan: Korea Theological Study Institute, 1994.

Kim, Sung-Won. "A Model of Moral Metaphysics Based on Yi T'oegye's Theory of Principle." Th. D. diss., Boston University School of Theology, 1994.

Kim, Yung Sik. *The Natural Philosophy of Chu Hsi (1130-1200).* Philadelphia: American Philosophical Society, 2000.

Knitter, Paul. *One Earth Many Religions.* New York: Orbis Books, 1996.

———. *No Other Name?: A Critical Survey of Christian Attitudes Toward the World Religions.* New York: Orbis Books,1985.

Kraft, Victor. *The Vienna Circle: The Origin Neopositivism.* Translated by Arthur Pap. New York: Philosophical Library, 1953.

Kum, Jang-Tai. *Hankuk yuhak ui Ihai.*[Understanding of Korean Confucianism]. Seoul: Minjok Munhwa Sa, 1989.

Kung, Hans. *Global Responsibility: In Search of a New World Ethic.* New York: The Continuum Publishing Company, 1996.

Land, Steven J. *Pentecostal Spirituality.* Sheffield: Sheffield Academy Press, 1993.

Lansing, John W. "The Nature of Whitehead's God." *Process Studies* 3 (Fall 1973): 144.

Leclerc, Ivor. *Whitehead's Metaphysics: An Introductory Exposition.* New York: Macmillan Company, 1958.

Lee, Byong-Do. *Hanguk Yuhaksa* [A History of Korean Confucianism]. Seoul: Asia Munhwasa, 1987.

———. *Yulgok ui saengae wa sasang* [Yulgo's Thoughts and Life] (Seoul: Suhmundang, 1984

Lee, Jong-Ho. *Yulgok: Inkan gwa sasang* [Yulgok: Man and Thoughts] (Seoul: Hyunamsa, 1984

Lee, Jung-Young, ed. *Ancestor Worship.* New York: The Edwin Mellen Press, 1988.

———, ed. *Emerging Theology in World Perspective: Commentary on Korean Minjung Theology.* Mystic, Conn: Twenty-Third Publications, 1988.

Lee, Ki-baik. *A New History of Korea.* Translated by Edward W. Wagner with Edward J. Shultz. Seoul: Ilchokak Publishers, 1984.

Lee, Peter K. H., ed. *Confucian-Christian Encounters in Historical and Contemporary Perspective.* Lewiston, NY: Edwin Mellen Press, 1991.

Lee, Sang-Un. *Hankuk-ui-yuhak-sasang* [Confucian Thought of Korea]. Seoul: Samsung Publishing Company, 1988.

Lee, Young-Kyung. *Yulgok Yulrisasang ui Insongnonjok Tamsaik* [A Study of Yulgok's Ethical Thoughts from a Perspective of Human Nature]. Pusan: Saejong Publishing Company, 2001.

Lehman, K. and A. Raffelt, eds. *The Practice of Faith: A Handbook of Contemporary Spirituality.* New York: Crossroad, 1986.

Leys, Simon., trans. *The Analects of Confucius*. New York: W. W. Norton & Company, 1997.

Liu, Shu-Hsien. *Understanding Confucian Philosophy*. Wesport, Conn.: Praeger Publishers, 1998.

Mark, Setton. *Chong Yagyong: Korea's Challenge to Orthodox Neo-Confucianism*. Albany: State University of New York Press, 1997.

Martin, David. *Tongues of Fire*. Oxford: Basil Blackwell Ltd, 1990.

McDonagh, Sean. *To Care For the Earth: A Call to a New Theology*. London: Cassell Publishers Ltd., 1986.

McGrath, Alister E., ed. *The Blackwell Encyclopedia of Modern Christian Thought*. Malden, MA: Blackwell Publishers, 1993.

———. *Christian Theology: An Introduction*. Malden, MA: Blackwell Publishers,1999.

Mellert, Robert B. *What is Process Theology?* New York: Paulist Press, 1975.

Minjokkwasasangynkuhoe [Study Group on Nation and Thoughts], ed. *Sadanchiljongnon* [Four-Seven Debates]. Seoul: Suhkwangsa, 1992.

Moffett, Samuel Hugh. *Christianity in Modern Korea*. New York: Friendship Press, 1962.

Moltmann, Jurgen. *Was ist Heute Theologie?* Freiburg: Herder, 1988.

———. *The Source of Life*. London: SCM Press, 1997.

Moon, Cyrus Hee-Suk. *A Korean Minjung Theology: An Old Testament Perspective*. New York: Books, 1985.

Moran, Patrick Edwin Moran. *Three Smaller Wisdom Books*. Lanham: University Press of America,1993.

Musser, Donald W., Price. Joseph L., eds. *A New Handbook of Christian Theology*. Nashville: Abingdon Press, 1992.

Needham, Joseph. *Science and Civilization in China. Corrected Reprinted* *ed.,*Cambridge: Cambridge University Press, 1954, vol.2.

Neville, Robert Cummings. *Behind the Mask of God.* Albany: State University of New York Press, 1991.

———. *Boston Confucianism: Portable Tradition in The Late-Modern World.* Albany: State University of New York Press, 2000.

———. *Creativity and God: A Challenge to Process Theology,* New ed. Albany: State University of New York Press, 1995.

———, ed. *The Human Condition A Volume in the Comparative Religious Ideas Project.* Albany: State University of New York Press, 2002.

———, ed. *The Religious Truth A Volume in the Comparative Religious Ideas Project.* Albany: State University of New York Press, 2002.

———. *A Theology Primer.* Albany: State University of New York, 1991.

———, ed. *Ultimate Realities A Volume in the Comparative Religious Ideas Project.* Albany: State University of New York Press, 2002.

Ng, On-Cho. *Cheng-Zhu Confucianism in the Early Quing.* Albany: State University of New York Press, 2001.

Nobo, Jorge Luis. *Whitehead's Metaphysics of Extension and Solidarity.* Albany: State University of New York Press, 1986

Odin, Steve. *Process Metaphysics and Hua-yen Buddhism.* Albany: State University of New York Press, 1982.

Oh, Sai-Jong. "An Essay for the Making of Theology of Rites" (in Korean). *Theology and Context* 5 (September 1995): 282-320.

Palmer, Spencer J. *Confucian Rituals In Korea.* Berkeley: Asian Humanities Press, 1980.

Panikkar, Raimundo. *The Intra-Religious Dialogue.* Bangalore, India: The Asian Trading Corporation, 1984.

Park, Andrew Sung. *A Wounded Heart of God.* Nashville: Abingdon Press, 1993.

Park, Jong-Chun. *Ki-o-ga-si-nun Hananim* [The Crawling God]. Seoul: The Methodist Theological Seminary Press, 1995.

Park, Keun-Won, ed. *Kidogkyo wa Kwan-hon-sang-jae* [Christianity and the Ceremonies of Coming of Age, Marriage, Funeral and Ancestral Worship]. Seoul: Chonmangsa, 1984.

Philopson, Sten M. *A Metaphysics for Theology.* Uppsala, Sweden: University of Uppsala Press, 1982.

Poewe, Karla, ed. *Charismatic Christianity as a Global Culture.* South Carolina: University of South Carolina Press, 1994.

Price, Lucien. *Dialogues of Alfred Whitehead.* New York: New American Library, 1964.

Rahner, Karl. *Foundations of Christian Faith.* Translated by William V. Dych. New York: The Seabury Press, 1978.

————. *The Practice of Faith: A Handbook of Contemporary Spirituality.* New York: Crossroads, 1983.

Rouner, Leroy S., ed. *Religious Pluralism.* Nortre Dame: University of Nortre Dam Press, 1984.

Ryu, Hong -Ryul. *Hankuk Chonju Kyohoe Sa* [A History of Korean Catholic Church]. Seoul: Catholic Press, 1962.

Ro, Young-Chan. *The Korean Neo-Confucianism of Yi Yulgok.* Albany: State of New York University Press, 1989.

Root, Wade Clark. *A Generation of Seekers: The Spiritual Journey of the Baby Boom Generation.* New York: Harper Collins, 1994.

Rule, Paul A. *K'ung-tzu or Confucius? The Jesuit Interpretation of Confucianism.* Winchester, MA: Allen & Unwin Inc., 1986.

Russell, Bertrand. *My Philosophical Development.* London: Unwin Books, 1975.

————. *Portrait from Memory.* New York: Simon and Schuster, 1956.

Ryu, Tong-Shik. *P'ungryudo wa hankukshinhak.*[The Way of Elegance and Korean Theology]. Seoul: Chonmangsa, 1992.

———. *The Christian Faith Encounters The Religions of Korea.* Seoul: Christian Literature Society of Korea, 1962.

Schillebeeckx, Edward. *The Eucharist.* London: Seed and Ward Ltd.,1977.

Sherburne, Donald W. *A Key to Whitehead's Process and Reality.* Bloomington: Indiana University Press, 1996.

Smart, Ninian. *Worldviews.* New York: Prentice-Hall, Inc., 2000.

Smith, Wilfred Cantwell. *The Meaning and End of Religion.* London: Harper & Row, 1978.

———. *The Faith of Other Men.* New York: The New American Library, 1965.

Song, Choan-Seng. *Third-Eye Theology: Theology in Formation in Asian Setting.* New York: Orbis Books.

Song, Sok-Ku. *Yulgok Sasang Yonku* [Study on Yulgok's Thoughts]. Seoul: Hyoungsol Publishing Company, 1994.

Song, Young-Bae, and others, eds. *Hanguk yuhak qwa iki cholhak* [Korean Confucianism and the Philosophy of Principle and Material Force]. Seoul: Yaemoonsowon, 2000.

Sudbrack, John. *Spiritual Guidance.* New York: Paulist Press, 1983.

Suchocki, Marjorie Hewitt. *God Christ Church: A Process Guide to Process Theology.* New York: The Crossroad Publishing Company, 1989.

Suh, David Kwangsun Suh. "American Missionaries and A Hundred Years of Korean Protestantism." *InternationalReview of Mission* 74 (January 1985).

Suh Hwadam, *Hwadamjip* [Complete Works of Hwadam] .3 vols. Seoul: Saegye-sa, 1992.

Suh, Nam-Dong. *Minjung-Shinhak- ui-Tamku* [In Search of Minjung Theology]. Seoul : Hankilsa, 1986.

Sullivan, John. *Spiritual Direction.* Washington D.C.: ICS Publications, 1980.

Swidler, Leonard, ed. *Toward a Universal Theology of Religion.* New York: Orbis Books, 1987.

Taylor, Rodney L. *The Confucian Way of Contemplation.* Columbia, SC: University of South Carolina Press, 1988.

———. *The Religious Dimensions of Confucianism.* Albany: State University of New York Press, 1990.

The Ecumenical Patriarchate, assisted by the Worldview Fund for Nature. "Orthodoxy and the Ecological Crisis." Istanbul: The Ecumenical Patriarchate, 1990.

The Korean Association of Oriental Philosophy, ed. Doyang Cholhak ui boncheron gwa insongnon [Study of Ontology and Human Nature in Oriental philosophy]. Seoul: Yonsae University Press, 1982.

The Hankyoreh Newspaper (Seoul). 27 June, 1998; 28 August, 1998.

Tracy, David. *Plurality and Ambiguity: Hermeneutics, Religion, Hope.* Chicago: University of Chicago Press, 1987.

Tucker, May Evelyn. and John A. Grim, eds. *Worldviews and Ecology Religion, Philosophy, and the Environment.* New York: Orbis Books, 1994.

Tu, Wei-Ming. *Centrality and Commonality: An Essay on Confucian Religiousness.* Albany: State University of New York Press, 1989.

———. *Confucian Thought: Selfhood as Creative Transformation.* Albany: State University of New York Press, 1985.

Twiss, Summer B. and Bruce Grelle, eds. *Explorations in Global Ethics.* Boulder, Cl: Westview Press, 1998.

Wakefield, Gordon, ed. *Westerminster Dictionary of Christian Spirituality.* Philadelphia: Westminster, 1983.

Whang, Jun-Yon. *Yulgok Cholhak ui Ihai.* [Understanding of Yulgok's Philosophy]. Seoul: Sokwang-Sa, 1995.

Wicks, Robert J. *Handbook of Spirituality for Ministers.* New York: Paulist

Press, 1995.

Williams, Daniel Day. "How Does God Act?." In *Process and Divinity*, eds. W. Reese and E. Freeman. Lasalle: Open Court, 1964.

Wolfteich, Claire E. *American Catholics Through the Twentieth Century: Spirituality, Lay Experience and Public Life.* New York: The Crossroad Publishing Company, 2001.

———. "Graceful Work: Practical Theological Study of Spirituality," *Horizons* 27 (Spring 2000): 7-21.

Wolski, Joann. *Women's Spirituality: Resources for Christian Development.* New York: Paulist Press, 1986.

World Council of Churches. *Baptism, Eucharist, and Ministry.* Geneva: World Council of Churches, 1982.

Yao, Xinzhong. *Confucianism and Christianity: A Comparative Study of Jen and Agape.* Sussex: Sussex Academic Press, 1996.

———. *An Introduction to Confucianism.* Cambridge: Cambridge University Press, 2000.

Yi, Jong-Ho. *Yulgok: Inkangwa sasang* [Yulgok: Man and Thoughts]. Seoul: Hyunamsa, 1984.

Yi, Pyong-Do. *Yulgokui saengaewa sasang* [Yulgok's Thought and Life]. Seoul: Suhmundang, 1984.

Zhu, Xi. Zhuzi yulei [朱子語類, Conversations of Master Zhu, Arranged Topically]. Beijing: Zhonghua, 1986.

Index

Actual Entity, 15-41, 81-5, 142
Actual Occasion, 18, 19, 20, 21, 36, 38, 39, 81, 84, 88
Ahn, Hyang, 45
Alderink, Larry J., 103
Allen, Ronald J., 132
Analects, 44, 47
Ancestor Worship, 8, 45, 92, 96, 97, 98, 116-27
Anonymous Christian, 144
Anthropocosmic, 106, 117, 135
Apostle's Creed, 120
Apophatic Prayer, 115
Appenzeller, Henry G., 92
Balasuriya, Tissa, 124
Baptism, Eucharist, and Ministry, 122, 123
Barth, Karl, 106
Berthrong, John, 33, 49, 52, 98, 101
Bible Study, 105, 110, 111, 144
Book of Changes, 71, 73
Brown, Arthur Judson, 94
Buddhism, 1, 3, 6, 43, 44, 45, 47, 48, 68, 93, 94, 95, 96, 113, 133, 146
Chan, Wing-Tsit, 49
Chang, Tsai, 56, 159, 107, 108, 109
Che (t'i), 55
Cheng, Chung-ying, 79
Chil-jong-po-sa-dan, 71, 73
Ching, Julia, 88, 99, 102, 113, 133, 134, 145
Cho, Yong-Gi, 93, 112
Choson Dynasty, 1, 2, 45, 46, 53, 58, 59, 75, 78, 97
Ch'ondo Ch'aek, 47
Christ, Jesus, 4, 11, 100, 106, 109, 110, 119, 120, 123, 124, 125, 139

Chou Tun-I, 56
Clark, Donald, 92, 95
Christian, William, 9, 21, 23, 24, 27
Christian Liturgy, 115, 116, 121, 122, 123, 144
Christianity, 1, 2, 3, 4, 5, 6, 8, 9, 11, 33, 34, 43, 91, 92, 93, 94, 95, 96, 97, 99, 100, 102, 103, 104, 105, 106, 109, 113, 119, 120, 121, 125, 133, 139, 141, 142, 144, 145, 146, 147
Christocentrism, 121
Chung, Chin-Hong, 121
Chung, David, 91
Chung, Edward, 46, 55
Chung, Hyun-Kyung, 132
Chung, Tsai-chun, 58
Clooney, Francis X., 145
Cobb, John, 9, 13, 14, 34, 80
Co-creator, 86, 130, 142
Communion of Saints, 116, 120, 122
Comparativist, 145
Comparative Theology/Religion, 6, 145, 146
Confucius, 44, 45, 49, 102, 133, 134, 135
Confucianism, 1, 2, 3, 4, 5, 6, 9, 43, 44, 45, 46, 48, 49, 58, 88, 91, 93, 95, 96, 97, 99, 101, 102, 103, 104, 105, 107, 108, 115, 117, 119, 126, 129, 130, 131, 132, 133, 134, 135, 141, 144, 145, 146, 147
Confucian Pneumatology, 147
Conversation, 16, 110, 111
Concrescence, 8, 17, 18, 19, 22, 23, 26, 28, 29, 30, 31, 32, 35, 36, 37, 39, 41, 81, 82, 86, 118, 129, 142
Confucian-Christian Dialogue, 1, 2, 3, 4, 6, 8, 11, 12, 80, 81, 96, 140, 141, 142, 143, 144, 146
Confucian Spirituality, 2, 3, 101, 102,

127, 132
Confucian Vision, 117, 138
Consequent Nature, 18, 35, 36, 37, 38, 40, 86, 87, 142
Contemplation, 102, 111, 112, 113, 115, 134, 144
Corinthians, 100, 123
Cosmoanthropic Vision, 131
Cosmology, 2, 4, 5, 6, 7, 8, 11, 13, 17, 18, 19, 23, 27, 30, 33, 38, 41, 43, 44, 47, 49, 56, 57, 58, 67, 69, 71, 78, 79, 81, 82, 85, 87, 88, 101, 102, 103, 104, 11, 129, 131, 132, 140, 141, 142, 143, 144, 147
Creativity, 8, 18, 28, 32, 33, 36, 38, 39, 41, 86, 88, 142
Datum, 15, 18, 21, 23, 27, 28, 29, 30, 32, 35, 36, 40, 82, 86, 87, 135
Day, Gardiner M., 120
Descartes, 14, 15, 20, 129
Dae-dong-sa-hoe, 138
Dao (tao, way), 2, 10, 50, 64, 70, 72, 75, 76, 77, 108, 113, 114, 129, 130, 138
Daoism, 1, 6, 43, 38, 113, 129, 130, 133, 146
Dao Mind, 64, 76, 77, 138
Deuteronomy, 108
Dipolarity of God, 35, 142
Door, Donal, 134
Driscoll, Michael S., 120
Dynamic, 8, 15, 17, 18, 20, 22, 33, 52, 54, 55, 56, 59, 60, 62, 66, 69, 75, 78, 83, 84, 85, 88, 99, 103, 104, 117, 118, 129, 130, 142, 143
Ecological Crisis, 103, 104, 128, 130
Eco-Spirituality, 127, 128, 129, 144
Ephesians, 119
Eternal Object, 7, 8, 18, 19, 23, 24, 25, 27, 30, 32, 35, 36, 37, 41, 79, 81, 82, 83, 84, 85, 86, 129, 142, 143
Eucharist, 116, 120, 122, 123, 124, 125, 126, 127
Exclusivistic, 3, 141
Exodus, 119

Ezekiel, 106
Feminist, 132, 133
Filial Piety, 43, 44, 46, 50, 98, 108, 117, 118, 119, 122, 125, 126, 127, 136, 146
Fink, Peter E., 123
Ford, Lewis, 9, 40, 86
Fung, Yu-lan, 48
Galilea, Segundo, 100
God and the World, 19, 33, 37, 38, 40, 85, 86, 87, 130
Gratton, Carolyn, 115
Great Learning, 44, 47
Griffin, David, 9, 13, 104, 130, 132
Gutierrez, Gustavo, 100, 134
Han, Chul-Ha, 95
Han, Young-Jo, 53
Harris, Maria, 100
Hebrew Bible, 137, 138
Hebrews, 107, 122
Holmes, Urban T., 111, 115
Hosinski, Thomas E., 14, 18, 33
Hume, David, 14, 15
Hwadam, 8, 46, 56, 57, 59
I-bal-ki-su, 55
I-il-bun-su, 8, 61, 62, 63, 64, 143
I-ki-ho-bal, 55, 75
I-ki-ji-myo, 8, 61, 66, 67, 69, 70, 143
Inclusivism / Inclusivist, 144
I-tong-ki-guk, 64
Interreligious Dialogue, 3, 9, 11, 102, 141, 144, 146
Interreligious Spirituality, 1, 2, 3, 6, 7, 11, 81, 91, 100, 102, 140
Isaiah, 138, 139
Jayon (thus-so of things), 60
Jen (in), 114, 118
Jongjwa (ching-tso), 113
Judeo-Christian, 104, 119
Kalton, Michael, 5, 64, 74
Kang, Wi-jo, 126
Kant, 15
Kelleher, Margaret Mary, 99

Index

Keum, Jang-Tae, 43
Ki-bal-yi-seung, 8, 61, 72, 75, 76, 143
Kim, Duk-Whang, 92
Kim, Ha-Tae, 95, 101, 109
Kim, Heup-Young, 105
Kim, Kyoung-Jae, 3, 78
Kim, Yung-Sik, 49
Kingdom of God, 96, 124, 139, 146
Korean Church, 2, 3, 5, 8, 9, 11, 92, 93, 94, 95, 98, 102, 103, 116, 121, 134, 140, 142
Knitter, Paul, 104
Koryo Dynasty, 44, 45
Kun-ja (chün-tzu), 131
Kwok, Pu-lan, 132
Kyung (ching), 95, 107, 108, 109, 110, 138
Lee, Jung-Young, 91, 92, 95
Lee, Ki-Baik, 44, 91, 92
Leibniz, 20, 26
Li (yi, principle), 8, 9, 10, 49, 50, 51, 53, 55, 57, 58, 60, 65, 78, 80, 87, 143
Locke, John, 14
Logos, 103, 106, 107
Luke, 119
Luther, Martin, 121
Man-on-bong-sa, 137
Martin, David, 94, 96
Matthew, 106
Mellert, Robert B., 27
Mencius, 47, 49, 74, 75, 76, 105, 107
Metzner, Ralph, 128, 129
Micah, 134, 137
Minjung Theology, 95, 96, 124
Mu-geuk (wu-ch), 87
Nash, Jmes, 128
Negative Prehension, 27, 28, 29, 30
Neo-Confucianism, 1, 2, 4, 9, 10, 11, 43, 44, 45, 46, 48, 49, 53, 56, 57, 58, 60, 62, 72, 78, 80, 2, 88, 101, 109, 132, 133, 142
Neo-Confucian Cosmology, 8, 43, 47, 57, 58, 67, 71, 78, 81, 87, 88, 142

Neville, Robert, 51
Odell, M., 126
Organismic, 4, 13, 14, 22, 79, 80, 104, 129, 139, 142
Palmer, Spencer J., 43
Panentheism, 34, 79, 85, 88, 142
Park, Jae-Soon, 124
Park, Jong-Chun, 125
Pentecostalism, 94, 146, 147
Philippians, 106, 108
Philosophy of Organism, 4, 13, 15, 17, 18, 19, 79, 80
Platonic Form, 24
Positive prehension, 27, 28
Prayer, 5, 99, 100, 111, 112, 113, 115, 121, 144
Preaching, 105, 106, 107, 110, 111, 144
Prehension, 8, 15, 18, 19, 21, 23, 25, 26, 27, 28, 29, 30, 32, 37, 38, 39, 40, 41, 126, 142
Price, Lucien, 16
Primordial Nature, 18, 35, 36, 37, 38, 40, 86, 87, 142
Principe, Walter, 100
Process-Confucian Spirituality, 3, 127, 132
Process Cosmology, 5, 6, 7, 8, 13, 17, 18, 19, 23, 27, 30, 33, 38, 41, 82, 85, 87, 103, 104, 117, 129, 132, 140, 141, 142, 143, 144, 147
Processive, 2, 4, 41, 104, 129, 139, 142
Process Metaphysics, 18, 19, 33, 34, 80, 81, 85, 86, 142
Process Philosophy/Theology, 1, 2, 4, 5, 7, 9, 13, 15, 21, 79, 85, 142
Protestant, 3, 11, 92, 93, 94, 96, 97, 102, 105, 110, 111, 112, 115, 121, 122, 133
Proverbs, 108, 119
Pyun, Sun-Hwan, 95
Qi (ch'i, ki), 8, 10, 48, 49, 50, 53, 56, 57, 58, 59, 60, 62, 75, 78, 79, 81, 83, 143, 147
Qi Monism, 8, 56, 59
Rahner, Karl, 134, 144
Reformation, 4, 120, 121
Relational, 2, 4, 14, 18, 27, 35, 41, 104, 115, 129, 139, 142
Religious Pluralism, 1, 3, 5, 11, 80, 81, 97, 100, 102, 140, 141, 144

Ricci, Matteo, 91
Ro, Bong-Rin, 93
Ro, Young-Chan, 106, 108
Romans, 105, 106
Russell, Bertrand, 16
Ryu, Tong-Shick, 95, 146
Sailers, Don E., 116
Sa-dan-chil-jong-non, 8, 74
Sa-sung-ja, 107
Schneiders, Sandra M., 99, 100
Schwartzbaum, A. M., 126
Self-Cultivation, 2, 5, 68, 75, 77, 99, 105, 109, 112, 113, 114, 131, 135
Shang-ti, 109, 146
Shim (hsin), 105
Shimsong, 95, 146
Shin-dok (shen-tu), 113
Socio-political Spirituality, 132, 133, 134, 135, 136, 139, 144
Sola Scriptura, 111
Song, Choan-Seng, 125
Songhak chibyo, 47
Speculative Philosophy, 14, 15
Spirituality, 1-11, 58, 78, 81, 88, 91, 98-106, 110, 111, 112, 114, 115, 117, 118, 121, 122, 126, 127, 128, 129, 132, 133, 134, 135, 136, 139-147
Spiritual formation, 2, 9, 11, 102, 105, 115, 118, 140, 147
Spirituality of Liberation, 134
Shamanism, 3, 6, 94, 95, 96, 133, 146
Subjective aim, 17, 31, 35, 36, 130, 142
Subjective Form, 15, 19, 23, 27, 28, 29, 30
Suchocki, Marjori H., 14, 18, 114, 118, 125
Suh, David Kwangsun, 94
Sung (ch'eng), 77, 95, 106, 107, 109, 110
Sung-ja, 107
Superject, 21, 28, 29
Taeji (great ultimate), 8, 10, 50, 51, 143

Theology of Kyung, 95
Theology of Sung, 95
Tien (heaven), 109, 146
Tongsung Kido, 112
Tracy, David, 111
Tu, Wei-ming, 101, 106, 112, 119, 131, 135
Tucker, Mary Evelyn, 104, 129, 130
Underwood, Horace G., 92
Western Inscription, 108
White, Lynn Jr., 103, 129
Whitehead, Alfred North, 1-9, 11, 13-41, 78-88, 103, 110, 114, 116, 117, 118, 129, 130, 139, 142, 143, 144
Williamson, Clark M., 132
Wolfteich, Claire, 100
World Council of Churches, 122
Worldview, 2, 6, 7, 13, 14, 17, 18, 58, 103, 104, 128, 129, 130, 141, 145
Wuthnow, Robert, 98
Yin-Yang, 49, 71, 72, 73, 87, 129, 143
Yi, Seung-hun, 91
Yi T'oegye, 8, 46, 47, 48, 53, 54, 55, 60, 67, 74, 75, 77, 78, 136
Yi Yulgok, 1, 2, 4, , 5, 6, 7, 8, 9, 11, 41, 43, 46, 47, 48, 49, 53, 55, 57-85, 87, 88, 106, 107, 108, 109, 113, 117, 118, 129, 130, 131, 136, 137, 138, 139, 142, 143, 144
Yulgok Chonso, 154
Yun, Sung-Bum, 95
Yong (yung), 55, 136
Zhongyong (chung-yung), 107, 109, 135, 138
Zhu Xi (Chu Hsi), 4, 8, 9, 10, 45, 48-53, 55, 56, 59, 62, 64, 71, 72, 73, 79, 80, 84, 87, 89, 106, 108, 114, 136

About The Author

Chung Soon Lee is a pastor of the First Congregational Church of Waverley-Senuri, UCC, and an adjunct professor of religious studies at Merrimack College. He has earned Th.D. with a major in Comparative Theology, Religion, and Spirituality from Boston University. Prior to that, he also obtained M.Div. and Ph.D in Systematic Theology from Mokwon (Methodist) University in South Korea. In addition to his ministerial and teaching experience, he has been participating in the ecumenical movement, social justice issues, the minjung theology movement, and inter-religious dialogue both in Korea and the U.S.A.

Made in the USA
Coppell, TX
22 November 2020